The World's Great
Adventure
Motorcycle Routes

First published in January 2012

A catalogue record for this book is available from the British Library

ISBN 978 1 84425 945 8

Library of Congress catalog card no 2011935258

Published by Haynes Publishing,
Sparkford, Yeovil, Somerset BA22 7JJ, UK
Tel: +44 1963 442030 Fax: +44 1963 440001
E-mail: sales@haynes.co.uk
Website: www.haynes.co.uk

Haynes North America Inc.,
861 Lawrence Drive, Newbury Park,
California 91320, USA

Designed by Lee Parsons

Printed in the USA by Odcombe Press LP,
1299 Bridgestone Parkway, La Vergne, TN 37086

Dedication

With a demanding full-time role in the sports marketing industry much of this book was put together in the evenings and at weekends, and this would not have been possible without the unwavering support of my family, so I dedicate this book to my wonderful wife Tanya and daughter Hannah. Thank you for all your terrific support and encouragement throughout.

Simon & Lisa Thomas – www.2ridetheworld.com

The World's Great
Adventure
Motorcycle Routes

The essential guide to the greatest
motorcycle rides in the world

Robert Wicks

Foreword by **Kevin & Julia Sanders**

Contents

Julia Sanders

It was in the 1990s when Julia and I shipped a 1989 BMW R80GS out to the USA. The plan was to ride the Pan American Highway to Ushuaia, Tierra del Fuego. It was barely 15 years ago, but there were no mobile or satellite phones, no GPS but a new thing called an 'e-mail address'. Just to find information about riding the Pan American was a struggle, as was buying maps good enough to navigate with. We ended up contacting the *BMW Members of America* magazine for advice and got some lovely handwritten letters, one telling us not to go to Mexico as it was 'too dangerous'. We could have ridden and stopped there, as many do. Fear of the unknown can be paralysing. But curiosity, thankfully, got the better of us. By no means were we the first riders to be lured by the Pan American, but that made it no less our own personal motorcycle adventure.

Adventure rides are not about having an easy or comfortable experience. By its very definition, adventure involves real exposure to risk, where the outcome is uncertain and where you are putting yourself out there, beyond your regular routine and your comfort zone.

Often adventure motorcycling can mean the challenge of a dirt road, but it doesn't have to. You can, in fact, ride from Alaska to Patagonia and take a route that sticks to the asphalt almost the whole way, but it doesn't mean it's not an adventure. Ask anyone who has haggled for hours at a border post, got caught up in an earthquake in Peru, slid down the road after hitting an alpaca or faced a gun-toting Nicaraguan policeman for heading the wrong way down an unsigned one-way street!

Even political unrest can stop you in your tracks. We've been held up in Quito, Ecuador after a bloodless coup ousted the president and we've had to divert a whole group of riders away from Osh in Kyrgyzstan when violence erupted, forcing the government to flee – adventure enough without a dirt road in sight! Of course dirt roads have a unique attraction. Often they are remote, across regions of the world less travelled, through pristine wilderness and unfamiliar terrain. Shown as a 'rideable road' on a map, the Pamir Highway (in Tajikistan) or the Tibetan Plateau, as examples, offer erratic road conditions – sand and gravel, altitude and cold.

These are roads through regions where nature is not your friend. Dust storms, snow-laden passes, swollen river crossings, mud and landslides are regular occurrences. Even finding the basics of shelter, fuel, water and food can be a struggle. There is no established 'gringo trail', no expat bars or bohemian eateries, no internet cafés, no cosy backpacker hostels. Not only is your riding tested, but also your negotiation skills, your ingenuity and your problem solving. Your ability to keep smiling when your bike is battered, your insides are churning and you cannot make yourself understood – these experiences are the stuff of great motorcycling memories. Turn the pages and you will find some of the world's finest adventure rides. We have been privileged enough to ride some, but certainly not all of them. Some of these rides may have been your dream for many years; others are hidden gems. Some are classic, long-distance, epic journeys, while others are little-known back roads that will inspire and challenge in equal measure. Not everyone has the opportunity to get on a bike and head for the horizon, but many can if they make it their priority to do so. These adventure rides are waiting for you, so what are you waiting for?

Kevin and Julia Sanders
January 2012

Introduction

I recall talking to Horizons Unlimited founder, Grant Johnson, two years ago and asking his thoughts about a book on the world's great adventure routes. He was sceptical at best and wasn't sure it was possible, given the scale of the undertaking. 'Where on earth would you start on something like that?' I recall him asking. Others shared his concerns. I could have stopped believing at that point, but I decided to press on and enlisted the help of some friends. These are not just any friends, but a rather special group of like-minded individuals who have contributed in various ways to what you now hold in your hands – the fourth title in the acclaimed Haynes *Adventure Motorcycling* series.

At a record 264 pages and more than 400 photos, this is unlike any adventure motorcycling book ever produced. The contributions come from some of the best-known names in the field, as well as from a number of people who had never previously put pen to paper.

Over the past two years, a considerable amount of time has been spent identifying and researching countless routes and then setting about finding the best contributors. Working with a large number of writers proved challenging at times and the book could, in fact, have been twice or even three times the size. Finally, choosing which routes to include proved one of the most challenging tasks and my study at home was rapidly transformed into what is best described as the 'war room' with countless maps, atlases and charts being pored over long into the night.

For the really adventurous there are epic transcontinental routes covering thousands of miles, but there are also some short, must-see trails for those not wanting to venture too far afield. Similarly, some routes are described in significant detail while others simply give a flavour of what to expect and tell more of the story through the accompanying images. The end result is more than 30 of the greatest adventure motorcycling routes in the world, and arguably the best collection of adventure motorcycling photography and maps ever assembled.

My sincere thanks go to each and every one of the contributors for making this book a reality: Kevin and Julia Sanders, Alan Whelan, Joe Pichler, Craig Carey-Clinch, Nick Sanders, Craig Marshall, Krzysztof Samborski, Sam Manicom, Sumit Tyagi and Harish Daita, Adam Lewis, Walter Colebatch, Rob and Pete West, Andreas Hülsmann, Mike Hyde, Simon Race, Ilker Ecir, Eythor Orlygsson, David French, Ramona Schwarz, Oliver Ruck, Sam Correro, Brian Clarke, Chris Smith and Liz Peel, and Roger Pattison. Their writing and accompanying photography will inform, excite and inspire.

I am also very grateful for the assistance I received from the editorial team at Haynes – Mark Hughes and Lee Parsons – who have supported the development of this book since its inception.

I hope you enjoy the read….

Robert Wicks
January 2012

Chapter 1

Epic Transcontinental

Anyone wanting to contemplate a significant journey should consider one of the three 'Epic Routes' described in this chapter. In the first instance, Alaska to Tierra del Fuego, or more precisely, Prudhoe Bay / Deadhorse to Ushuaia, is the longest. Through Central and South America the route follows the Pan American highway and broadly speaking will see you riding through the USA, Canada, Mexico, Guatemala, El Salvador, Honduras, Nicaragua, Costa Rica, Panama, Colombia, Ecuador, Peru, Chile and Argentina. Veteran adventurer Walter Colebatch says: *The biggest challenge for this route is overcoming the Darien Gap, a formidable section of the Pan American highway in Panama, filled with jungle and drug smugglers.*

The second of the 'Epics' is from Europe to Cape Town in South Africa. For the purists, the route begins in Nord Kapp, the most northerly point in Europe, but for most people heading to Africa, riding across Europe is secondary to the main goal of this route, the north to south crossing of Africa. A reverse journey heading north is also worth considering. There are two broadly grouped 'routes' through Africa; an eastern route though Kenya and the western route through Nigeria. The eastern route is more predictable and probably safer although recent developments in the north of Africa, in particular Egypt, may influence your decision. The western route involves crossing the Sahara, and dealing with unstable countries around The Congo.

The final 'Epic' comprises a ride between somewhere in Europe to Vladivostok. Colebatch adds: *Purists will turn this into an Atlantic to Pacific ride and will insist on beginning on the Atlantic, but for most the crossing of Europe is of secondary importance to the crossing of the worlds biggest continent – Asia.* For the first half of the journey, there are many different variations of the route, but these are increasingly taking in the more interesting Central Asian 'Stans' described in considerable detail in the Asia chapter. Beyond the Stans lies Mongolia and then the route follows the Trans Siberian Highway to Vladivostok. As travel in and around China becomes easier, the opportunity to divert south and head to Beijing and Shanghai is also a worthwhile consideration.

Though not described in too much detail here, a 'shorter Epic' could be the run from Europe to Chennai in India. The route is curtailed due to the impassability of Burma. Says Colebatch: *In an ideal world this route would continue on to Singapore and perhaps at some stage in the future it will be.* Of all the Epic Routes this takes in the fewest number of exotic countries – once Europe is left behind, the route goes through Turkey, Iran, Pakistan and India. One of the great challenges of this route is dealing with the elusive Iranian visa.

Whatever route you decide to consider, be safe in the knowledge that by taking on one of these you will join a small group of intrepid global adventurers who have completed a trans-continental ride! ∎

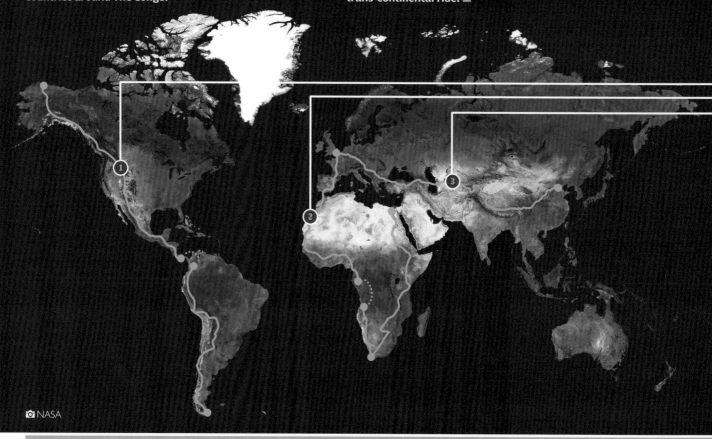

NASA

Routes

Trans Americas

Five months along the Pan American Highway

Kevin and Julia Sanders

Riding the full length of the Americas is a massive motorcycling achievement and the longest north/south or south/north route possible in the world. No wonder it is considered to be such an epic journey. Often referred to as riding the 'Pan American', this colloquialism reinforces the concept that there exists a road called the Pan American Highway that runs from the top of Alaska to the tip of Argentina. Up and down the two continents there are sections of road that make up the Pan American Highway. But the reality is that such a single road does not exist. So if you're off motorcycling this route, don't get too hung up about the 'Pan American'. The reality is that there are a lot more interesting roads to ride on your journey than sticking to this name.

For most, the Trans Americas is a north to south journey, normally begun by freighting your bike into Anchorage, Alaska. There is no reason why you can't start in the south, but somehow starting in the north just feels right. The other good reason is that Ushuaia is a much better place to celebrate your achievement than Prudhoe Bay – Prudhoe Bay is a dry town!

North America
North to Prudhoe Bay

Sitting right at the top of Alaska is just one road. It is called the Dalton Highway (and locally known as the Haul Road) and was built in 1974 to service the oil pipeline, opening to the public only in 1994. It has to be an essential part of any transcontinental ride. Nowhere else in the world have we killed our engines at the side of the road and heard the stomp and grunt of thousands of migrating caribou, viewed in complete silence the grazing *Star Wars*-esque musk-ox, or felt the prickle of fear and wonder at a mother bear and cub crossing the road only a few hundred metres ahead.

The Dalton's challenges are its dirt and gravel road surface with sections that are constantly churned up by graders, unpredictable wintry weather (even in summer), huge thundering trucks that kick up blinding dirt clouds, gallivanting wildlife and lack of services. On leaving Fairbanks, it is a two-day ride to Prudhoe Bay and your convenient stopping point for food and fuel part way through the first day is at the Yukon River, about 135 miles (217km) north of Fairbanks. A few miles on is the Hot Spot Café, but there is no fuel here. Another 55 miles (89km) further along and you'll cross the Arctic Circle, around 190 miles (305km) from Fairbanks, with a lay-by on your right, containing 'The Sign'. The obvious break point to the journey is Coldfoot Camp, another 65 miles (105km) north of the Arctic Circle. It's a motley collection of Portakabin-style buildings, where camping is definitely the cheapest way to stay over. Grub at Coldfoot is a magnificent 'all you can eat' buffet, but at a price.

From Coldfoot you are presented with 240 miles (386km) of remote road where fuel and food are not

←← **The Valley of the Gods, Utah.**

← **Inside the Arctic Circle on the Dalton Highway.**

↑ **Following the oil pipeline on the Dalton Highway.**

available. The only permanent form of human existence is denoted by the constant presence of the oil pipeline and oil pumping stations, which are off limits.

If you've reached Deadhorse, Prudhoe Bay without dropping your bike then well done, as this is fairly commonplace and we've had to airlift a few riders out in recent years. Prudhoe Bay is not the most welcoming of places and resembles a *Mad Max* film set. Fuel is sourced from massive barrels, alcohol is banned and camping is not welcome. Bears do live here – they roam through the inhabited areas and have attacked campers. If that's a bit too much adventure, be prepared to shell out upwards of US$190 for a room.

South through Canada and to the Mexican border

Heading south, the Alaskan Highway is the obvious route and is popularly considered part of the Pan American. The start/end point of the Alaskan Highway is Delta Junction (Alaska). You have to continue your ride on the Alaskan

to start with, but as it's also the choice of excessively large recreational vehicles you do need to get off it as soon as you can. There are some great alternatives. First, the Klondike Highway via Chicken to Whitehorse, followed by the Stewart-Cassiar Highway. Picking these much quieter wilderness routes gives you the best chance of seeing bears roadside, idyllic lakeside swimming opportunities and isolated pine cabins for rest at night.

While the Stewart-Cassiar is paved all the way through now, there are still some side roads you can take to get even further off the beaten path. The road down to Telegraph Creek quickly becomes a challenging, narrow, muddy road. Alternatively, further south take the right-hand turn to Lava Bed National Park, a mix of dirt and asphalt, which runs across an ancient lava field. The Stewart-Cassiar offers plenty of campsites in the provincial parks along its route.

A trip down the Cassiar would not be complete without a side excursion to Hyder – the southernmost town in Alaska and reached via Stewart. This tiny outback town has two very special attractions – first, watching the grizzly bears feast on spawning salmon at Fish Creek (go in August) and second, riding the tiny dirt road to the most incredible viewpoint overlooking the spectacular Salmon Glacier.

Continuing south, although it's on the tourist trail, take the Icefields Parkway through Canada's Jasper National Park, then divert through Kootenay National Park. It is classic road riding, against stunning and pristine backdrops and drops you only a few hundred miles shy of Waterton National Park. It's easy to overload on forests, lakes, mountains and glaciers by this stage, but head for the tiny Chief Mountain border crossing for the Going to the Sun Road and you will be left in awe.

In the USA, you can take your pick of roads from north to south. The western USA is recognised as the best area to ride, and if you like beach life then maybe the Pacific Coastal Highway is the route for you. However, we'd recommend sticking to the Continental Divide area, taking you through less inhabited, less congested areas. Selecting some of the USA's incredible national parks, then linking them through the squiggliest, green-edged roads means that you won't go far wrong. It also brings greater opportunities to try some of the dirt trails.

The US national parks in peak season are always going to be busy but if you try them at the end of September and beginning of October you're on to a winner. The Continental Divide route can take you through Yellowstone, Arches, Canyonlands, Mesa Verde, Monument Valley (not an official US national park, but an iconic stop) and the Grand Canyon. A tip for the Grand Canyon is to go to the North Rim (not the South) and visit the canyon at its narrowest part by heading for Toroweap Overlook, along a dirt road, which is left just off Highway 389. This road does require a good grasp of technical slow manoeuvring skills to wind your way across some smooth rocky outcrops towards the canyon's edge. You'll be rewarded by the best view of the Grand Canyon, devoid

of any other visitors, and the chance to ride your bike as close to the edge as you dare.

The great thing about the Continental Divide route is that there are some of the best motorcycling roads to link them all up. Favourites are Red Mountain Pass on the San Juan Highway, Beartooth Pass (Highway 212), and Highway 128 to Moab and Highway 191 south from Moab. Another gem is the Mokee Dugway, an 18-mile (29km) loop through the Valley of the Gods, just north of Mexican Hat, Utah. This is a great single track dirt road through mini-Monument Valley and definitely better riding than the real deal.

Officially the southern point of your US journey, if you are a Pan American Highway junkie, should bring you to Laredo, where the 'Inter-Americana' spans 3,400 miles (5,470km) between here and Panama City. If you've taken the Continental Divide route, Laredo is a long way east, therefore pick a small border crossing through the mid section of the USA/Mexico border (avoiding the infamous El Paso/Ciudad Juarez).

Mexico

It would be utter madness to stick to the official 'Inter-Americana' Highway in Mexico. Much of it is dual carriageway roads which, while fast, are ugly, the domain of large Mexican trucks, and will cost you a fortune in tolls. Besides that, on its way it will dump you in Mexico City, the congestion and pollution of which reduces your ride to a battle of wits that will leave you frazzled. At all costs, avoid getting caught up in Mexico City – there is such a huge choice of delightful roads that are far away from the Pan American.

The famous adventure riding route of Northern Mexico is Copper Canyon, of which the most common section is the ride down to Batopilas. Take the right-hand turning from Highway 23, signed La Bufa/Batopilas for 50 miles (80km) of paved and dirt road deep into the canyon. It starts out

◀ **Going to the Sun Road.**

◀ **Toroweap Overlook on the Northern Rim of the Grand Canyon.**

→ Antigua,
Guatemala.

as a new asphalt road for around 15 miles, through scented pine forest which peters out when it reaches the top of the canyon, by which time it has narrowed to a single dirt track, with sheer cliff drops.

You'll largely be in first gear the whole way down, up on the pegs, negotiating tight hairpin bends and avoiding rusty trucks coming up the other way and wanting all of the road! By the time you reach the bottom, the temperature will have rocketed, giant cacti line the route and there's a wooden bridge to traverse to the other side of the canyon. Batopilas is a charming Mexican village, with a variety of accommodation, and it's worth spending a day there to relax before heading back out again.

Maintaining a highland route keeps you in the Sierra Madre and your way will be dotted with colonial gems such as Zacatecas, San Miguel de Allende and Guanajuato. Diverting to the Pacific will put you on Highway 200, the coastal route. It has delightful pockets of riding, but they compete with big tourist places like Acapulco. We prefer the inland routes, and the rides over the Sierra Madre Oriental are stunning, albeit marred by the ever-present obstacle of topes. Topes are road humps used all too frequently on the smaller roads through villages. Miss seeing one of them and you could be off your bike.

⬇ Copper
Canyon in
Mexico.

A ride through Mexico would not be complete without taking some time to visit at least one Mayan archaeological site. We tend to avoid the Yucatan Peninsula as the terrain is flat and the riding tends to be dull as a result. Stopping at the UNESCO gem of Palenque is the best of the best and is located in the previously volatile Chiapas region, home

to the Zapatistas rebels. Riding through the Zapatista heartlands is more spectacular mountain riding that will bring you to San Cristóbal, a small colonial town and an easy point from which to enter Guatemala.

Central America

In the end, Mexico will funnel you down to the tiny countries of Central America, where the Pan American is the artery linking them together. Due to the small size of these countries, one of the big adventures in Central America is haggling your way through the quick succession of borders. Fixers are a way of life here, so swallow the few bucks, help out the local economy and use them – they will make your life easier and you can practise your Spanish banter.

Although Central America provides less opportunity to divert from the main highway, where it does exist, it's worth taking. The Guatemalan Highland route from Chichicastenago up to Sacapulas and across to Coban is a refreshing, cool ride through small indigenous villages and mostly dirt road, but it is subject to landslides in the rainy season. It also gives the option of avoiding Guatemala City – a hideous riding experience.

From Guatemala to Honduras, taking the Copan Ruinas border crossing is a far more pleasant experience than the main Pan Am crossing and places you perfectly next to one of the greatest Mayan sites in Central America. In Honduras, diverting through the mountains via La Esperanza keeps you to quieter, rougher roads and immersed in local culture.

During Costa Rica's high season you'll want to stay away from the beach resorts which are packed full of American package holiday tourists. Heading for Arenal gives you more opportunities to take the unpaved roads via Dos de Tilaran and Rio Chiquito. When you get to Lake Arenal you can try the dirt trails and go anti-clockwise around it.

From Costa Rica, crossing into Panama from the remote northern border provides not only a hair-raising railway bridge to negotiate but also drops you on to one of the best motorcycling roads in Central America, from Changuinola to the junction to Chiriqui Grande. Take the opportunity, because your ride to Panama City inevitably means dual-lane Pan American Highway for the final 200 miles (320km) or so, crowned only by the magnificent Bridge of the Americas, spanning the Pacific entrance to the Panama Canal and your own personal reaction to the milestone 'halfway there' (or thereabouts!). Panama City presents the last remaining challenge of the Pan American Highway – 'The Gap'!

The Darien Gap

Soon after Panama City, anyone hoping for the fast lane to Tierra del Fuego, at the far end of South America, is on a road to nowhere. East of the Panamanian capital, the highway finally dissolves into mud at the small town of Yaviza. There is then an 'as the crow flies' gap of some 54 miles (87km) to the start of the road in Colombia.

HISTORY OF THE PAN AMERICAN HIGHWAY

The concept of a road connecting the North and South American continents was first proposed at the Fifth International Congress of American States held in Santiago in 1923, but it was never originally envisaged to build a road going from the very northern tip of Alaska to the very southern shores of Argentina. The intention was to provide a system of roads that would link the countries of North and South America, being beneficial for economic and other reasons. American literature from the 1930s, including *The Rotarian* magazine, shows hand-drawn maps of the original concept, starting from Fairbanks in Alaska and finishing in Buenos Aires. Back in those days, there was no need to plan a road further north than Fairbanks or further south than Buenos Aires.

For decades, efforts have been made to facilitate this missing link in the Pan American Highway, but these have always been thwarted by environmentalists, citing possible extensive damage to the local ecosystems. Chances are, this tiny section of road will never be finished.

There are a few people who have managed to traverse the Gap overland. In 1975, Robert L. Webb completed the first motorcycle crossing of the Darien Gap, using a Rokon motorcycle. Before him there were a couple of bikers, the more infamous of whom was Danny Liska, who rode from Alaska to Argentina between 1959 and 1961. Liska did freight his bike from Panama to Medellin, but he continued his journey overland on foot through the Darien, to meet up with his bike. In 1985, Ed Culberson went from north to south through the Darien on an R80GS called 'Amiga', and Helge Pedersen took his R80GS 'Olga', from south to north. In 1995, Loren Upton became the first man to cross the Darien Gap totally overland on a motorcycle (another

⬇ **The Banana Bridge marks the border crossing between Costa Rica and Panama.**

In the north, attempting the Dalton Highway is best done from mid-June to mid-August. Even during this summer period we've encountered snow and freezing temperatures – but we've also got sunburnt. Outside these core times, the weather becomes increasingly unpredictable.

At the other end of the world, Patagonia is best visited from November through to March. Again, even during their summer period, there can be snowstorms. Very strong crosswinds are another hazard and these can blow in at any time.

Other extremes are the hurricane and rainy season in Mexico on the Caribbean side and in Central America from August through to October. Ride in the rainy season and the upside is that it's quiet and accommodation is great value. The downside can be flash floods and mountain landslides.

Finally, the Andes. The rainy season is from January through to March. If you want those stunning deep blue skies and crisp white salt flats to ride across, avoid this time.

Rokon). The point here is that Upton never used a canoe, boat or other method to get his bike through – it was all done overland and took 49 days.

Current conditions through the Darien make it pretty much suicidal for any normal traveller to attempt a crossing. Most riders will opt for airfreight over 'The Gap', for while is it more expensive, it is more reliable and significantly less hassle than going by sea. Ride out to Tocumen International Airport, about 10 miles (16km) east of Panama City, and rather than turning right for the passenger terminal, head left and follow the ring road to the old airport to reach the cargo section. Your best bet is to approach Copa, the Panamanian airline, or Girag, the Colombian airline. Costs have escalated over the years. Back in 1999, we spent US$350 getting our bike flown to Quito. Now you are looking at over US$1,000 plus handling charges at the destination.

South America

In South America, a ride that remains on the Pan American ticks the box of traversing the continent without really getting to the heart of it. There is no doubt that in Colombia and Ecuador, the Pan American will seduce you with its curves, grind the edges from your panniers and provide you with ten bends a minute. Then, just to be temperamental, it'll throw in the random challenges of Latino life – reckless drivers, suicidal livestock, landslides, potholes and officious military checkpoints. In other words, it'll give you exactly what an overland motorcycle adventure should be about. Once you have passed Cuenca in Ecuador, you can stick with the Pan American, descending to the flat terrain of endless banana plantations to cross into Peru at the main, rather chaotic border post of Huaquillas, or stay on the smaller mountain roads to the tiny, mostly unused crossing at Macara. The latter is infinitely preferable, the road being more remote and uncongested, and it will test your cornering ability to the limit on swooping bends and tight hairpins.

You could decide to stick to the Pan American all through Peru. It's a long paved road through mainly desert terrain, forming a ring road around Lima and then spitting you out south of Tacna to cross into Chile. We'd recommend that you pick the Pan Am sections where you can see the ancient desert cultures of Chan Chan in the north and Paracas and Nasca in the south, but as much as possible divert into the Andes. The Andes roads will deliver quintessential South America, on a combination of road surfaces. In the Northern Andes try the Cajamarca, Kuelap, Chachapoyas and Jaen loops, while in the Southern Andes there is the traditional gringo circuit of Cusco and the Sacred Valley, Puno and Lake Titicaca, and Arequipa. Another classic dirt road is the tiny Canyon del Pato to Caraz. While the destination towns are crammed with

← **Canyon del Pato in Peru.**

package tourists, the roads in between are yours alone, winding among magnificent snow-capped and glacier-laden mountains, with the remnants of Inca and pre-Columbian archaeological sites visible from the road.

From Peru, northern Chile will deliver over 1,000 miles (1,600km) of excellent straight (some consider, dull) tarmac roads through the Atacama Desert. Although the title of being the 'driest desert in the world' leads many to want to tick that box, it's common for others, at this point, to stay at altitude and continue from Puno into Bolivia.

Taking the Chilean route will plunge you through abandoned mining ghost towns, some of the best desert terrain on the trip and a magnificent coastal ride sandwiched between goliath freefalling cliffs and the Pacific Ocean. Chile is a modern country, with order and rules (don't try and bribe a policeman here), vast steel and glass service stations, everyday credit card use and good infrastructure – a bit of a reverse culture shock when coming from Peru! At this point, after thousands of miles on the road, some riders enjoy this familiar feel to recalibrate their senses.

Diverting into Bolivia, one of the poorest countries in South America, will keep you immersed in the indigenous culture and rural mountain life, but also provide your first glimpse of the shimmering white salt flats, bright green turquoise lakes and deep red volcanic vistas of that country. There's no doubt that Bolivia offers the greatest adventure riding opportunities – there's the 'Road of Death' from La Paz and the routes to Uyuni. You can get back into Chile to see San Pedro de Atacama over Paso de Jama, or continue through northern Argentina and take the main crossing of Los Libertadores to Chile. The latter takes you past Aconcagua, and then down a huge number of hairpin bends descending from the mountains on the Chilean side.

Once south of Santiago, you can zigzag the Andes border between Chile and Argentina to take advantage of

the Lake District, honing your dirt riding skills on a network of unpaved roads. Link up the national parks of Tolguaca and Conguillo, then head to the border between Pucon and Junin de Los Andes, which runs past the still smoking Volcan Villarrica and Volcan Lanin – and remember that volcanoes in Chile are active and explosive.

Patagonia

Patagonia – code name for an adventure traveller's playground, with two of the most spectacular rides of South America – the Carretera Austral and southern Ruta 40 (from the town of Perito Moreno to the junction for El Calafate).

Joining the Carretera Austral from the branch road that

⬆ **Following the Pacific coast in Chile.**

⬇ **Carretera Austral in Patagonia.**

Ruta 40 in Argentina.

leads from Esquel (Argentina) to Fuetalufu (Chile) avoids the need to take ferries on the northern section. This is a route that has something for everyone but without compromising anything. It's an adventure, a challenge, a pleasure, an inspiration all along its winding path. It has a bit of everything.

Although largely unpaved, you can still find perfect tarmac bends near Cerro Castillo, while at other times it is a precariously narrow, severely cambered dirt road, with tight blind bends. The contrast is as extraordinary as the beauty of this region. The whole road is set against a jaw-dropping landscape of jagged mountain peaks, tumbling waterfalls, temperate rainforests, hanging glaciers and bright turquoise lakes. Most of the ride isn't technical and a good road rider should be fine, as long as the eyes don't stray away too long to look at the scenery! Mercifully,

other traffic is virtually non-existent. You may have to compete with unpredictable weather as bright blue skies can give way to low cloud and torrential downpours, even in the best months.

There's just enough infrastructure so you don't have to worry unduly about fuel – Copec, the Chilean fuel giants, ensure the area is sufficiently served. While there is only one town of any size along its length, Coihaique, the small villages have cafés and basic lodgings and there's plenty of opportunity to find rough camping spots. Taking the route around Lago General will take you into Argentina at the Chilecito crossing, setting you up perfectly to join Ruta 40 south.

The Patagonian section of Ruta 40 is a great route from the town of Perito Moreno to the right turn to El Calafate. It cuts through the Patagonian Desert and, towards the southern end, the glimpses of snow-capped Andes peaks and iceberg-laden turquoise lakes are breathtaking. But the challenge of this dirt road, with its high crosswinds, rutted tracks and deep gravel, is quickly becoming the stuff of myth. Linking together isolated *estancias* (ranches) in some of the most remote parts of Argentina, this once proud pioneering track is being upgraded to blacktop. There are a few precious years of challenge left, so get on with it!

Services are few and far between. You can pick up fuel in Baja Carcoles or Tres Lagos and beyond that there will perhaps be some to spare if you get to an *estancia*. Even peak season for Ruta 40 means passing just one or two vehicles a day – it's that type of isolation amid such a vast landscape that gives you a close connection between man and machine. It's only the two of you out there and the bike is your lifeline to warmth and shelter.

So finally you are nearing the end of the journey. Drop in to view the Perito Moreno Glacier, just outside El Calafate, and then head towards Tierra del Fuego. There's a short 20-minute ferry ride from Punta Delgada to Puerto Espora, a final compulsory dirt stretch from Cerro Sombrero to the border with Argentina at San Sebastien,

Carretera Austral in Patagonia.

and then its tarmac all the way to Ushuaia. By this stage, you'll probably be thankful of the easy run in.

When you get to Ushuaia, you'll be greeted by the 'Welcome to the most Southern City in the World' sign, but the real finish is not until you are at Bahia Lapataia, some 18 miles (29km) beyond Ushuaia in Tierra del Fuego National Park. There the sign declares 'Aqui finalisa Ruta 3'. If you make it to this point then you've reached the end of the road and you'll have joined the small number of motorcyclists who have notched up the full length of this legendary journey.

How long do I need?
Some riders take years and never finish; our Guinness World Record™ was 34 days. Less than three months and you've set yourself a reasonably demanding schedule, with not much time off, and some long days of riding ahead of you. Depending on the route you choose, the total distance from top to bottom is the best part of 19,000 miles (30,500km); on a three-month schedule on average that's over 200 miles (320km) a day, every day.

If you want to do the Trans Americas within a six-month sabbatical period, that's nicely achievable. You'll have a relaxed schedule with the ability to take time off the bike. Obviously anything more than that and you can really start to detour from a north to south run.

Which bike to ride?
Other than the top of Alaska and barely a hundred dirt miles in Chile, it's possible to ride from the top to the bottom on asphalt. It can therefore be treated as essentially an 'on-road' trip. Pretty much every type of bike has done the route – Harleys, the Honda C90 and Goldwings, not to mention all genres of small, medium and large dual-purpose bikes.

Your choice is largely dependent on whether you are going to go off the beaten track on to the dirt and gravel roads, largely through the Andes and Patagonia. Your schedule is a big factor too, as it will be a compromise between the miles you need to cover in the time you have available and your comfort. Long distances on a 125cc day after day are not to be undertaken lightly! Another thing to consider is the availability of parts or servicing; it's much easier to get a BMW GS or a Honda sorted in Latin America that it would be a Suzuki or Triumph.

Getting a motorcycle there
If you're starting at the top, you can airfreight your motorcycle out to Anchorage for around £1,450 (subject to fuel charges). This includes crating the bike (one way) through James Cargo (www.jamescargo.com). USA customs are based in the passenger airport terminal and the freight company can supply the necessary paperwork for you to do the temporary import yourself. However, you must have applied for EPA approval of your motorcycle temporary import in advance (see www.epa.gov). Make sure you have your original V5 and your passport as well.

↑ **Snow hampers progress on the border between Argentina and Chile.**

If you're starting at the bottom, most people will come into Buenos Aires; some to Santiago. Flying a bike into either of these destinations can cost upwards of £1,650 (or around £795 by sea). Latin American clearance procedures are considerably more onerous than those in Alaska and you will still have destination handling charges to pay.

What about motorcycle insurance?
While you'll not get a UK company to provide you with even the minimum third party cover for the Americas, it is a compulsory requirement for most countries. Brokers like Motorcycle Express in the USA (www.motorcycleexpress.com) or Alessie (www.alessie.com) can provide cover, albeit at a hefty price. Certain countries such as Nicaragua, Costa Rica and Colombia will only recognise local third party insurance and you will have to buy this as well at the border, or at the nearest border town.

What paperwork do I need?
Your original passport, original motorcycle title/registration document, original driving licence and original international driving permit are necessary. Copies of all these documents will make your life much easier at borders. You do not need a carnet de passage. Always have a travel/medical insurance policy valid for riding a large cc motorcycle.

How safe is it?
In all the time we have travelled through the Americas, petty crime is the only issue we have encountered – street scams that lift a wallet or snatch and grab a camera. In all situations, with a bit more care and attention, the problems could have been avoided. Don't let scaremongering or sensationalised news make you think it is more dangerous than it really is. And don't listen to your friends at home who will commence the 'what if' campaign.

Fuel availability
Access to fuel is generally very good, with the longest

distance between stops on the north to south route being the Dalton Highway in Alaska. Quality of fuel is now much better and, unless you are unlucky, the lowest octane that you have to use is 90 within the Andes in Peru and Bolivia. However, once in Latin America, get into the habit of filling up whenever you can. Strikes are not uncommon, reducing fuel availability and leaving smaller filling stations empty.

Our pick of the best adventure motorcycling roads in the Americas (from north to south!)

- Dalton Highway (Alaska)
- Stewart-Cassiar Highway (Canada)
- Beartooth Highway (USA)
- Highway 128 to Moab (USA)
- Copper Canyon (Mexico)
- Changuinola to Chiriqui Grande (Panama)
- Bogota to Medellin (Colombia)
- Canyon del Pato (Peru)
- La Paz to Coroico (Bolivia) *the most dangerous road in the world*
- Nasca to Cusco (Peru)
- Carretera Austral (Chile)
- Southern Ruta 40 (Argentina)

← **The ferry across the Magellan Straits towards Tierra del Fuego.**

ABOUT THE AUTHORS

The husband and wife team of Kevin and Julia Sanders founded GlobeBusters in 2002. The pair are double Guinness World Record™ holders for the Fastest Circumnavigation of the World by Motorcycle and the Trans Americas by Motorcycle. Coupled with this, Kevin and Julia have notched up hundreds of thousands of miles riding around the world, from Siberia to Colombia, Iran to Australia, Finland to Bolivia and back home to the UK. GlobeBusters was founded as the first overland motorcycle expedition company in the UK, specialising in taking riders on amazing journeys in unusual destinations.

The GlobeBusters Trans Americas Expedition in 2005 was a milestone – it brought together a team of motorcyclists to ride from Alaska to Argentina, taking over 19 weeks and covering more than 22,000 miles. Until GlobeBusters operated the eight month around the world ride 'Discover our Earth' in 2010, the Trans Americas was the longest assisted motorcycle expedition ever undertaken. This expedition was featured globally on the National Geographic Channel, as a six-part TV series *The Ride – Alaska to Patagonia*.

This success, together with a growing portfolio of destinations, has rapidly established GlobeBusters as one of the world's leading operators of supported motorcycle expeditions and attracted partnerships with leading names such as BMW Motorrad (for whom GlobeBusters is a Travel Partner), Cotswold Outdoor, Metzeler, Scottoiler, Metal Mule and Castrol.

GlobeBusters remains at the forefront of the assisted motorcycle overland expedition sector and continues to innovate and create new routes worldwide. No other company can give you the same quality of experience.

All photographs courtesy of Globebusters

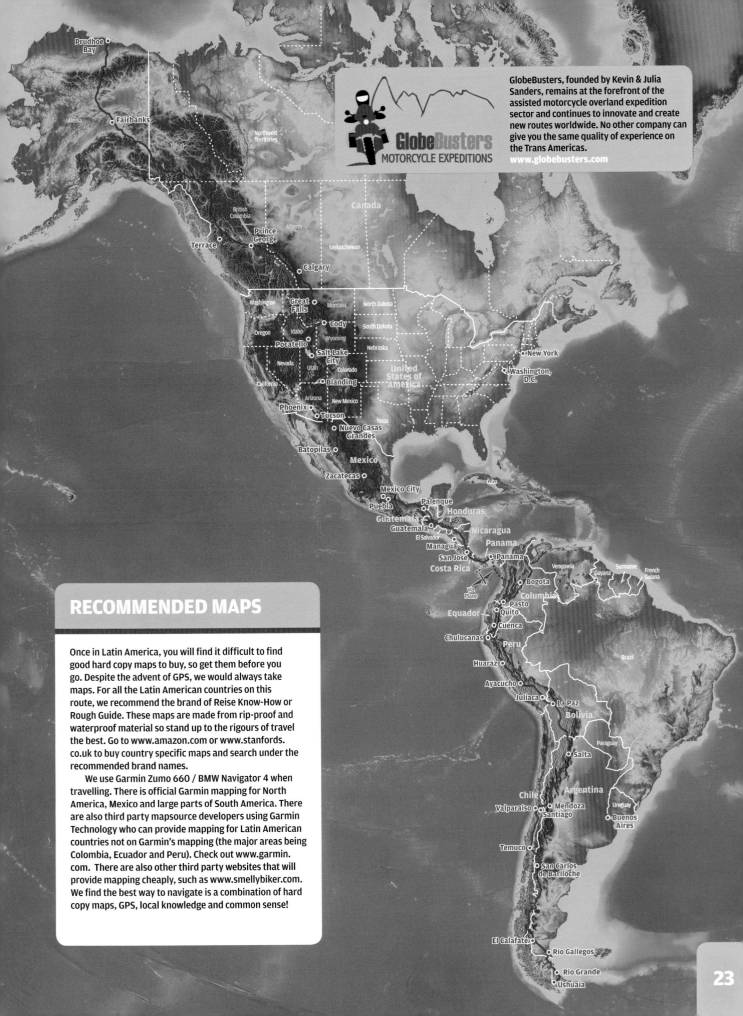

GlobeBusters, founded by Kevin & Julia Sanders, remains at the forefront of the assisted motorcycle overland expedition sector and continues to innovate and create new routes worldwide. No other company can give you the same quality of experience on the Trans Americas. www.globebusters.com

GlobeBusters
MOTORCYCLE EXPEDITIONS

RECOMMENDED MAPS

Once in Latin America, you will find it difficult to find good hard copy maps to buy, so get them before you go. Despite the advent of GPS, we would always take maps. For all the Latin American countries on this route, we recommend the brand of Reise Know-How or Rough Guide. These maps are made from rip-proof and waterproof material so stand up to the rigours of travel the best. Go to www.amazon.com or www.stanfords.co.uk to buy country specific maps and search under the recommended brand names.

We use Garmin Zumo 660 / BMW Navigator 4 when travelling. There is official Garmin mapping for North America, Mexico and large parts of South America. There are also third party mapsource developers using Garmin Technology who can provide mapping for Latin American countries not on Garmin's mapping (the major areas being Colombia, Ecuador and Peru). Check out www.garmin.com. There are also other third party websites that will provide mapping cheaply, such as www.smellybiker.com. We find the best way to navigate is a combination of hard copy maps, GPS, local knowledge and common sense!

Trans Africa

Across the world's second largest continent

Alan Whelan

It has been said by people who have ridden the major overland routes that Africa is the toughest: the climate, scarcity of food, road surfaces, potential for disease, ever-changing political situations and sometimes baffling red tape at borders can all be challenging. If dealing with these matters puts you off, you may not fully appreciate the joys of riding through this extraordinary continent. But if you go with an optimistic nature and an open mind, prepare yourself for the ride of your life. When describing Africa it is easy to fall into the trap of praising or cursing with a broad brush; but every country – and ethnic group – is different and, in my experience, much more varied than the countries of Europe. Some (or many) things on your African trip will not go as planned, so prepare to live on your wits, use your nous and, above all, keep a sense of humour. Enjoy it – when are you going to do this again?

Which route?

With a couple of hiccups, I rode a Triumph Tiger 955i from Lancashire in the UK to Cape Town in South Africa in five months. I travelled solo and did not take a mobile phone or GPS; rather, I took the three (essential) Michelin maps of Africa (if I got lost I asked for directions), a tent (that I never erected), and two metal panniers mostly filled with stuff I never used.

It was cheaper to ride the west coast but there were other obstacles, predominantly the weather (it is wetter on the west side) and the greater number of borders to cross. While many countries on the continent remain politically volatile, there can be no ideal route down to Cape Town so you must assess the situation in each country before travelling. Having said that, a lone European traveller in a remote part of the jungle is unlikely to attract much attention during civil unrest because that is often centred in the towns.

The usual east coast route begins in Egypt, follows the Nile through Sudan, then goes over the stunning mountains of Ethiopia into Kenya from where you can, if you wish, take the tarmac road through Tanzania, Malawi and Mozambique all the way to the Cape. Travelling east to west in Central Africa is extremely difficult due to poor roads and the prolonged civil war in the Democratic Republic of Congo (DRC) and unrest in southwestern Sudan.

My route took me through France to Spain where I took a ferry to Morocco and – more or less – rode the west coast of Africa to Cape Town. My intention was to apply for visas on the road for the country to which I was headed. By and large this was a good strategy because it is difficult to plan exactly the dates when you will enter and exit every country. Also, visas are often cheaper on the road or at the border posts than from the foreign embassies in your home country.

The otherworldly desert

Morocco is a fascinating country – Fez, Marrakesh, Casablanca, the names alone weave a spell over the traveller – the roads are excellent, the food is great and the locals are hospitable. Apart from the ancient cities, stand-out features are the High Atlas mountains, a romantic vista of snow-capped peaks and lush valleys. By the time you reach the south of the country you will be riding through the western edge of the Sahara. This will be your opening challenge. Unfortunately, my first experience of riding on sand wore out the clutch and I was stranded for four days in an encampment while I waited for someone who could repair it. Then it was on to Mauritania, a less developed country – with just as much sand. The road is mesmeric...

In my peripheral vision I am aware of the monochromatic beige of the landscape that does not change for hour after hour. Above, the blue is so oppressive I try not to look up. In front, the strip of black tarmac and the broken white line become as unreal as a video game. The vastness of the landscape forces me back inside my own mind. An occasional camel or black figure is not enough to return me to human-scaled certainty. The muscles in my limbs are so tired and locked in position and the drone of the engine so uniform that my mind plays strange games and I start to believe I can step off the bike whenever I choose. I overlook the fact that I'm actually travelling at 120 kilometres an hour. I am going to sleep.

← **The road to Timbuktu.**

⬇ **Riding in the Atlas mountains.**

Fried clutch in Western Sahara.

If you were to pick a place that represents the cusp between North Africa and black Africa it would be Nouakchott, capital of Mauritania. On the dusty streets you will see a fascinating mix of Arab and Wolof, Muslim and Christian, city and desert people.

After the otherworldliness of the desert, Senegal, the next country south, is thrillingly real. The border crossing at Rosso is every bit as traumatic as its reputation; instead, you may wish to head for Diama nearer the coast. Visit Dakar if you want to hear some terrific live music. Then I headed for Gambia, which is English-speaking, laid back and an ideal place to recharge your batteries after the desert miles.

From here you could continue down the coast through southern Senegal into Guinea-Bissau, Guinea, Sierra Leone and Liberia. These are notoriously unstable countries (especially around election times) so you should check the Foreign Office website for up-to-date information.

From the Gambia coast I rode inland back through Senegal and into Mali, a dry, blistering country that feels as though you are tip-toeing on the surface of the sun.

Riding north, the terrain changes back to semi-desert and the default personality of the people is reserved and courteous. Beyond the town of Kayes I found the dirt road to the capital, Bamako, very tough and I was beaten, both mentally and physically. It was the first time I felt out of my depth.

> *Breathless, I find some shade and park up for a drink, but the water is now so hot I can't even put it to my lips. If I am to continue I must get fresh water. As soon as I realise I am without it, it is my only thought. I consider whether it is still possible to turn back to fill the jerry can in Kayes and continue on later. I have to make a decision soon otherwise it will be too late. But there is also something within me that wants to reach the point of no return so that I am forced to continue. Besides, the idea of going back down this track scares the hell out of me.*

Don't be afraid to ask for help when you need it. You will come to prize every interaction with people along the way, especially if you travel alone. My experience showed me that once people understand the craziness of your quest, they will want to help.

From Bamako, the long road to Timbuktu passes through the flood plain of the Bani River over narrow causeways, temporary lagoons and wide rivers to one of the highlights of the trip – Djenné. Every building in this beautiful town is built from the same material – mud. Djenné is also worth visiting for its main architectural feature, the magnificent mosque, the largest mud structure in the world. There is an organic atmosphere within the narrow alleyways, which makes it a memorably harmonious place. Sand underfoot and the blistering sun complete the biblical scene.

Welcome to Nigeria

Originally I had planned to ride through Niger and Chad to reach Cameroon, but the first two countries were in turmoil so I went south through Burkina Faso and Benin to Nigeria. Even in Africa, Nigeria has a fearsome reputation for crime and fraud, so I arrived at the border post with more than my usual share of adrenalin pumping through me. But I was introduced to another side of this remarkable country. People stood on the side of the track and applauded my arrival in their villages; this went on for many miles. Imagine that happening the first time you ride through Croydon, or Newcastle, or Ealing Broadway! I could not reach a town that night and was shown to a pastor's house by a group of children who said they had never seen a white man before. Nigerians are loud and colourful and, it has to be said, have a different concept of personal space from northern Europeans. But if you accept that people are usually trying to help you, and you can deal with a dozen checkpoints a day, Nigeria will stay with you forever.

Roads up to this point on my trip were often poor

dirt or tired tarmac with potholes within potholes. But there was little to compare to the remote border post into Cameroon at Mfum where there was no road to speak of, just a mud slick. The six-month rainy season had extended into November for the first time anyone could remember. For the only occasion on my trip I asked a local to ride with me on his little bike and I was glad I did. A trip that we estimated would take three hours took us four days. I dropped the bike at least 30 times and even the two of us often could not extract it from the Velcro-like mud. We met someone stranded in a four by four who said he had been stuck for three weeks! Three or four times a day we had to negotiate our way past gangs of teenagers who required a 'dash' for our safe passage. My clutch wore out again and I spent a night in a mud hut with a large family. This is from day three in the mud...

↑ **A fuel stop in Senegal.**

← **The appalling road in Mali from Kayes to Bamako.**

↑ **The beautiful town of Djenné in Mali.**

➜ **Boriya in Nigeria.**

Nothing, sweet Jesus, nothing prepares me for what we encounter halfway to Kumba. We stop our bikes on the edge of a swamp. The road looks as if it has been churned in a giant food mixer and left to set for a month. In between mountainous ruts lies a menacing, viscous goo. People are staring awestruck. There are no discernible dry spots to aim for, and the surrounding jungle is too dense for even the most determined machete-wielding gang to cut a path through.

Serendipity should see you through

By this stage you may be thinking 'This is too much like hard work', but the feeling of overcoming these obstacles with ingenious locals is what will make the trip for you. If you want a completely predictable journey, there's always the regular Sunday ride out to the local tea wagon.

Serendipity plays a large part in an African overland trip, which is another word for not knowing what's coming next. And long may it be the case; unpredictability is one of Africa's many virtues. After four days in the mud, I reached Yaoundé and by chance was invited to sit in with the judges on the Cameroon version of *The X Factor*. I spent some time repairing my bashed-up bike, eating and recuperating, and set off once again.

The next country south is Gabon, which is 95% rainforest – and that means it rains a lot of the time – but 10% of the land is given over to conservation so there are good opportunities to see wildlife in the parks – much of the rest is killed for bush meat. The road in the north of the country is smooth as a desk, built for the huge loggers that roar down to the coast, but in the south of the country the roads are poor and the villages crumbling.

In southern Gabon I had an unscheduled encounter with a herd of goats in the road that smashed up the bike and me too. I spent more than a week in hospital and a month recuperating. This is obviously an unfortunate and rare occurrence, but proves that (a) even in the jungle someone found me and brought me to a bush hospital (where the nursing excelled that of the NHS), and (b) a serious accident need not stop you if you are determined enough.

Five weeks later I returned to the site of the bike crash, repaired the Triumph with make-do parts and the help of a mechanic with just a pair of pliers in his hand, then carried on.

From Gabon I crossed the border into the Republic

After just two hours on the Mamfe Road in Cameroon.

of Congo, one of my favourite countries on the trip for friendliness and hospitality. Congo is very wet, with lots of deep standing water on the tracks. My advice is to take your time and copy the locals. On one memorable day I dropped the bike in four feet of water, then got stranded when I wedged the bash-plate on a rock with water up over my boots, and later broke down (the bike, not me) in the middle of another long stretch of water. I was helped out of every predicament by locals who had come to my aid. I spent that night in a welcome shack with a man who gave up his bed for me.

Traditionally, the route continues to Brazzaville, across the Congo River to Kinshasa in the DRC and on to Matadi where you can apply for the Angolan visa. But when I reached Dolisie in Congo I learned that both the road and the railway tracks were washed away. Consequently, I took a train to Pointe Noire – a memorable diversion – and flew the bike to Namibia.

Arriving in Namibia is a surreal moment for everyone who travels through Africa. After months of living on your wits and experiencing lifestyles you may have thought

unlikely in the twenty-first century, Namibia is orderly, calm and a shock to the system. There are tarred highways, brand names, and everything seems to work. Even though you may be desperate for a hot shower and steak and chips, I guarantee you will miss Central Africa. But there's still much to enjoy: the Etosha National Park in the north of the country, the Skeleton Coast and the Fish River Canyon in the south are all spectacular sights.

South Africa too has terrific game parks and is for the most part westernised, although the townships are no-go areas at night. Your last stretch to Cape Town will be riding on tarmac roads through the Western Cape Province, a beautiful landscape of farms, vineyards and mountains that boost the spirits after so much jungle. The most southerly point of Africa is Cape Aghulas, two hours from the city. Then there's only about 15,500 miles (25,000km) to ride back home.

Extracts from *African Brew Ha-Ha* by Alan Whelan, published by Summersdale.

CAPE TOWN TO CAIRO ROUTE

For anyone with the time and a desire to see the eastern side of the African continent, this is a good route to consider and can, of course, be reversed if you're heading south.

From	To	Miles	Cumulative	Km	Cumulative
SOUTH AFRICA					
Cape Town	Johannesburg	872	872	1,400	1,400
Johannesburg	Pietersburg	201	1,073	322	1,722
Pietersburg	Beitbridge	136	1,209	218	1,940
ZIMBABWE					
Beitbridge	Masvingo	176	1,384	282	2,222
Masvingo	Harare	182	1,566	292	2,514
Harare	Hyamapanda	161	1,728	259	2,773
MOZAMBIQUE					
Nyamapanda	Tete	90	1,817	144	2,917
Tete	Turn off 17km before Zobue	64	1,881	103	3,020
Turn off 17km before Zobue	Dedza	118	1,999	189	3,209
MALAWI					
Dedza	Lilongwe	53	2,052	85	3,294
Lilongwe	Salima	66	2,118	106	3,400
Salima	Nkhata Bay	200	2,318	321	3,721
Nkhata Bay	Mzuzu	30	2,348	48	3,769
Mzuzu	Border crossing near Kyela	161	2,509	259	4,028
TANZANIA					
Border crossing near Kyela	Mbeya	82	2,592	132	4,160
Mbeya	Iringa	245	2,837	394	4,554
Iringa	Morogoro	212	3,049	340	4,894
Morogoro	Chalinze	52	3,101	84	4,978
Chalinze	Korogwe	119	3,220	191	5,169
Korogwe	Moshi (Kilimanjaro)	171	3,391	274	5,443
Moshi (Kilimanjaro)	Arusha	55	3,446	88	5,531
Arusha	Namanga	93	3,539	149	5,680
KENYA					
Namanga	Nairobi	121	3,660	195	5,875
Nairobi	Isiolo	163	3,823	261	6,136
Isiolo	Marsabit	170	3,993	273	6,409
Marsabit	Moyale	156	4,149	250	6,659
ETHIOPIA					
Moyale	Mega	72	4,221	116	6,775
Mega	Awasa	269	4,489	431	7,206
Awasa	Addis Abeba	112	4,601	179	7,385
Addis Abeba	Gonder	271	4,872	435	7,820
Gonder	Metema	138	5,010	222	8,042
SUDAN					
Metema / Gallabat	Gedaref	97	5,107	155	8,197
Gedaref	Wad Medani	141	5,248	227	8,424
Wad Medani	Khartoum	117	5,365	187	8,611
Khartoum	Atbara	194	5,559	312	8,923
Atbara	Abu Hamed	144	5,703	231	9,154
Abu Hamed	Wadi Halfa	230	5,933	369	9,523
EGYPT					
Wadi Halfa	Aswan	Ferry across Lake Nasser			
Aswan	Luxor	133	6,066	214	9,737
Luxor	Asyut	185	6,251	297	10,034
Asyut	El Minya	173	6,424	277	10,311
El Minya	Cairo	153	6,576	245	10,556
Cairo	Alexandria	140	6,717	225	10,781

Note: Cape Town to Cairo route information provided by Robert Wicks.

TOP TIPS FOR A GREAT AFRICAN ADVENTURE

- Travel alone.
- Expect your plans to change on the road. The reality of your expectations, your route, the terrain, and a thousand other considerations will mean you will have to alter your plans. It's called adventure.
- Africa moves at its own pace, and cannot be rushed. There is joy to be found everywhere.
- Don't worry about not finding food, water and petrol. If there are people about you will find all three – although they will rarely be 100% pure.
- Don't make your bike so heavy that you cannot pick it up alone. I guarantee you will ignore this advice and regret it. I did – and I did!
- Don't camp, especially if you travel alone. Stay in cheap hotels (more income for the local economy) and it will give you plenty of opportunities to meet people.
- Don't procrastinate, just do it.

ABOUT THE AUTHOR

Alan Whelan trained as a journalist and now works as a copywriter, PR consultant, ghost writer and travel writer. Brought up in a London Irish household, his overriding ambition as a child was to travel. He moved to New York City aged 20, where he worked on the Lower East Side for five years, and he has been travelling ever since. He now lives in Lancashire with his South African wife, three cats and a Triumph Tiger.

Currency

Like the euro in Europe, many countries use a common currency. The West Africa CEFA franc is used in Benin, Burkina Faso, Cote d'Ivoire, Guinea-Bissau, Mali, Niger, Senegal and Togo. The Central Africa CFA franc covers Cameroon, CAR, Chad, Republic of Congo, Equatorial Guinea and Gabon. Having said that, it is easy to find yourself with either too little or too much local currency in any particular country. As far as western currencies are concerned in West Africa, euros are favoured, then come US dollars and lastly British pounds. I brought a Visa card and found that about half the countries I visited had an ATM in the capital city. The east coast route has less French influence so you will be less dependent on euros and more reliant on US dollars.

Red tape

The first piece of red tape you will deal with is the carnet de passage, a kind of passport for the bike that, while it is not required in every African country, will ease your passage through customs. The carnet in the UK is administered through the Royal Automobile Club; other countries have similar organisations.

There is a small cost for the documentation, but the major financial implication is the bond that must be left with the RAC before you leave, which is levied to ensure

you return with the bike. You will then be repaid most of the money – if you don't get a final customs stamp at a UK point of entry you will not get your money back.

The amount of the bond is set by the countries you visit and is expressed as a percentage of the value of your bike. If the countries you plan to travel through set carnet figures of 100%, 150% and 200%, you only pay the highest figure. At the time I travelled, the bond for Egypt was 800% (a prohibitive £32,000 in my case), which forced me to travel down the west coast.

Visas can be bought on the road, usually in capital cities for the next country. Specialist travel insurance is essential. Many policies will not cover you for countries that are subject to Foreign Office warnings. A serious accident in a blacklisted country could ruin your trip – and even bankrupt you if you have to be repatriated.

Bike choice

Perhaps the major consideration when planning the trip will be which bike to ride. Regardless of personal preference for particular marques, your prime consideration should be the overall weight of the bike and luggage. Go light and you should be all right. I did not seriously consider this factor when I planned my trip and I lived to regret it. I rode a heavy Triumph Tiger to Cape Town, but on a later 4,000km ride through West Africa I rode a 150cc single cylinder machine. Which bike do you think was easier to pick up, skims over gravel roads, handles in the mud and wheels into hotel bedrooms? There are some downsides, of course, notably comfort and speed, but my feeling is that more frequent stops bring you closer to the people you are there to meet, so unless you want to break a record of some kind, take your time.

Communications

I did not take a mobile phone, but coverage is spreading all the time so you may wish to bring one. Also, GPS coverage is much better than it was. I wrote a blog for friends and family to follow my travels – while bandwidth is still slow and can be intermittent, there are lots of internet cafés in sizeable towns.

➔ **The edge of the desert.**

➔➔ **The Kumba Road in Cameroon.**

All photographs courtesy of Alan Whelan

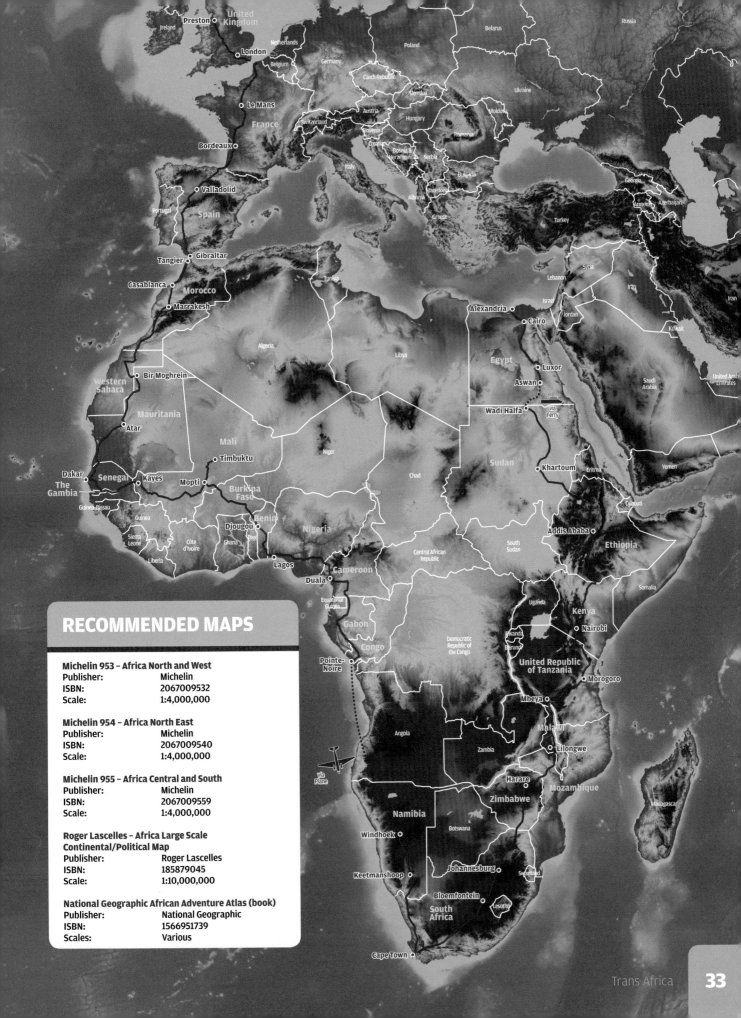

RECOMMENDED MAPS

Michelin 953 – Africa North and West
Publisher: Michelin
ISBN: 2067009532
Scale: 1:4,000,000

Michelin 954 – Africa North East
Publisher: Michelin
ISBN: 2067009540
Scale: 1:4,000,000

Michelin 955 – Africa Central and South
Publisher: Michelin
ISBN: 2067009559
Scale: 1:4,000,000

**Roger Lascelles – Africa Large Scale
Continental/Political Map**
Publisher: Roger Lascelles
ISBN: 185879045
Scale: 1:10,000,000

National Geographic African Adventure Atlas (book)
Publisher: National Geographic
ISBN: 1566951739
Scales: Various

London to Beijing

An Asian adventure on the Silk Road & Tibetan Plateau

Kevin and Julia Sanders

Back in 2008, Kevin was ready for a new challenge and decided he wanted to fulfil a long held ambition of riding his bike across Tibet. The journey would also be the backbone of a new GlobeBusters Expedition, Silk Road & Everest. We both went on our research ride in 2009 and followed it up by leading two team of riders on London to Beijing in 2010 and 2011. It remains the most extreme ride that we have either undertaken, because the challenge of the roads is not even half the battle!

There isn't one road that makes up 'the Silk Road', there's a network of ancient trading routes, so when we planned our first ride across Asia we included some must-see destinations along the way. The Terracotta Army in Xi'an, Shaanxi Province in China was a must. Kashgar and the Central Asian jewels of Samarkand and Bukhara are all major Silk Road centres, so we threw those in for good measure too. But our ride needed to be more than a dot to dot of World Heritage Sites – it is, after all, about the journey!

So the idea was to blast to Istanbul, gateway to Asia and a place where suddenly home feels a long way away. From here, we'd cross Turkey and Georgia to Azerbaijan, hitch a ride over the Caspian Sea and enter Central Asia. At this point, there were a few major routes we wanted to include in our Silk Road journey. The Pamir Highway in Tajikistan (running the Afghan border and claimed as the second highest international highway in the world), the Tibetan Plateau past Mount Kailash, on to Everest Base Camp and the Potala Palace in Lhasa, and finally the descent of the Tibet-Sichuan Highway to Chengdu.

'Stay away from the Black Sea,' my Turkish pal, Kazim,

↑ **Cappadocia, Turkey.**

had warned. With his advice we headed east on single track roads, through tiny Ottoman villages and beyond them to the faint snow-capped peaks. Route 260 from Kangal to Erzincan and the road to Ispir and Yusufeli are both excellent routes, with a World Heritage Site at Divrigi, a small river crossing after Ispir, gorges, single track roads and ruined castles.

From Turkey there are two choices of route to get you to Turkmenistan. Either you enter Iran, ride to Tabriz and run the Caspian Coast or you travel through Georgia and Azerbaijan with a ferry across the Caspian Sea to the port

← ← **Xinjiang Province, China.**

← **Yusufeli, Turkey.**

→ **Turkmenistan – riding here means travelling with an approved guide.**

of Turkmenbashi. The latter carries the advantage of not requiring a carnet de passage at a 500% duty rate that is stipulated by Iran. The former avoids an unpredictable sailing across the Caspian.

In 2003, we rode in and out of the tiny country of Georgia within a couple of days. It's a place where ancient churches litter the countryside and 800 years of decline have left nothing but crumbled structures, shadows of their former glory. The roads are no different, with potholes that surely rank among some of the best (biggest) in the world. You need to be up on the pegs because unless you're crawling along at ten miles an hour you'll be slamming through plenty. Tbilisi brought a chaotic, free-for-all on the roads and a presidential coup. It wasn't the first uprising during our global riding travels and it certainly won't be the last.

'AZERBAIJAN BORDER 500m – GOOD LUCK.' We hoped that this Georgian road sign meant GOODBYE, but peering down a narrow border bridge to an AK47-wielding guard, protecting a metal barrier into Azerbaijan, left us wondering. The border was dull, with a begrudging indifference to travellers. In the customs office we were asked if we would like a cup of tea, as three officials smoked. It cost us five bucks and we left with bike permits that only allowed us 72 hours' transit time in Azerbaijan. Just 72 hours on a temporary bike permit is absolutely standard practice, allowing no time to explore the country, just a mad dash to the capital of Baku, the port that serves the Caspian Sea.

↓ **Georgia has suffered years of decline, leaving a crumbling infrastructure.**

Once there, it was another race to get on board a ferry as soon as possible so that customs could stamp out the bike within the ungenerous time limit. We use the term 'ferry' loosely, however – it was a rusting hulk, devoid of passengers. It is down to riders to secure their bikes below, so you will need to have straps with you. Ensure you also have with you enough food and water

for 48 hours (the journey is only around 16 hours but it is common to be stuck at sea for ages waiting to dock), sleeping bags and anything to make the journey seem more pleasurable – books, music, alcohol…

Turkmenistan is a police state. It's a paranoid country that forces all foreigners to travel with an approved guide and you will need to arrange this in advance. Unless you like dodging camels, the riding is uneventful and across a lot of desert. The country boasts the 'Mouth of Hell' – a massive flaming crater, the result of a Russian gas drilling explosion. A night-time visit is a refreshing take on health and safety. With no barriers around the 328ft (100m) drop into the inferno, we asked our guide how many tourists had fallen in. She laughed and said: 'It is forbidden to speak of these things.'

Like Turkmenistan, Uzbekistan does not offer the most

exciting of riding, but it is the stomping ground of Genghis Khan, Alexander the Great and the land of the ancient Silk Road cities. Thousands of years of civilisation rest in Khiva, Bukhara and Samarkand. Between the cities are vast desert expanses dotted with occasional teahouses. No matter where we stopped, pots of green tea and fresh

warm bread were delivered to the table and the smell of grilled meats and freshly cut coriander wafted around.

It would be easy to dismiss these two countries as unadventurous based on the riding alone, but this would be short sighted. Riding in this part of the world is a real challenge: try navigating around when what few signs exist are meaningless to English speakers, when GPS has no mapping, where no one understands English, where the largest monetary note that exists is worth 50p, where fuel shortages and electricity cuts are rife, where you run the gauntlet of police checkpoints every day, where in the summer months temperatures can reach over 40°C (104°F). The riding may be on largely straight roads, but travelling is anything but straightforward. And the further east you go the more challenging these issues become. A few local words, a practised point and smile technique, a picture of your family, the offer of a cigarette and a firm handshake with police (take the time to remove your gloves and show your face) ease the way. That said, all these challenges melt away to mere niggles when the riding goes from average to awesome. Welcome to

↙↑ Uzbekistan still shows evidence of Soviet control.

↑ **Tajikistan –
home to some of
the best riding in
the world.**

Tajikistan – adventure motorcycling nirvana awaits.

Tajikistan is home to the Pamir Highway, one of the highest altitude roads in the world and the remote Wakhan Valley running the border with Afghanistan. If BMW made roads, this is what they would have carved out for the GS. Even without obstacles, this dirt road is a remote, breathtaking single track winding past tiny villages and over high passes. Add to this the river crossings, landslides, minefields, heavy snow and with Afghanistan sometimes a mere 65ft (20m) to your right, this road is what adventure biking is all about.

We always stop for a while in Dushanbe, the capital city, to stock up and check over the bikes before continuing on to the Pamir Highway. At this point the bikes have clocked up just over 6,000 miles (9,660km) and this is the halfway point. Given what is to come, you don't want to leave Dushanbe without ensuring the bikes have some major attention, including new knobbly tyres, and that you get extra supplies. Dushanbe also happens to be the last point for any 'easy' communication home for a while.

When plotting a route from Dushanbe, don't be

fooled by the maps. The M41, a thick red line, is not what it appears and there does not seem to be an alternative. The M41 is not a motorway. You need to check the best route to Kalaikhum before you leave. In 2009 the M41 was still closed due to snow, so we took the route via Kulyab. In 2010 the road via Kulyab had collapsed and we were forced on to the M41. There is no easy route to Kalaikhum – either way will turn into a goat track or a muddy quagmire, with the road climbing to altitude and clinging to the side of a cliff face, and you'll not avoid a river crossing either.

Landslides are almost as common as river crossings. On our second day on the Pamir, two separate slides had blocked the road. One was impassable until an ancient grader had done five hours' worth of pushing and scraping. Then within hours a massive truck blocked the route, grounded on another landslide it couldn't get over. You can see very quickly how hard it is to predict travel in the Pamir Mountains.

Khorog is the main town of the region, offering a range of accommodation from staying with local families to the

exclusive Serena Inn. Stock up again in Khorog. From here, there are two choices: to stay on the M41 or divert to the Wakhan Valley. We decided on the latter. The Wakhan is a must – the rough dirt road running the valley is only separated from Afghanistan by a small river, and on a clear day you can see straight across Afghanistan to the towering snow-laden peaks of the Hindu Kush, marking the border with Pakistan.

The valley is part of the ancient Silk Road, which was travelled by Marco Polo, and it is littered with mighty crumbling fortresses. At this point on the journey we were as remote as it gets and, but for the motorcycles, modern life was a distant memory. Take the five-mile (8km) side trip up to the thirteenth-century Yamchun Fort – the steep gravel switchbacks and narrow tracks are a challenge but worth it for the breathtaking panorama. Along this road many small villages house families that will offer you accommodation for the night. Take up the offer – it's an amazing insight into the local culture and much warmer than trying to camp.

After rejoining the M41, it's tarmac all the way to Murgab until you reach the border and the Kyzyl-Art Pass. On our first ride this way, the Kyzyl-Art Pass was deep in snow, with only slushy ruts providing guidance for the bikes. At over 13,100ft (3,992m), this is the type of physical activity you want to avoid. Wheels spun vigorously, feet paddled furiously over the ruts and we fought for breath. It took us all day to get to the Kyrgyzstan border, arriving just before another snowstorm blew in. We were exhilarated and exhausted at the same time. We were attempting this crossing in the first week in May and it was just too early.

We were once lucky enough to spend a week riding in Kyrgyzstan before taking the Torugart Pass into China. Kyrgyzstan feels very different from its counterparts. Lacking military checkpoints and over-zealous police, it made for fluid riding through beautiful mountain scenery.

But when I arrived there in 2010 it was a very different story. Civil unrest had turned violent in the south and our planned route ran straight through the areas where locals with AK47s were running around randomly shooting at people. The political instability of this region is another factor in its adventure appeal, but we only spent one night in Kyrgyzstan and avoided the volatile area by diverting directly over the Irkeshtam Pass into China.

Both the Torugart and the Irkeshtam Passes lie at high altitude. They are tough, unpaved and remote, with their difficulty dictated by the unpredictability of the weather. For the Irkeshtam, in 2010, that meant blizzard conditions, thick fog and an unidentifiable road. A late winter

⬆ **Approaching the Tajikistan/ Kyrgyzstan border**

⬅ **There's no avoiding river crossings in Tajikistan.**

THE BEST TIME TO TRAVEL

If you are going over the high mountain passes and travelling at high altitude you need to be doing this between June and August; any earlier and the weather becomes very unpredictable. During the mid-year window the Kyzyl-Art Pass between Tajikistan and Kyrgyzstan and into China from Kyrgyzstan over the Irkeshtam or the Torugart Pass into China can still be snowbound. However, leave the journey too late and the temperatures going into Xi'an, which is in a low-lying area, will be over 35ºC (95ºF) with almost 100% humidity.

presented the biggest motorcycle challenge we had ever faced. Among our team, there were 40 bike drops over a distance of 40 miles (64km) and it took us more than seven hours to cross the pass. These passes present as big a physical barrier to entering China as the country's long and protracted bureaucratic processes.

If you do get to the border with China (and many independent travellers do), just popping into the country with your bike is not going to happen without some exceptional luck. Many have tried, and you can find one or two people saying that they got through – often entering to ride the Karakoram Highway and out to Pakistan – but in all likelihood you will be turned back. So if you are intent on going, make sure you have your arrangements sorted out in advance using one of the specialist agencies.

Getting to ride in Tibet is another layer of complication and bureaucracy – again best sorted out for you by an agency. Even before you get close to the provincial border, there are large military checkpoints guarded by officials wielding guns. Without the right documents, you're simply sent back.

In Western Tibet you are way off the tourist trail – and

riding here is not for the ill-prepared biker. The roads are almost always dirt, gravel, sand, mud or still under construction. The altitude and freezing temperatures compound the difficulty. The air is dry, which irritates the lungs, and this can lead to a hacking and debilitating high altitude cough. Dehydration is a common problem, while getting a good night's sleep is almost impossible. There are no evening comforts, either – no hot showers, no comfy beds and no familiar food.

We have tended to find that these conditions hamper riders more than their bikes. The big BMW GS bikes take it all in their stride, never bothered by some of the most extreme riding conditions we have faced. Wipe off three inches of snow in freezing temperatures and they still start first time. Throw them down the road and they still start first time. Pound them through potholes, force them across rivers, take them to over 17,388ft (5,299m), fill them with the lowest quality fuel you can find – throughout all our rides to Beijing none of them falter.

But for all the challenges that Tibet throws at you, the rewards truly exceed expectations. Take the road to Everest. It snakes below the Himalayan ranges, with countless switchbacks and cliff tunnels, to a green and fertile valley, before it climbs back up to 17,060ft (5,200m). Guidebooks will often say: 'The view of Everest is best from the Tibetan side.' It seems too understated to describe Everest as a 'view', particularly when the challenge of riding towards it totals thousands of very unpredictable miles. Everest is iconic – a momentous milestone, breathtaking, awe-inspiring, humbling and hugely emotional. When our team arrived for the first time, we were on top of the world.

It would be a big mistake, though, to reach Lhasa and think you've cracked Tibet. A bit like reaching the summit of Everest – at the summit you're only halfway there because the most dangerous part is getting down.

→ **Breathtaking scenery in Kyrgyzstan.**

In this instance, getting down means the Tibet-Sichuan Highway (known as the G318), except that it's not so much getting down as still riding narrow dirt roads and traversing numerous high passes before a final descent from Kangding. In the 260 miles (418km) from Zuogong to Litang alone, there are five enormous passes, ranging between altitudes of 12,880ft (3,926m) and 16,699ft (5,090m). It's no wonder that this stretch of road is reckoned as one of the most dangerous on the planet.

The wonder of riding one of the most remote regions in the world sizzles away on reaching Eastern China. People are everywhere and temperatures push 40°C (104°F). A small unknown name on the map turns out to be a city of five million people. With this comes chaos through every city, town and village. This is intense 'combat motorcycling'. Along with the people comes industrialisation and pollution. Coal-powered electricity stations dot the landscape and visibility is hampered by thick yellow fumes.

After the remoteness of the Tibetan Plateau, it can take a while to get your head attuned to these riding challenges, especially when faced with the random, chaotic and suicidal actions of other road users. Unlike people in other developing countries, the Chinese have not even adopted a road strategy based on the primeval instinct of staying alive. Cyclists, mopeds, cars, trucks, three-wheelers, donkeys and carts do whatever they want, in any place, at any time, at whatever speed they can, in any lane, hard shoulder or pavement, and irrespective of both direction and others around them. The initial instinct is pure, unadulterated road rage when yet another nutcase speeds out of a minor road without stopping, heading straight into your path. Despite the fact that speed limits are sporadically signalled on the road, you soon realise that they don't need them. The whole environment is so 'hit and miss' (literally), that your own self-preservation slows you to a speed that would earn you a good citizen award at home.

In the final weeks, Eastern China can deliver the Tiger Leaping Gorge, giant pandas, the Terracotta Army and Beijing with the Forbidden City, the Bird's Nest Olympic Stadium and the Great Wall. But it all comes at a price.

↑ **Glimpsing Everest, Tibet.**

↑ The Rongbuk
Monastery lies
5,100m up in the
mountains of
Tibet.

→ Potala Palace
in Lhasa, Tibet.

The onslaught on the roads is relentless and riding becomes a battle of a very different kind.

The Silk Road is the essence of motorcycle adventure travel. It takes you out of your comfort zone completely – to regions where English is not spoken, where western-style food is rarely available, where the writing is completely unintelligible, where you cannot afford to be ill or injured, where freedom of movement is restricted and political stability can be a smokescreen, where credit cards don't work and you can't flick open your mobile and expect it to work. Where even what we consider to be the fundamentals – clean drinking water, hot water for showers, nutritious and filling food – are not guaranteed. And all this without even riding your bike! Getting fuel is never certain and being able to sort your bike out for yourself if it goes wrong is essential. It's an unpredictable road journey – extremes abound, whether it's the late winters and snowbound passes or natural disasters such as landslides and earthquakes. This is motorcycle adventure travel at its best. What more could you ask for?

How long do I need?
The route can be completed in three months – any less and it becomes a real struggle, with no time off the bike to sightsee and do other activities. You can always take considerably longer, although your main constraint will probably be time on your tourist visas for the Central Asian countries.

Which bike to ride?
This particular ride is a fair few notches up the extreme adventure ladder, so kitting out your bike correctly for the journey is key. Kevin used the BMW R1200GS Adventure with aluminium panniers, fuel injector protector, steering stop, headlight protector, extra HID lights and a louder horn (the final two being a safety measure to be

seen and heard in chaotic Asian traffic). The bike was also upgraded to a Hawker Odyssey battery. Engine protection bars, hand guards, bash plate and cylinder head protection come as standard.

Servicing and maintenance
Ensure your bike is fully serviced and fitted with new tyres before you start the journey. Kevin ran with Metzeler Tourance road tyres all the way to Dushanbe (Tajikistan) and then switched to Continental TKC80s for the remainder of the journey. He also carried a minor service kit and changed oils and filters at the same time as the tyres. There were no mechanical issues with any of the bikes on this journey and there was only one puncture.

↑ **City traffic in China.**

← **Enjoying the Fo Ping Mountain Road, China.**

Getting a motorcycle there

There are no obvious points to where a motorcycle can be freighted along this route. These countries are not major international air-freight hubs and as such any air freight tends to be prohibitively expensive. One option is to ship into Bishkek in Kyrgyzstan, but it is not cheap and the process of releasing the bike at the airport required a local fixer. This is really a ride it from start to end journey.

Paperwork

Your original passport, original motorcycle title/registration document, original driving licence and original international driving permit are necessary. Copies of all these documents will make your life much easier at borders. You do not need a carnet de passage unless you are going to go through Iran. To ride legally in China, you will need to have a temporary Chinese driving licence and your motorcycle will need to have a temporary Chinese registration. In addition to this, you will need to have an approved Chinese guide and your route must have been pre-authorised in advance by all the relevant authorities. Your guide will then make sure you stick (more or less) to the authorised route. The only way to do this is to go through a specialist Chinese agency – Google 'self drive motorcycle china' to get a list of them.

Visas

For a UK citizen, you currently need visas for Azerbaijan, Iran, Turkmenistan, Uzbekistan, Tajikistan, Kazakhstan, Kyrgyzstan and China. As of 2010, Azerbaijan, Iran and Turkmenistan all require 'Letters of Invitation' from a tour agency or hotel to accompany a visa application; the other countries named do not need this requirement. All these countries have an embassy in London and you can visit the various embassy websites for the most up-to-date requirements. For a three-month journey, you can get all your visas before you leave and this is highly recommended. However, time limits for applications mean that often, for long journeys, you will be forced to get visas en route.

For Tajikistan, when you apply for your tourist visa from the embassy, remember also to request a GBAO (Autonomous Gorno-Badakshan Region) permit to allow you travel on the Pamir Highway. It costs an extra £50 and is stamped next to the visa. Without this, you will be turned back.

For further advice on visas, use a specialist visa agency.

Motorcycle insurance

A UK insurer will be able to give you the necessary EU cover and most should be able to provide a Green Card

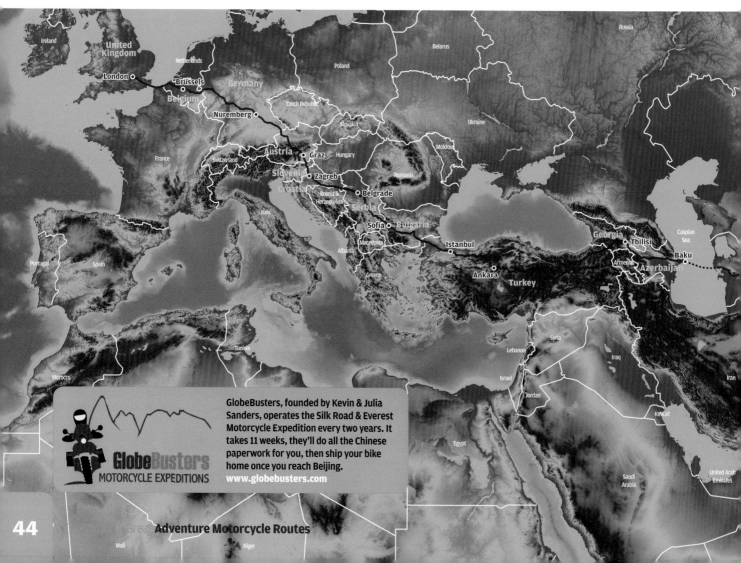

GlobeBusters, founded by Kevin & Julia Sanders, operates the Silk Road & Everest Motorcycle Expedition every two years. It takes 11 weeks, they'll do all the Chinese paperwork for you, then ship your bike home once you reach Beijing.
www.globebusters.com

Adventure Motorcycle Routes

as proof of insurance in Turkey and Iran. After that you are on your own. In Central Asia it is hard even to find out what the legal requirements are. Azerbaijan and Turkmenistan will make you buy third party cover at the border. The upshot is that in most of Central Asia, you are self-insuring. In China, the agency that does your paperwork will normally include third party cover as part of the package.

Fuel availability

Access to fuel is generally good up to Dushanbe (Tajikistan), although from time to time fuel pumps may not work due to electricity shortages. On the Pamir Highway you will need to buy fuel from locals and out of barrels. This is also true for the western part of the Tibetan Plateau. You need to check any fuel you buy to ensure it does not look contaminated, and maybe strain the fuel if it looks suspect.

Communications

Internet access is not easy once in Central Asia, Xinjiang Province and Tibet (other than Kashgar and Lhasa). Mobile phone signals in China were excellent, even in the remote regions of Xinjiang and Tibet. If you want to keep in touch with home regularly, consider taking a SPOT

device. For the remote parts of the trips, where mobile phones won't get a signal, pressing the SPOT device each night will send a reassuring message back home to friends and family that all is well. The SPOT device also offers a Search and Rescue Package. See www.findmespot.com for more details.

RECOMMENDED MAPS

We will always take hard copy maps when travelling and buy them before leaving the UK. Within the Reise Know How range (distributed by www.stanfords.co.uk), you can get maps for Turkey, Central Asia, Kazakhstan, China West, Tibet and China East.

There are also increasing amounts of GPS mapping for many countries. We use a Garmin Zumo 660 or BMW Navigator 4. Official Garmin products are available for Turkey and China, but not much else. However, there are other suppliers of digital mapping, which are free or at a nominal fee (but are unofficial and not supported by Garmin), such as OpenStreetMap or SmellyBiker. Horizons Unlimited (www.horizonsunlimited.com) also provides information such as GPS waypoints on certain Asian routes thanks to independent travellers sharing their information.

📷 All photographs courtesy of Globebusters

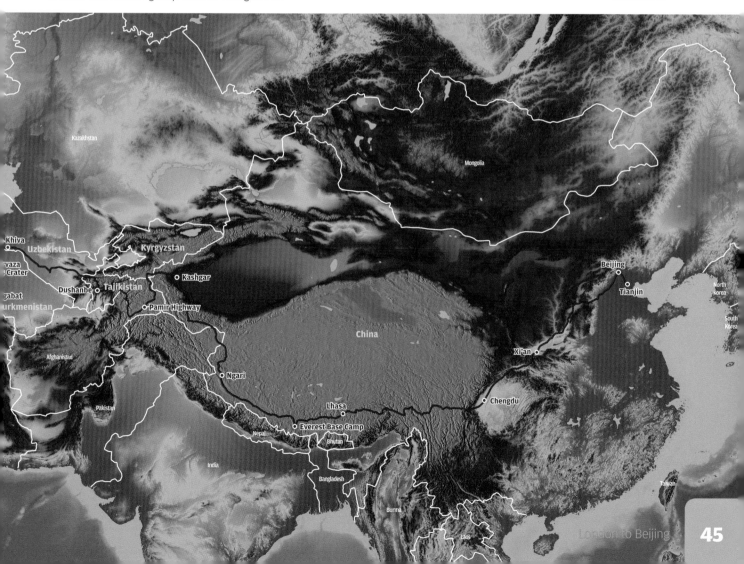

A group of 53 countries make Africa the planet's second largest continent and the second most populous, with just over a billion people. Riding in or across Africa is the epitome of adventure motorcycling. Ongoing political instability in different parts of the continent means things are constantly changing – borders open and close without warning and tensions move to new areas overnight.

The most notable geographical features include the world's longest river system – the Nile. Running north from its source in the highlands of southeastern Africa, it flows for 4,160 miles (6,693km) ultimately to drain into the Mediterranean. Any riders attempting an eastern transcontinental run will find the Nile to be an integral part of their journey. On the same side of the continent lies the Great Rift Valley, a dramatic depression in the earth's surface approximately 4,000 miles (6,400km) in length. It extends from the Red Sea area near Jordan all the way south to Mozambique. It's a series of geological faults caused by huge volcanic eruptions that subsequently created what we know today as the Ethiopian Highlands, with a series of perpendicular cliffs, mountain ridges, rugged valleys and very deep lakes along its entire length. Many of Africa's highest mountains front the Rift Valley, including Mount Kilimanjaro and Mount Kenya.

Africa also plays host to the world's largest desert. At 3,500,000 square miles (9,065,000km2) the Sahara covers almost one-third of the continent. At about a quarter of its size, but no less forgiving, is the Kalahari Desert covering much of Botswana, the southwestern region of South Africa and all of western Namibia. Desert riding needs a light bike, excellent navigation skills and, ideally, some previous experience.

For those in search of jungle adventure, the Congo River Basin in central Africa dominates the landscape of the Democratic Republic of the Congo, neighbouring Congo, Angola, Cameroon, the Central African Republic and Zambia. This fertile basin contains almost 20% of the world's rainforest.

Closer to Europe, the Atlas Mountains run from southwestern Morocco along the Mediterranean coastline to the eastern edge of Tunisia and provide excellent and highly accessible riding from Europe. ■

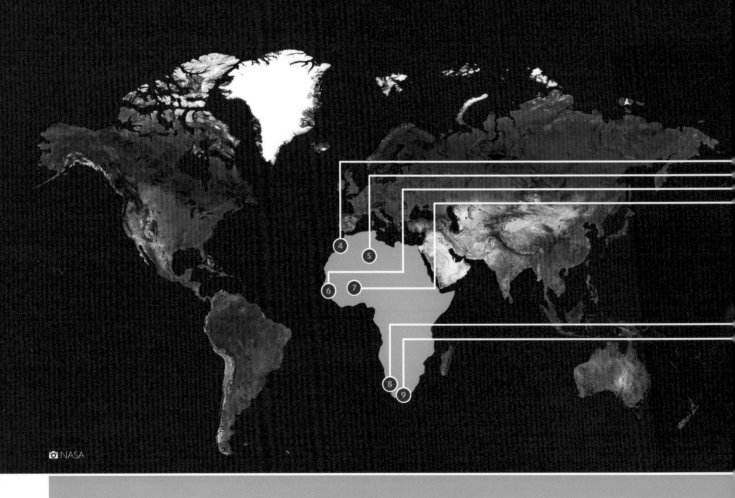

NASA

Morocco
Adventures in the Maghreb

Robert Wicks

Morocco is undoubtedly one of the most popular adventure riding destinations, given its close proximity for mainland Europeans, and no carnet is required. It's relatively inexpensive and the country offers some phenomenal routes, sights and cities that are best explored by motorcycle. Morocco is also a good gateway for expeditions headed down the west coast of Africa and further inland to places like Timbuktu.

Situated on the extreme northwestern corner of Africa, Morocco is bordered by Mauritania to the south and Algeria to the east. The country's varied geography includes no fewer than four separate mountain ranges, in addition to lush river valleys, beautiful sandy coasts and wide expanses of desert. Immediately south lies the disputed region of Western Sahara – one of the most sparsely populated territories in the world. The three most prominent mountain ranges, which run parallel to each other from the southwest to the northeast, are the Middle Atlas, the High Atlas and the Anti-Atlas, and together make for some excellent and varied adventure riding. In the southeast, Morocco's mountain ranges yield to the desolate expanse of the Sahara. Long winding rivers carve their way through deep granite gorges while a series of watercourses, terraced fields and almond groves lie scattered around tiny Berber villages constructed almost entirely of local stone and timber.

A ferry from Algeciras in southern Spain to the enclave of Ceuta (Sebta) is the best way to cross from Europe to Africa. Border formalities are simple and once across the Straits of Gibraltar the adventure really begins. Areas in the north of the country tend to be more expensive than the south and this works in your favour as the best adventure riding lies to the south, so my view is not to lose too much time in the north. There are essentially two ways to head south, with your immediate goal being Marrakesh and then over the Atlas Mountains to Ouarzazate, a town which lies on the south side of the range and is described by locals as the 'door to the desert'.

The coastal route is faster and more direct whereas the longer inland route takes you through Fez and provides a more enjoyable introduction to the country. As you head south there are isolated pockets of an age-old culture that has seen little change over the centuries.

ROUTE OPTIONS

OPTION 1 – COASTAL ROUTE

From	To	Route	Miles	Km
Ceuta (Sebta)	Tetouan	N13	24	38
Tetouan	Tanger	N2	33	53
Tanger	Larache	N1	51	82
Larache	Rabat	N1	85	137
Rabat	Casablanca	N1	63	101
Casablanca	Marrakesh	N9	149	240
Marrakesh	Ouarzazate	N9	127	204
TOTAL			530	855

OPTION 2 – INLAND ROUTE

From	To	Route	Miles	Km
Ceuta (Sebta)	Tetouan	N13	24	38
Tetouan	Ketama	N13 / N2	103	165
Ketama	Fez	N8	95	154
Fez	Azrou	N8	51	83
Azrou	Khenifra	N8	51	82
Khenifra	Kasba Tadla	N8	68	109
Kasba Tadla	Beni-Mellal	N8	24	38
Beni-Mellal	Marrakesh	N8	120	194
Marrakesh	Ouarzazate	N9	127	204
TOTAL			661	1,067

← **Morocco is a visual feast and a photographer's paradise.**

← **Heading over the Atlas Mountains to Ouarzazate.**

⬆ **No sir, that is not the Grand Canyon.**

As you approach Ouarzazate you'll begin to notice many prominent Kasbahs which make for a great welcome and photo opportunity. The town is a starting point for excursions across the Draa Valley. Ouarzazate is also a renowned film-making location. The likes of *Lawrence of Arabia* (1962), *The Living Daylights* (1987), *The Last Temptation of Christ* (1988), *The Mummy* (1999), *Gladiator* (2000), *Kingdom of Heaven* (2005) and Martin Scorsese's *Kundun* (1997) and *Legionnaire* (1998) were shot in the area and it's still possible to see the sets of some of the movies that lie abandoned in the desert.

Use Ouarzazate as a base for a couple of days to gather supplies, prepare your bike and gain some valuable off-road riding practice, because the entire journey will have been on sealed routes up until now. The 'Bikershome', run by Peter and Zineb is a wonderful retreat for any exhausted rider. The following route is based on a large loop, taking in some of the best off-road adventure riding the south has to offer, as well as a number of sights that will make this a most memorable ride.

Retrace your steps, heading northwest out of

Ouarzazate. Stop at the fortified village of Ait Benhaddou – a UNESCO World Heritage Site – before heading south on the N10 towards Taznakht. Route markers are not always the easiest to spot so take care before making a turn. This is a short 40-mile (65km) run and should take no more than an hour. Head 53 miles (85km) west to the small town of Taliouine. Turn southwest out of the town and ride off road for 53 miles (85km) to Igherm in the Anti-Atlas Mountains. You can refuel here and there is a reasonable campsite.

From here you need to aim for Tata, and you can follow the main road south and then east, or head across country along the valley of the Oued Tata. This is a splendid ride and the descent towards Tata is spectacular. Take a break at Souk Tleta de Tagmoute which lies about halfway to Tata.

From Tata head west to Foum Zguid, a run of about 94 miles (152km). On this stretch of the route you are less than 30 miles (48km) from the border with Algeria. There's not much to see or do in Foum Zguid, but replenish your fuel and water.

Continue west on the off-road track towards the bustling town of Zagora. This is a great ride as you track the famous ridge known as the Jebel Bani. Several roads are being improved in Morocco while a number of previously marked 'tracks' are being prepared for asphalting; this is one of them. It's easy to want to ride quickly and make progress on what looks like a well-prepared surface, but adjust your tyre pressures accordingly and be conscious that the stones are sharp – as I learnt to my peril with a big blow-out in the rear tyre that took three plugs and a large helping of cement to fix. Ask for Mohamed 'Gordito's' repair shop in Zagora for any bike-related ailments. The owner is always thrilled to see bikers coming by and is extremely helpful. His workshop is adorned with stickers and memorabilia from every desert rally in the last ten years, testimony to his skill. Very fine dust from the desert seems to get into everything so use every opportunity to clean your filters and give the bike a good going-over before heading off again.

If you have the time, consider a one-day 90-mile (145km) excursion on your bike to Mhamid, which lies due south of Zagora. It's a scenic ride and is literally the 'end of the road'. There are excellent dunes surrounding Mhamid so leave your panniers and non-essential gear in Zagora and have fun in the sand.

To the north of Zagora lies the Drâa Valley, one of the highlights of the route. This ribbon of palmeraies, rural settlements and fortified red kasbahs runs from Ouarzazate in the west to Zagora in the east. The longest river in Morocco, the Drâa, originates in the High Atlas before reaching the Atlantic north of Tan Tan, although it often dries up and rarely manages to make it all the way to the coast. Main attractions include the majestic Ksar of Tamnougalt and Timidert Kasbah.

Midway along the valley, take a right turn at Tansikht

(GPS: N30 41 03.37 W 6 10 55.42) and follow the track east for 24 miles (38km) to Nekob. Contine west, passing through Mellal and Tazzarine, before heading north to Alnif where you can refuel. The road surface improves from here for the 42-mile (67km) run to Rissani. Along parts of the route the country seems almost forgotten in time, with primitive habits and cultures, vast amounts of subsistence farming – and some spectacular scenery.

Aim for the bustling market town of Erfoud which lies at the south of the Ziz Valley before making a run to Errachidia in the north. Although water flow is intermittent

↑ **Don't look down!**

↓ **Big adventure bikes like the BMW 1200GS Adventure and KTM 990 Adventure are well suited for Morocco.**

→ **Even camels stop to take in the view.**

→→ **Riding partner Greg Baker thinks he's getting an offer on the KTM.**

↓ **Some good technical riding skills were needed to negotiate this part of the track near Tailouine.**

along the Ziz riverbed, its watercourse has long been used to facilitate human transit through this mountainous region. Errachidia is one of the most famous and ancient Moroccan cities, known for its friendly people and cultural sights.

The final leg of the journey is a 188-mile (303km) run southeast to Ouarzazate. Along this stretch lie some unforgettable sights – the famous Todra and Dades Gorges as well as Lake Isli and Lake Tislit, high up in the

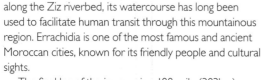

Atlas Mountains. The lakes are best accessed by turning right at Tinerhir and heading through the Todra Gorge. Cleft by the Todra River, the cliffs of the Todra Gorge rise to 1,000ft (300m), and at its narrowest point it is barely 30ft (9m) wide. The lakes lie about 80 miles (130km) north of Tinerhir and the ride through the gorge is simply unforgettable, while a night or two beside the lakes will live long in the memory.

Retrace your steps from the lakes as far as Agoudal before bearing right to head back to the N10 route, but in order to do that you must ride through the Dades Gorge. This is a challenging mountain pass that is very narrow in places. Keep to the right-hand side of the track to avoid plummeting off the sheer drop on the left-hand side, and watch out for rocky outcrops that act like magnets for your panniers. Exit the Dades Gorge at Boumalne Dades and follow the N10 past wonderful kasbahs to your starting point of Ouarzazate.

Climate

The climate in Morocco is reliably dry, although the temperature varies considerably by season and area. While the southern and southeastern desert regions can reach extremely high temperatures during the hot summer months, the higher altitudes of the mountains are cool during summer evenings and freezing in winter.

Did you know?

- At 172,400 square miles (446,550km2), Morocco is just slightly larger than the US state of California.
- Morocco gained independence from France in 1956.
- The full Arabic name of Morocco is 'Al-Mamlaka al-Maghribiya', which translates as 'The Western Kingdom'.
- The official language of Morocco is Arabic; the Berber dialect and French are also spoken widely.
- A number of stone circles in Morocco serve as proof of its contact with the megalithic cultures of Atlantic Europe.
- The University in Fez, founded in AD 859, claims to be the oldest university in the world.
- Morocco is the 12th richest country in Africa.

📷 All photographs courtesy of Robert Wicks

ABOUT THE AUTHOR

Robert Wicks was born in South Africa and is the author of four books in the Haynes *Adventure Motorcycling* series. He is a brand ambassador for BMW and a regular speaker at adventure meetings.

Following a successful period in the media industry, his passion for travel and motorcycles saw him join the Superbike World Championship as head of marketing. He has also worked for Suzuki's factory race teams in MotoGP and British Superbikes. In 2009 he was appointed Chief Operating Officer of the Powerboat P1 World Championship in London.

He has travelled extensively to more than 50 countries, including Mozambique, Iceland, Peru and Japan. An avid outdoor enthusiast and keen photographer, Robert has successfully climbed to the summit of Mount Kilimanjaro and is a qualified paragliding pilot. 'This latest book has been a long time in the planning and I hope it inspires people to get out there and travel,' he says.

RECOMMENDED MAPS

742 Morocco National Map
Publisher:	Michelin
ISBN:	2061000428
Scale:	1:1,000,000

Morocco
Publisher:	International Travel Maps
ISBN:	0921463197
Scale:	1:900,000

Morocco
Publisher:	Insight Travel Maps
ISBN:	9812582312
Scale:	1:800,000

Trans Sahara

Across the world's largest desert

Joe Pichler

The Sahara (or 'Great Desert') is the largest 'hot desert' in the world and occupies approximately 10% of the African continent (the frozen continent of Antarctica is so dry that some scientists consider it a desert too). The greater Sahara stretches across Africa from the Atlantic Ocean in the west to the Red Sea and down to the highlands of Ethiopia, covering an area of over 3,630,000 square miles (9,400,000km2) – an area the same size as Europe or the United States. It receives less than three inches (7.6cm) of rain a year, and even in the wettest areas rain may arrive twice in one week, then not return for years. Sand dunes can reach 590ft (180m) in height.

The desert is principally divided into Western Sahara, the central Ahaggar Mountains, the Tibesti Mountains, the Aïr Mountains, the Tenere Desert and the Libyan Desert. The highest peak in the Sahara is Mount Koussi at 11,204ft (3,415m) in the Tibesti Mountains in northern Chad.

Not long ago I set out on an expedition to explore the Sahara, in particular the Tibesti Mountains in remote northern Chad. It was a trip filled with wonderful adventure, frustrating border crossings, news of landmines en route and the challenge of life in the desert where the temperature can swing from −6°C (21°F) before dawn to 48°C (118°F) at midday.

My route took me from Genoa in Italy to Tunisia and I then headed east to Libya. I'm lucky to have done my trip when I did, given all the turmoil Libya has experienced recently. I was hoping to head directly south to Chad, but the border was closed so I was forced back to neighbouring Algeria and then south to Niger, which in turn led me to Chad. Before I left home I had spent ages at home scanning maps and calculating GPS data so I was familiar with the area, but you cannot pre-plan for this kind of detour. It was complicated and frustrating, but certainly not uncommon in Africa.

As I crossed the Mediterranean on a boat called *Carthago* I discussed with some fellow-passengers the potential problems we might encounter entering Libya. According to some sources, entry into Libya at the time for those travelling solo was potentially a problem, even if one possessed a valid visa. Consequently we decided to join forces with two Bavarians and try our luck together at the border. Completing the entry formalities was a slow process, but finally one of the officers found a suitable plate to fix to my motorcycle and I was ready to enter the 'empire' of Muammar al-Gaddafi.

I headed for Sabha, the most important city in southern Libya. It is here that the Sahara Desert begins. Illegal

← **The minaret of the mosque in Agadez is 27m high and made of clay.**

↓ **A rough road leading to the Assekrem pass.**

Peter Buitelaar was born in Holland in 1956 and has been travelling in the Sahara since 1978. He has covered extensive routes in Morocco, Algeria, Niger, Burkina Faso, Mali, Ghana, Turkey, Syria and Jordan. Today Peter and his wife Zineb run the friendly 'Bikershome' guest house in Ouarzazate, Morocco.

- It is important to be flexible all the time – borders close at short notice and you will often have to modify your plans.
- You need a suitable bike for the dunes – the lighter the better.
- Desert sand is easier to ride in the morning (it compacts overnight). The later in the day, the drier it is and the harder it is to ride.
- Riding solo can be a special experience, but this is only advised for experienced riders. It's best to travel with at least one other person. Travelling alone affords the best feeling of freedom but when things go wrong you are on your own.
- Both you and your bike need to be in good condition before heading into the desert.
- Do not take more stuff than absolutely necessary, but don't head off without duct tape, tie-wraps, superglue and epoxy paste.
- Learn from the people you meet along the route, from the good and certainly from the bad.
- Be very selective whom you trust. Strangers who approach you with a 'Hello, my friend' are frequently just after your money.
- Be careful where and what you eat and drink.
- Be sure to always carry a good quality personal first aid kit.

passenger buses arrive in Sabha from southern African countries – a dangerous, week-long journey during which bus drivers often lose their way and passengers sometimes die from lack of food and water. The road was a monotonous stretch of asphalt flowing straight ahead to the far horizon. The villages noted on my map turned out to consist of little more than a few houses and a petrol station, but the petrol price of five (US) cents per litre was a real boost to my travel budget. Dunes on both sides of the road become more frequent and larger, and after a rather boring journey I finally reached Erg Ubari (also called Awbari), which lay like a huge sea of sand before us.

Ubari is exactly that – a huge sand dune sea in the Fezzan region of southwestern Libya, close to the border with Algeria. Most of the face of the Sahara Desert stretching across northern Africa is bare stone and pebbles rather than sand dunes, but there are exceptions – sprawling seas of multi-storey sand dunes known as 'ergs'. A large outcrop of Nubian sandstone separates the Erg Ubari sand from the Erg Murzuq (or Murzuk) further south.

With the luggage safely stowed at the campsite in Tkerkiba, it was time to mount my Pirelli MT21 tyres and head off to try my first ride in the dunes. Riding in the dunes requires a reduction in tyre pressures so I dropped mine to around 18psi (1.24bar). Finally, in the late afternoon, I climbed the first dune at high speed – it was easier than I thought – but the trickiest part was finding the right speed to reach the top but at the same time avoid being catapulted over the top of the dune by carrying too much speed.

Fascinating scenery in the Hoggar Mountains.

← ✈ **Tuareg live in the northern part of Niger in the Air region.**

The beginning of October didn't appear to be the main travel season in Libya – there was no one else about when I headed off to explore the Ubari Lakes, a group of about 20 lakes set amid a landscape of towering dunes and the palm-fringed oases of the Ubari sand sea. Most of the lakes are highly carbonated, enabling swimmers to float easily without exerting any effort. The salt content of the water is high, nearly five times saltier than sea water.

I set off early in the morning, loaded with only my essential items – 10 litres of water, my sleeping bag and a few bites to eat. Amid the dunes, I noticed for the first time that the long hours of preliminary work I'd done at home were invaluable. Thanks to the GPS I didn't encounter any problems finding the right route to the lakes. When I got to Lake Mandara I was rather disappointed – the lake was dried up (as a result of drought and artificial drainage) and the abandoned lakeside houses were slowly deteriorating into a dreary sight. Despite that, I found the riding was excellent and a return leg past Um el Ma, 'the mother of water', was a highlight, with massive dunes, some reaching over 328ft (100m), remaining a fond memory.

I'd expected difficulties obtaining fuel and oil in Chad and just to be on the safe side I did an engine oil change in Libya before heading south to landlocked Chad – one of the poorest and most corrupt countries in the world and

sometimes referred to as the 'Dead Heart of Africa'.

Upon reaching Al Qatrun on the border with Chad, I discovered that Tubus rebels had laid landmines on countless tracks and that it would be foolish to proceed without a guide. I set about finding an escort to help me cover the 435 miles (700km) to Zouar, an oasis in the Tibesti Mountains in northern Chad. But even the locals seemed reluctant, given the risks, and my only chance to continue my journey was to move in convoy with one of the heavily overloaded trucks heading south. Each day at least two trucks hauling thousands of litres of petrol,

↑ **When riding the bike in the sand, good off-road tyres are needed.**

↓ **Camel caravans transport the salt from Tegguidda-n-Tessoum to Ingal.**

ABOUT THE AUTHOR

Joe Pichler took his first major motorcycle trip in 1984, riding a Yamaha Tenere 600 around the Mediterranean, and it was on this trip that he says he was 'infected by the dangerous travel virus'. Since that trip he has ridden more than 186,000 miles (300,000km) and visited every continent. From 1986 to 1998 he made use of the proven technology of the single cylinder Suzuki DR600 and DR650. In 1999 he switched to the sporty KTM 620/640 Adventure and in 2004 to the new V2 cylinder 950/990 KTM Adventure. On most trips he is accompanied by his wife Renate, who rides pillion. 'With the new KTM Adventure, travelling has become a lot more comfortable, but certainly no less adventurous,' he says. For further information visit www.josef-pichler.at

people and luggage left Al Qatrun for Niger, but it would be a week before a truck heading to Zouar departed.

I was very frustrated but there was no way round it – I had to change my route and head west into Algeria. Unlike Libya, where at least from time to time I met some fellow-travellers, I was very much alone on the road in Algeria. The route I planned would head to Tamanrasset, an oasis city in southern Algeria in the Ahaggar (Hoggar) Mountains and the main city of the Algerian Tuareg. These

are some of the most beautiful mountains in the Sahara, yet they are exceptionally barren. Tamanrasset was originally established as a military outpost to guard the trans-Saharan trade routes. It is here that some of the world's highest known temperatures have been recorded. The Museum of the Hoggar, which offers many exhibits depicting Tuareg life and culture, is certainly worth a visit.

Along the route a good asphalt road, named the N3 on some maps, has finally replaced the much feared and damaging corrugated 102-mile (162km) track from Djanet to Zaouatallaz. Fuel availability is mixed and at the gasoline station in Zaouatallaz I could only find diesel so I scoured the village and bought 10 litres in a rusty can.

I had planned to camp at Fort Serouenout southwest of Illizi but this formerly abandoned fort is now an active military station and I was forced to make alternative arrangements. I headed instead for Ideles, the route to which was littered with wrecked cars from the 1970s and 1980s. Much to my delight, I found plenty of gasoline here – and wonderful fresh bread in the bakery! Illizi itself is one of the gates to the Tassili N'Ajjer National Park, where one can find caves situated under the sands containing prehistoric drawings dating from 6000 BC.

The route continued to take me south, on a tough track from Hirhafok to Assekrem and the Tin Taratimt Pass, followed by a 248-mile (400km) run in a single day to In Guezzam on the border with Niger. One still has to be extremely cautious in the area between Algeria and Niger. The Algerian exit formalities were handled correctly and quickly in stark contrast to the corrupt frontier police in Assamakka, Niger, who sit in their tin hut drinking beer from

➜ **Navigation in Libya is a bit difficult.**

early morning. They tried to explain to me that I would not be able to continue my journey until the next day because the head of the office was not available and no one else was authorised to sign my documents. Two hours later, after some careful negotiation, I was on my way, albeit with a lighter load. My passport showed all the necessary stamps and I quickly headed for Arlit, some 372 miles (598km) to the southwest; this is an area that has seen attacks on travellers in the past so I made sure to keep my wits about me.

The route I'd planned would head southwest towards Niamey, the capital of Niger, then north to Gao in Mali and finally on to Timbuktu. Before leaving Niger I decided on a side trip to Tegguidda-n-Tessoum, 55 miles (90km) from Ingal. The track was in catastrophic condition – deep sand and ruts frustrated me so much that I almost gave up and headed back to base. After some long hours in the deep sand the tiny oasis of Tegguidda-n-Tessoum in the southern part of the Sahara appeared on the horizon.

I set up my tent just in time as the dry and dusty Harmattan started to blow. These strong winds carry huge dust clouds across the desert that can severely limit visibility and even block out the sun for several days. Local folk claim that people and animals become increasingly irritable when this wind has been blowing persistently. That may be so, but I was more than happy having reached the end of my 6,200-mile (10,000km) journey through the Sahara, and sat on the terrace of the Grand Hotel on the banks of the Niger River enjoying the sunset and a bottle of beer.

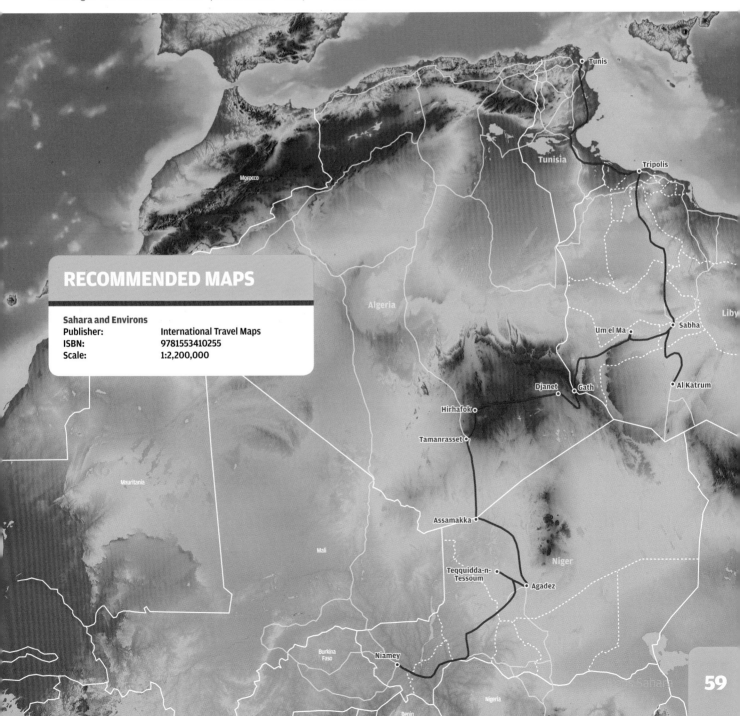

RECOMMENDED MAPS

Sahara and Environs
Publisher:	International Travel Maps
ISBN:	9781553410255
Scale:	1:2,200,000

ROUTE: 6

West Africa
Trans Sahara to mysterious Guinea-Bissau

Craig Carey-Clinch

In 2005 I had what would be for many people the adventure of a lifetime when I rode from London to the Gambia in West Africa in the company of friends. We crossed the Sahara Desert, experiencing the wonders and beauty of Africa as well as riding some of the best routes on offer anywhere. Three years later Barbara Alam and I headed back to West Africa, this time to research a route for a GlobeBusters expedition, which we successfully led later that year. This time we planned to push further southwards, to unknown Guinea-Bissau.

A visit to the Moroccan border in Ceuta used to involve several hours of arguing with hustlers, queues and general chaos. This time, a mere 20 minutes and we were on our way into Morocco. Our destination was Chefchaouen, the beautiful and ancient Berber stronghold, where among the high peaks we later enjoyed the wonderfully spiritual atmosphere of the narrow winding lanes and colours of the medina.

The following day, the road took us first to the Roman ruins at Volubilis, vast, awe-inspiring and one of the most extensive of Roman remains that can be found. After an evening in the market town of Azrou we headed into the heart of the awesome High Atlas Mountains, climbing steeply winding roads and switchbacks, past vast reservoirs and ever higher until the snow-covered peaks gleamed ahead of us. Our goal was the waterfalls at the Cascades D'Ouzoud, a truly beautiful sight in the warm afternoon sun.

After a coastal break in the old Portuguese port of Essaouira, we headed south via twisting coastal roads and into the towering peaks of the Anti-Atlas. The road wound around towering peaks and past ancient kasbahs until we reached the town of Tafraoute, where we enjoyed an evening meal against the backdrop of the jagged granite ranges.

Entering the Sahara was the next big landmark. We rejoined the main road south and after a short section of hills, the desert vista opened out before us as the road headed out into the rocky and hilly 'Hamada'. After 100 miles (160km) of following huge inland folds in the country, we took our night's rest in the town of Tan Tan before continuing our journey south, sea on one side, desert on the other.

We crossed into Western Sahara, a disputed territory watched over by the UN, and scene of massive investment from a Moroccan government keen to consolidate its hold on the country. Dakhla felt like the last place on earth, a lonely and remote town at the end of a long strip of dune-filled land which reaches out into the ocean, offering dramatic vistas as the final miles are ridden. But good food is on offer and a quiet beer can be enjoyed at the Regency Sahara hotel.

It was another early start for our final day in Western Sahara, a planned dash for the border with Mauritania, aiming to deal with customs formalities before lunchtime closure. A poor set of tracks led us in all directions through the minefield that sits on the border of the two

countries. Finding the right path is not easy; straying too far off can have the worst kind of consequences.

The loneliest section of the desert has to be the 320-mile (515km) ride between Nouadhibou and Nouakchott. The first 150 miles (240km) are blank, flat and empty, but after this the dune sea encroaches as the sand of the Azeffal and Akchar makes its presence felt in rolling clean yellow vistas. The road fires arrow-straight through most of this European-quality highway, tempting the rider to nail the throttle hard back. But to do so means missing the sheer majesty of the open desert.

From Nouakchott we headed south, through the western edges of the Trarza dunes, which on this southern edge of the Sahara are covered in low forests of spiny acacia. Nearing the River Senegal and the border of Mauritania the land came to life, with tall plants and numerous trees appearing in all directions.

The entire feel of the ride changed upon entering Senegal, as conservative Arabic transformed into exuberant black African. There were busy street markets in every village we passed through, the people dressed

↑ **Stealing space on the Banjul ferry, Gambia.**

← **Loaded like a block of flats – a research trip two-up means extra kit.**

↑ Leaving Guinea-Bissau.

in vibrant colours discoursing with each other in animated fashion. Our journey took us along the Senegal River route, around the north of the country. This long and variable road is some way off the beaten track for tourists and runs through a country that changes by the hour – from river plains and sugar plantations to undulating low hills covered in acacia trees. Ouro Sogui was our destination, an impoverished transit town at a large crossroads that can take the traveller either south to the Mali border or west into the blazing cauldron of the Ferlou Plains.

An early start the following day and our wheels took us south along a worsening road. But this was to be a pleasant ride as the ground rose into a range of low rounded hills, covered by trees and brown grass. The sentinel figures of huge baobabs dotted themselves across the landscape. The road curved smoothly around hills and past mud hut villages, where children ran out towards us, waving and shouting.

Leaving Senegal and entering Mali was a relaxed process. A policeman insisted on being photographed with the bike before we were allowed to set off on the road to Kayes.

Kayes was chaos. Parked convoys of trucks, checkpoints, roads thronged with people, badly driven wrecks of cars. We noted the run-down colonial buildings and street traders sharing space with newer commerce and cashpoint machines. Despite its impoverishment, the town has plenty to attract the traveller. The markets are great, with a large variety of goods. Nearby are the Chutes de Felou waterfalls and the old French fort at Medine.

Returning to Senegal, the ride took us through rolling hills and out into the central Senegal plain, with its extensive forests and exotic wildlife. We arrived in Tambacounda as the afternoon heat once again set in. This battered-looking town is a major regional centre

↑ A pathole
or two!

↘ The infamous Tamba
to Kaolack road.

GUINEA-BISSAU

Population:	1,586,000
Capital:	Bissau
Area:	13,948 square miles (36,125km2)
Roads:	2,734 miles (4,400km)
Paved/unpaved:	280 miles/2,454 miles (450km/3,950km)
Language:	Portuguese, Crioulo, African languages
Religion:	Indigenous beliefs, Muslim, Christian
Currency:	CFA franc
Life expectancy:	45
GDP per capita:	US$700

▨ Guinea-Bissau lies on the Atlantic coast of Africa. It is bordered by Senegal to the north and Guinea to the south and east.

▨ The climate is tropical and generally hot and humid, with monsoon rains from June to November.

▨ Guerrilla warfare liberated a mix of ethnic groups from Portuguese rule in 1974. In 1994 the country's first multi-party elections were held. An army uprising four years later led to a bloody 1998–9 civil war, which caused severe damage to the nation's infrastructure. Political instability continued, with a military coup in 2003.

▨ Guinea-Bissau is among the world's least developed countries, with most people engaged in subsistence agriculture and fishing – cashew nuts are the main export crop.

▨ The flag of Guinea-Bissau is derived from the flag of the republic of Ghana, which served as an inspiration as Guinea-Bissau fought for independence.

▨ Guinea-Bissau and the Cape Verde Islands were a single country until 1980 when a coup which succeeded only in Guinea-Bissau ended the union between the two countries.

▨ Guinea-Bissau's most famous son is Amilcar Cabral. Revolutionary and philosopher, Cabral led the fight of Guinea-Bissau and Cape Verde for independence from Portuguese colonial rule. Sadly, a year before independence in 1972, he was assassinated by persons believed to be agents of the Portuguese government.

and transport hub, with several fuel stations, banks and other businesses.

Nothing had prepared us for the 100 miles (160km) of deep potholes, ruts, shattered tarmac, car-sized trenches, broken lorries and heavy congestion that we were to face the following day on the road to Kaolack. This was a motorcycling challenge *par excellence* as we wove about, mixing with other traffic, chewing diesel fumes and acknowledging the friendly shouts from drivers of broken-down trucks.

Our next destination was Banjul in the Gambia. The ride took in a part of central Senegal that ran near the coastal marshes and swamps. Packed with exotic birds and small traditional villages, the sometimes rough road to the border turned out to be one of the nicest rides in Senegal. Banjul lies at the south side of the mouth of the Gambia River and is reached via one of the poorly maintained ferries that ply the water. Too many vehicles

ABOUT THE AUTHOR

Craig Carey-Clinch is one of the best known lobbyists in motorcycle industry-related political issues, both in the UK and Europe. A published writer, journalist and ex-RAF engineer, Craig is also an experienced transcontinental motorcyclist who has undertaken several overland journeys by motorcycle, including three crossings of the Sahara to promote awareness of the charity Motorcycle Outreach, of which he is a director. He also led a GlobeBusters adventure to Senegal and Mali. His most recent journey was a coast to coast crossing of Canada during 2011. His company, Rowan Public Affairs, offers a range of strategic marketing and policy support services to the motorcycle world.

Casamance region. The reputation of the area, due to sporadic 'separatist' action, puts many people off visiting a place of remarkable beauty. Vast jungle-like forests line the roads, which wind their way through extensive greenery and across picturesque rivers. Passing through Ziguinchor, with its easy relaxed atmosphere and numerous colonial buildings, we took a quiet road to the border, where there was little comment from officials as we passed through.

Guinea-Bissau is still reeling from the disastrous civil war of 1998 to 1999, plus three bloody coups that took place in quick succession. But its villages were quiet and picturesque, set under groups of tall trees, and on the higher ground of the dense tropical countryside. Groups of people sat around talking – and sometimes staring in disbelief as we rode by.

Bissau City, the capital, seemed more familiar than many West African towns. Road-building had been taking place and the main road into town was a dual carriageway, with several new buildings springing up among the ruins of the humidity-stained Soviet-style blocks which had been heavily damaged during the war.

That evening we walked around the compact and quiet city centre. The focal point was the presidential palace, which was heavily shelled during the war and stands as a silent reminder of times to which the surprisingly upbeat locals do not want to return. As we headed back to our

were crammed aboard, people occupying every inch of space, as the overloaded ferry inched its way across the river, propelled by knocking and belching diesels.

And so to Bissau. Leaving the Gambia and entering Senegal once more we rode south into the tropical

➜ ➜ **The Presidential Palace in Bissau City.**

➜ **Ferry in Guinea-Bissau – more overcrowding.**

RECOMMENDED MAPS

Morocco and Western Sahara – Morocco National Map
Publisher: Michelin
ISBN: 2061000428
Scale: 1:1,000,000

Morocco
Publisher: Reise Know-How Verlag
Stanfords catalogue no: 140898
Scale: 1:1,000,000

Mauritania – Mauritania Carte Generale
Publisher: IGN (Institut Geographique National)
ISBN: 3282118501410
Scale: 1:2,500,000

Senegal – Senegal Carte Touristique
Publisher: IGN (Institut Geographique National)
Stanfords catalogue no: 115970
Scale: 1:1,000,000

Guinea-Bissau – Guinea-Bissau Carte Touristique
Publisher: IGN (Institut Geographique National)
Stanfords catalogue no: 36911
Scale: 1:500,000

National Geographic African Adventure Atlas (book)
Publisher: National Geographic
ISBN: 1566951739
Scales: Various

hotel, later that evening, the town came to life, with loud music coming from bars and groups of people gathering to socialise and laugh. We took a ride in a battered taxi, where music bellowed from broken speakers and frequent stops were made to pick up and drop fares.

As much as we wanted to stay longer, deadlines beckoned. Bissau was the furthest point of our expedition and all roads from now to Dakar would be ones we were retracing. We both felt sad to see Bissau City disappear behind us as we headed north along now familiar roads. It's a terrible shame that political unrest has once again returned to this beautiful, but exhausted, country.

📷 All photographs courtesy of Craig Carey-Clinch

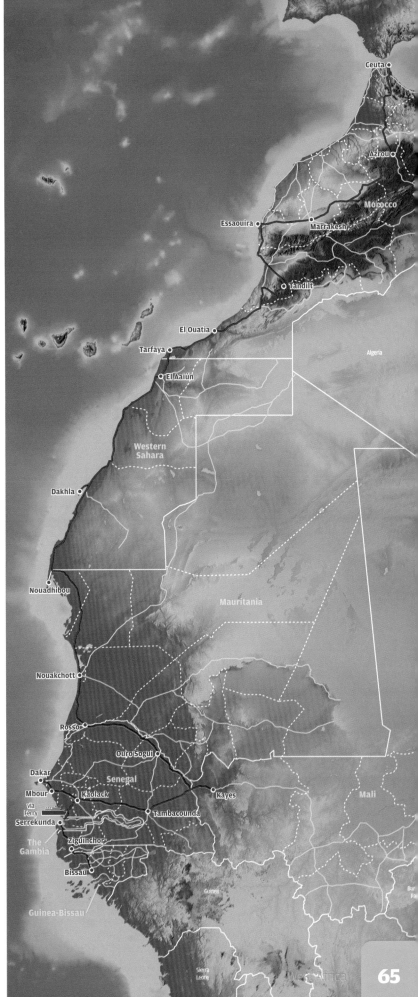

Timbuktu

Overland to Africa's fabled city on the edge of the Sahara

Nick Sanders

The mysticism surrounding the fabled city of Timbuktu is suggested in an old Sudanese proverb, which says: 'Salt comes from the north, gold from the south, and silver from the country of the white man, but the word of God and the treasures of wisdom are only to be found in Timbuktu.' The journey to Timbuktu has the cachet of a *grand voyage*. It is a rare trans-African journey to a place of legend, part of which I am sure will rub off on anyone capable of riding there.

Timbuktu lies in central Mali in northwest Africa, normally accessible from Europe via Morocco. Alternatively one can start from the Gambia or Senegal and head due east into Mali. This route describes a ride from the United Kingdom. One can obviously ride to southern Europe, but a good option to avoid the motorways would be to transport your bike to the south of Spain or Portugal and start the journey in earnest from here. Before we crossed the sea to the Spanish enclave of Ceuta we had ridden down from Lisbon to Setúbal and then along the primary north-south highway shadowing the autoroute to Portimao.

We sailed past Gibraltar and the ship took us quickly out to sea, cutting through white horses, until we could soon see the Rif Mountains of Morocco. We were soon riding south, across the edge of Ceuta and towards the Moroccan border. Passports at the ready, we were processed quickly and in a friendly fashion by Moroccan customs. The country is traditional and yet at the same time drawn to the modern world, a tree whose roots lie in Africa but whose leaves breathe in European air.

Away from the border we rode gently through the scruffy town of Mdiq, then on a ring road that allowed us to bypass Tetouan and head towards Chefchaouen, where rural Morocco starts. This is where the old sit until they die, watching. The younger men slap down chess pieces, hardly stopping to think between moves, while

boys gather their goats. Across the most verdant fields children always ran towards us as we rode past, shouting and waving, giving a false sense of familiarity.

Our route across the mountains had jumped over the Medium and High Atlas ridges. Crossing the Plateau de l'Arid on the high scrubby plains we were at 4,921ft (1,500m). It is here the oueds and gorges drain their melt water. The larger peaks of the High Atlas appear immediately behind Midelt en route to the Ziz Gorge, great massifs rising dramatically to 12,100ft (3,700m). Here Berbers irrigate small squares of land to cultivate potatoes, turnips, lucerne, corn and maize, all crops that grow well at high altitude. Flocks of goats and sheep are grazed for their milk, butter and wool. Some hamlets, clustered under overhangs, become more fortified, while kasbahs, with their crenellated towers, stand guard as a homily to a biblical way of life, abandoned as people move into the cities leaving the old and their old ways.

Marrakesh came and went. There's so much to find out about this pearl of southern Morocco. The history of

↑ Road hazards in Africa come in all shapes and sizes.

← A local tent provides respite from the Sahara sunshine.

← Heading south in Morocco near the Atlantic coast.

⬆ **Evidence of Africa's treacherous coastline.**

⬇ **African savanna is ideal adventure biking territory.**

After completing our paperwork we rode out of Morocco, entering territory administered neither by Morocco nor Mauritania – Western Sahara, one of the most sparsely populated countries on earth. A hard surface had never been laid but, apart from patches of sand, the dirt was firmly packed and deeply rutted.

We made good progress and soon the first buildings in Mauritania appeared, slightly set back from the rough road, manned by guards. We were ushered into a small room. The walls were roughly papered and yellowed with nicotine while the one table displayed an approximation of formalities: simple things like staplers and drawing pins, items that some of the larger African countries cannot make; paper was at a premium but the most essential piece of stationery was the rubber stamp, without which nothing happens. In reality there was no obvious procedure other than to be patient and polite.

The guard asked for a small *cadeau*, and to his credit wasn't threatening or even insistent. After a long day it was easier to give in than confront him with the ethics of taking a bribe. He probably hadn't been paid for months and, even if he had, it would be a small amount quadrupled by what he could cadge from tourists. Deeply south of what was formerly the Spanish Sahara, a sun-parched piece of arid land that only politicians wanted for colonial gain, we were pitched against a simple logic of life. I pay him a bit and he lets me through easily. I pay him nothing and perhaps all of us have to stay there for the night at our collective inconvenience.

the city is there on pitted walls, but it was the secrets that interested me, the ones behind closed doors. The next day we left Marrakesh and filed out past the Djemaa el Fna and the Koutoubia Mosque. The road leading to the Tizi 'n' Test Pass runs over the sedate but monotonous Haouz Plain to Tahanaoute and then up to the gorges of the Moulay Brahim.

The ride from Tan Tan was not tedious but there was little to see other than scrawny desert landscape. The road was straight, with kinks that veered lazily to the left and the right, either side of which scrappy small dunes sat hunched against a strong wind.

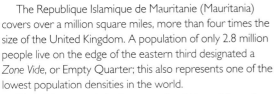

← I bet you
couldn't pour it
like this at home.

↑ It took a while
for the RAC man
to arrive.

The Republique Islamique de Mauritanie (Mauritania) covers over a million square miles, more than four times the size of the United Kingdom. A population of only 2.8 million people live on the edge of the eastern third designated a *Zone Vide*, or Empty Quarter; this also represents one of the lowest population densities in the world.

That night we rode to the campsite at Nouadhibou, the second largest town in Mauritania, whose major economic activity apart from fishing is the processing of iron ore. The campsite was pleasant enough and was the place where all the overland travellers break their journey. It is places like this, and not the guidebooks, that tell you about the way ahead.

Gas stations are sometimes 300 miles (480km) apart in Mauritania so we set about filling spare jerry cans. Sporadically, clay buildings — with corners of mud daub and corrugated roofs — gave credence to human participation in a landscape that, while beautiful, is yet so sparse that it is virtually invisible.

The next day after a breakfast of bread, butter and jam, washed down by hot milky coffee, we headed east in good spirits. Panniers were packed and reattached to bikes. Once again tyres and oil levels were checked, chains tensioned. We had gleaned enough information about the road surface to feel confident that all of our bikes would have sufficient off-road capability. Such simple summaries were all we needed to know. While adventure is about having knowledge it is not about knowing everything. Sometimes it is impossible to pinpoint when a catastrophe might occur.

We had now ridden 3,500 miles, crossed Morocco,

TIPS

- Roads in Africa change all the time – they are being improved in some areas but many are neglected and deteriorate at a rapid rate. Be aware of potholes.
- The piste with its hard-packed surface doesn't pose too many problems and the secret is to ride as light as possible.
- There is very little soft sand until the final stretch to Timbuktu and those stretches that exist are relatively short. Riding in the dry season makes it easier to cross – ride with confidence and you'll get through without any problems.
- Riding in Morocco is 'luxurious' compared to further south – hotels are good, the food is excellent and the people are friendly. Riding in Mauritania is harder than Morocco – not many motorcyclists pass through here, so expect curiosity without being hassled. The road will be hard piste for the most part, isolated and barren. Malian people are said to be among the friendliest in Africa.
- Apply early for your carnet – this is a legal requirement. It acts like a passport for your bike and indemnifies you against import duty charges.
- The Sahara Desert is at its coolest in the winter, very cold at night but may be as high as 30°C and more during the day.
- Much of Mali's surface area is taken up by desert and semi-arid land and thorny scrub known as the Sahel.
- Further south is the Savannah, the humid, greener subtropical grasslands.

Nick Sanders has been riding motorbikes since he was 16 years old. Since 1992, when he first rode around the world on an Indian Enfield 500cc 'Bullet', he has been riding professionally. His expeditions culminated in an historic recapture of his solo circumnavigation by motorcycle on a Yamaha R1 in 19 days. Since 1992 he has motorcycled around the world seven times, more than anyone else, his mileage totalling over 350,000 miles (563,000km). During this time he led a group of 22 riders across 17 countries and five continents, around the world.

In 1996 Nick rode the length of the Americas from Ushuaia to Fairbanks in 30 days as a training run for his first speed circumnavigation a year later. Subsequently he has ridden up and down the Alaskan Highway eight times, taken groups of riders on tours to North America, Europe and India, and is one of only two motorcyclists ever to guide riders around the world, the Holy Grail of motorcycle touring. Most recently he has ridden the length of the Americas a total of five times, failing in 2010 to beat the 21-day record by a few hours. In 2011 he will ride the length of the Americas a further three times.

Nick divides his time equally between his canal boat and Wales, where he lives with his two sons Willow and Juno and daughter Tatyana. For more information see www.nicksanders.com

⬇ **The holy grail of Timbuktu.**
📷 IStock

Mauritania and were deep in the Savannah region of the Sahara Desert. Edging closer to Timbuktu, we rode across roads of red piste. Soon we descended into Bamako, the capital of Mali. During a rest day, we planned the route to Mopti and then Douentza, the gateway village to the final piste and to Timbuktu itself.

The route out of Bamako was straightforward enough. The traffic flow was orderly and without incident and within 30 minutes we were back in the Sahel. As we rode deeper into Mali, east and then northeast, roughly following the river, denser vegetation grew along the banks which, without proper irrigation, soon thinned to sand and then road.

That morning, before we set off on the piste, we turned out of our hotel in Douentza, stopping on the quiet main road for coffee. This road that ran through the town was the main west-east arterial route between the capital, Bamako, and Gao in the far east of the country. The further away from the commercial centre of Mali, the fewer the trucks. Larger towns have police stations manned by men without fuel to run their jeeps; should a telegraph line be cut or short-circuited, as often happens, all communication ceases. We were in bandit country now, and we were vulnerable hostages to misfortune in the real sense. Hospitals would be so rudimentary as to be worthless should we need one. You can take the adventure out of the man but, sometimes, you cannot take the man out of the adventure.

If, on the track to Timbuktu, anyone should fall ill or simply fall, we would have to deal with the situation ourselves. Even if mobile phones were to detect a signal, whom would we call? Air-and-sea rescue services are not for ordinary folk in extraordinary overseas circumstances, and this is what separates adventure from something that only purports to be. There was something about the Wild West in our hearts as we sat astride our iron horses, and taking the next left was our way to Timbuktu.

The corrugated piste to the river crossed the Reserve des Elephants and the lakes around the halfway point at Bambara Maoundé, where we stopped for tea and goat stew. We didn't see any elephants or lakes, just more of the same, a plain of grass and thorny bush. We were riding in the direction of Bourem Inali by the river. From there we would board a ferry that would take us downstream briefly before landing at Gouriem, just 12 miles (19km) from one of the most mysterious cities in history.

Timbuktu is positioned 6 miles (9km) north of the port of Kabara on the Niger. Timbuktu was a trading post for gold and avoided the seasonal flooding by not being on the riverbank itself. Caravans, therefore, could trade throughout the year. As such, it was also linked to the major trading post of Gao by water and by land, with connections to Tunisia and Egypt. While trade was important to Timbuktu, so was food. Situated on the edge of the desert, the inhabitants needed access to fertile ground, and Djenné on the River Bani provided the city dwellers with fresh produce. Djenné, which lies 250 miles (400km) south of Timbuktu, is seasonally surrounded by water to become an island, making Timbuktu accessible only by boat. Gao, Timbuktu and Djenné were all *entrêpots* or commercial centres for traders, who brought

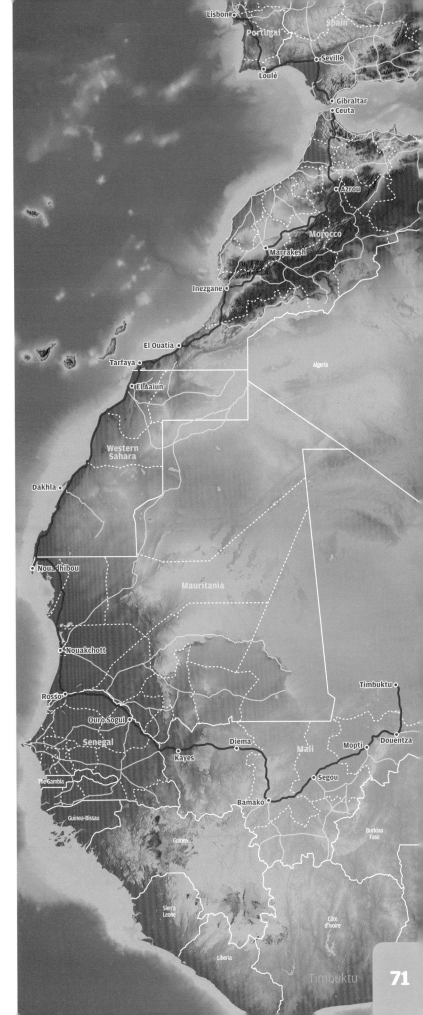

caravans from the north and south. Smaller boats called *pirogues* would ship salt to Djenné from Timbuktu and gold in the opposite direction. Timbuktu was a transit port for shipping and a magnet for explorers who came hoping to discover streets paved with precious metals and admire fine buildings, when there were none.

The final 150 miles (241km) to Timbuktu were tough. The hard corrugated road gave the last part of this adventure the appropriate blend of brown to make us all look like hard men. Dusty, unsealed, it was the red dirt of the journey. Everything was brown and red and green; no yellows, no turquoise, nothing chromatic ... not even a blue sky. To add to the realism, the pastel shades of what little colour there was had a gentle covering of dust.

Just 6 miles (9km) upstream from the lively port of Korioumé was the hamlet of Kabara. We boarded the river ferry in the dark and alighted under a full moon, still rising. The quays were astir with animated bustle, like Old Delhi at night.

We arrived at night in the city of Timbuktu, lending our entrée a thin veneer of romance. We had been patient, riding over bump and cranny to get to the journey's end. Even in the moonlight the town was in ruins, but as Felix Dubois, author of *Timbuktoo the Mysterious* once said: 'Its wretchedness is overpowered by life and movement.'

Today Timbuktu is little more than a dusty little shanty town. Three days' journey from Bamako and we had arrived. Some riders who had accompanied me on this trip had been outside their comfortable environment for too long. With experience, you learn to feel at ease within the envelope of reality you have around you, and after a while that comfort zone becomes supported. Africans know how hard it is for westerners to live their way, but they respect you for your efforts so long as you are prepared to try. Now all we had to do was ride back.

RECOMMENDED MAPS

Michelin 953 – Africa North and West
Publisher: Michelin
ISBN: 2067009532
Scale: 1:4,000,000

National Geographic African Adventure Atlas (book)
Publisher: National Geographic
ISBN: 1566951739
Scales: Various

Morocco International Travel Map
Publisher: International Travel Maps
ISBN: 0921463197
Scale: 1:900,000

Mali International Travel Map
Publisher: International Travel Maps
ISBN: 9781553413141
Scale: 1:2,400,000

Mauritania IGN Carte Generale
Publisher: IGN (Institut Geographique National)
ISBN: 3282118501410
Scale: 1:2,500,000

All photographs courtesy of Nick Sanders

ROUTE: 8

The Cederberg Adventure Route
Exploring the Cape's prehistoric landscape

Craig Marshall

In terms of adventure motorcycling routes in South Africa, the mountainous Cederberg region in the Western Cape Province is undoubtedly one of the best places. Perhaps it's a closely guarded secret among local riders, or it's simply not marketed extensively, but few international riders are acquainted with the Cederberg's jagged prehistoric landscape and undulating gravel roads. It's a region diverse in geological history and abundant with well-preserved Bushmen rock art, depicting animal hunting scenes and stick figures stained on the cave walls, and rock formations which were home to several South African hunter-gatherer tribes dating from between 3,000 and 6,000 years ago when elephants still roamed the area.

The region is mostly undisturbed and still looks like it did thousands of years ago. The gravel passes and valleys are very sparsely populated, with small settlements of subsistence farmers, possibly descendants of the inhabitants who enriched the cave walls with their distinctive rock art.

The Cederberg is most commonly accessed from the R303, a tarred secondary road, from Ceres and the town of Prince Alfred Hamlet, approximately 105 miles (170km) northeast of Cape Town.

About 8.5 miles (14km) north of the winelands town of Paarl, just off the N1 freeway, lies the quiet agricultural town of Wellington, a gateway to adventure. The notorious 14-mile (23km) long, narrow, tarred Bainskloof Pass between Wellington and Ceres follows the meandering gorge of the red stained and oddly named 'Witriver' (White River) towards Ceres. Red staining is a result of the high levels of tannin extruded from the run-off of rainwater through the Fynbos (natural Cape shrubland) covered slopes leading down into the deep gorge.

This is a great way to start your adventure – a windy and scenic tarred road through the Hawequas Nature Reserve. The road is uneven in places and a favourite with weekend adventure bikers en route to the majestic Cederberg mountain range. The twisty Bainskloof Pass ends where the road joins up with the R46, and again riders are rewarded with a great scenic gorge up and over Mitchell's Pass into Ceres, the citrus-producing headquarters of the region.

Once through Ceres and Prince Alfred Hamlet, the R303 heads towards the Cederberg Mountains via the amazing Gydo Pass. It's well worth a quick photo stop in the dedicated parking at the top of the pass to take in the vista of the entire Ceres Valley below. Some 17 miles (28km) further along the R303 is the small settlement of 'Op Die Berg' ('On the Mountain') where the bold signage will clearly point you to the right, to the Cederberg. From here it's a short 11-mile (17km) stretch of tarmac before the magic of Cederberg's gravel meets your tyres.

This unforgettable gravel road starts in a strange tilted landscape dotted with ancient chunks of rock protruding from the plains. The road rambles through valleys and over three spectacular passes for 29 miles (47km). Looking along the valley, riders are welcomed by the sight of Blinkberg Pass snaking its way over the horizon. The exquisite beauty that keeps visitors coming back is evident from the top of Blinkberg Pass, looking down on Varkkloof Pass and back up Grootrivierhoogte Pass as the undulation continues until, dipping through a small flat orchard of citrus trees spotted around the campsite, the bikers' favourite stopover is reached – the Cederberg Oasis. It is here that green lawns, ice-cold beer, massive steaks, a cool swimming pool and a variety of accommodation options await adventure bikers, rock climbers and hikers alike. In rainy seasons the gravel conditions are generally better and more hard packed, and several shallow river crossings are flowing.

The total distance from central Cape Town to the Cederberg Oasis is only 145 miles (233km) so if one leaves Cape Town early enough there is ample time to

← **The winding gravel ribbon into the Cederberg conservancy.**

← **The view from the top of Gydo Pass.**

→ **A regular visiting spot for bike tours.**

→→ **Bushmen paintings.**

↘ **A small water crossing in Eselbank.**

↘ **The descent into Wupperthal.**

have lunch, swim and relax before heading out in the cool afternoon sun to explore the prehistoric rock formations and Bushmen art.

Truitjieskraal and Rocklands rock formations and Bushmen art
GPS: S32 32.230 E19 19.493
About 1.5 miles (2.5km) north of the Cederberg Oasis is an unsignposted side junction on the left which leads up a steep track to the Truitjieskraal rock formations. The 2.2-mile (3.6km) track is moderately sandy in places, but very easy to ride. When arriving at the signboard and entrance gate you will need to use the supplied combination number for the lock on the gate. Shut and lock the gate once you have entered. The rock art at this site dates back 1,600 years to when Khoi San people lived a hunter-gather life in this prehistoric landscape.

Stadsaal Caves
GPS: S32 30.629 E19 19.081
Almost 4 miles (6.3km) from the Cederberg Oasis, at the Matjiesrivier junction, one can turn left and proceed for another 1.8 miles (2.9km) before arriving at the sign for Stadsaal rock formations. Some of the most spectacular rock formations shaped and sculptured by the wind over millions of years can be seen here.

Note: You need a permit to visit and this can be obtained from Dwarsrivier, Kromrivier farm or at the Cederberg Oasis.

To Clanwilliam
There are two main routes to Clanwilliam:

- The main gravel road past the Stadsaal Caves and via Uitkyk Pass through the Algerian Valley, down Nieuwoudt's Pass and through Kriedouwkloof Pass to the water's edge of the Clanwilliam Dam.
- The alternative, much less travelled route is a stunning 25-mile (40km) long track which leads up and over the Eselbank Plateau and down a steep trail into the quaint settlement of Wupperthal. This route is for experienced riders only, although beginners should cope if accompanied by experienced riders to assist them. The Eselbank section is a well-worn track sprinkled with loose rocks, sand patches, river crossings and the most amazing scenery any rider could wish for.

The going is moderately slow and technical, but once you are familiar with the terrain, it's really straightforward; just watch out for the intermittent sand patches. During the winter months (May, June, July) several river crossings and pools of water are present. The road is well used by the 4WD community so the most obvious track is generally always apparent. Always check the depth if you cannot see the bottom of a river or pool. The sand sections on this route are not a major issue and vary in depth from 2–8in (5–20cm) and up to 328 feet (100m) in length.

Eselbank Waterfall
GPS: S32 20.783 E19 13.429

The turn-off to the waterfall is exactly 14.7 miles (23.8km) from the Matjiesrivier junction. It is very easy to miss if you are not aware of it. It can be found just after the concrete bridge on the north side of the settlement of Eselbank, on the sharp left-hand bend. The cascade is very well hidden and first-time visitors can arrive at the crystal-clear cool rock pools above the waterfall and be unaware that only a few hundred feet away is the massive gorge dropping by more than 520 feet (158m).

Heading further along the route riders will encounter a series of very rocky, loose turns and one long deep sand patch before descending down the concreted trail into Wupperthal. The deep sand is at GPS: S32 18.782 E19 13.371. If in doubt, just use first gear, keep your tyres in the rut, prevent the front wheel from straying out of the rut and paddle with your feet to avoid dropping the bike.

Descent into Wupperthal
GPS: S32 18.172 E19 13.169

The beginning of the descent is moderately loose but not steep at all. Once you reach the concreted sections it's first or second gear all the way, as the steep track winds its way along the Eselbank Pass towards Wupperthal, which is visible from the top.

Wupperthal was previously a Moravian mission station, nestled in the bottom of the Tra-Tra Valley, and

THE CEDERBERG

The Cederberg derived its name from the endemic cedar tree, *Widdringtonia cedarbergensis.* In 2004 the Cederberg Wilderness received World Heritage Site status as part of the Cape Floristic Region. The Cederberg region is one of the best areas for ancient Khoi San (Bushmen) rock art in the world, with over 2,500 discovered locations.

Rules to observe when visiting the Cederberg
- Do not touch or damage rock art as this causes deterioration of the paintings.
- Do not interfere with plants or wildlife.
- Do not litter.
- Never discard cigarette butts as they can cause fires.
- No open fires are permitted, except at designated areas.
- Do not use soap or detergents in or near rivers and mountain streams.
- Access to outdoor recreational activities and attractions are subject to permits obtainable at various establishments.
- Stay on the gravel tracks when riding to prevent damage to vegetation.
- All fossils are protected as National Monuments and may not be disturbed or removed.

↑ **Vast, unspoilt and breathtaking – the Cederberg region offers postcard views in any direction.**
📷 Waldo van der Waal

← **Despite its isolation, the area is well protected and cared for.**
📷 Waldo van der Waal

→ **Striking rock formations under the bluest of skies – but in summer the heat can become unbearable.**
📷 Waldo van der Waal

ABOUT THE AUTHOR

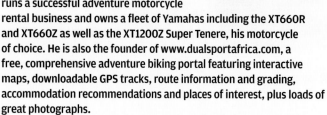

Craig Marshall is more at home on two wheels than his own two feet. He was involved in BMX racing as a youngster, mountain biking through his teens and currently prefers to use the throttle rather than pedal power. 'For riding fitness there's nothing like hitting the single track at high speeds on a mountain bike,' he says. His travels have taken him to most places throughout southern Africa. Craig runs a successful adventure motorcycle rental business and owns a fleet of Yamahas including the XT660R and XT660Z as well as the XT1200Z Super Tenere, his motorcycle of choice. He is also the founder of www.dualsportafrica.com, a free, comprehensive adventure biking portal featuring interactive maps, downloadable GPS tracks, route information and grading, accommodation recommendations and places of interest, plus loads of great photographs.

with its thatched cottages has remained much the same since 1830. The name 'Wupperthal' is derived from the Wupper River in Germany and Thal, meaning valley in German, from where two Rhineland missionaries, Theobald von Wurmb and Johan Gottlieb Leipoldt, arrived in the Cape in 1829.

The steep Kouberg Pass leads you out of Wupperthal and affords riders a look back at the steep descent into the town. The trail continues along easy gravel conditions via the Biedou Valley and up over the Hoek se Berg Pass, which also has a short tarred section. At the T-junction of the newly tarred R364, turn left to Clanwilliam and travel for 23.9 miles (38.6km) on the tar through the picturesque Parkhuis Pass and down into the town of Clanwilliam.

Clanwilliam
GPS: S32 10.540 E18 53.553
This quaint town is the only fuel stop until Citrusdal, so you will need to fill up here. The first visitors arrived in the area in 1662, and around 1725 Clanwilliam became a permanent settlement and grew into the friendly agricultural town it is today. It's regarded as the gateway

to the Cederberg for travellers coming along the N7 from Cape Town. Clanwilliam was first known as Jan Disselsvalleij, but its name was changed to Clanwilliam in 1814 by Sir John Cradock who named the town after his father-in-law, the Earl of Clanwilliam. The town is noted as being one of the oldest in South Africa.

Clanwilliam Dam

Running along the entire length of the Clanwilliam Dam is a stunning and very easy gravel road which is frequented by bikers, local farmers and tourists en route to the Algeria Valley in the Cederberg. Not far outside the town of Clanwilliam, the 23-mile (38km) gravel road begins. In the summer months (November to April) the gravel road can be a little sandy and the surface will be very loose, so inexperienced bikers should take caution. This leads riders to a four-way junction:

▧ Turning left will take one back into Cederberg via the Nieuwoudt Pass and through the Algeria Valley, up Uitkyk Pass and back to the Cederberg Oasis. This is a popular loop if you are spending three days in the Cederberg.
▧ Continuing straight ahead for 17 miles (27km) will take you to Citrusdal, another small farming community town and the last point where you can access the N7. If you continue straight out of Citrusdal on the gravel, the road comes to a dead end after 19 miles (30km) and you will have to return to Citrusdal to meet up with the N7 again.

Sadly, this is the end of the gravel surface roads; the scenic route through Porterville, Gouda and Wellington is all tarmac, as is the route up the windy R303 via three mountain passes – Elands Kloof Pass, Middelberg Pass and Buffelshoek Pass – and back to Op Die Berg. If you are in a hurry to get back to Cape Town, the quickest route from Citrusdal would be back on the N7 in a southerly direction.

The Route via Porterville to Wellington and the N1

From Citrusdal, riders can take a 12-mile (19km) run on the N7 south towards Piketberg. Soon after joining the N7 the road winds up and over the Piekenierskloof Pass, breaking through the Olifants mountain range and down into the flatlands of the Boland. A few miles after the bottom of the pass is a turn left and a 20-mile (32km) run towards Porterville, one of South Africa's best known paragliding locations.

The scenic R44 route follows the entire Olifants mountain range from Porterville through Saron and on to Gouda. At the junction turn right towards Wellington, which lies 25 miles (40km) ahead. The R44 continues through Wellington. At the junction, turn right towards Paarl and Stellenbosch: this leads back to the N1 and South Africa's 'mother city' of Cape Town. This is a 365-mile (589km) ride that can comfortably be completed in two or three days.

↑ Light sandy surfaces through Eselbank.

RECOMMENDED MAPS

Cederberg
Publisher: **Slingsby Maps**
ISBN: **9781920377090**
Scale: **1:160,000**

Cape Westcoast and the Cederberg
Publisher: **International Motoring Publications**
ISBN: **9781920115029**
Scale: **1:300,000**

The Garden Route

Off-road adventures along South Africa's famous coast

Craig Marshall

There is much to be said for the Garden Route – it includes the amazing Outeniqua and Swartberg Mountains and, of course, the epic Baviaanskloof, which is rated as the number one adventure ride in South Africa. Most motorcyclists and visitors to the Garden Route cruise up and down the tarred roads and even those are impressive through the countless mountain ranges. But it is the gravel mountain passes that are really the most impressive.

From the deep canyon of Prince Alfred Pass and De Vlugt, Rooiberg Pass, the old Historical Outeniqua (Montagu Pass) to the famous Swartberg Pass to the majestic collection of passes in Baviaanskloof (Grasnek Pass, Holgat Pass, Combrink's Pass and Nuwekloof Pass) – this is South Africa at its very best. Our route begins in the town of George, established back in 1776 by the Dutch East India Company as an outpost for the provision of timber.

George to Knysna
Old Seven Passes Route – part tar, mostly gravel
GPS: S33 58.127 E22 29.239

Passes: Zwartrivierhoogte Pass – Kaaimansgat Pass – Silver River Pass – Duiwelskop Pass – Hoogekraal Pass – Karatara Pass – Homtini Pass – and you can add Phantom Pass down into Knysna to make it eight if you like.

Our route begins at the Saasveld Road on the eastern side of George. To access the road coming from the N2 in either direction, take the Garden Route Mall, or N12 off-ramp and travel towards George for 1.7 miles (2.7km) before turning to the right at the traffic lights into Saasveld Road.

The first 6 miles (10km) is tarred and then at Kaaimansgat Pass it changes to gravel. The entire route is very easy gravel and can be ridden by all riders of all levels, and also with a pillion rider. The gravel section is 3.5 miles (5.6km) and then you will arrive at a T-junction: turn left towards Karatara and travel for 7.7 miles (12.4km) and the gravel returns again. The next 17 miles (28km) is all gravel and certainly the most interesting through Hoogekraal Pass, Karatara Pass and Homtini Pass.

After 5.5 miles (8.8km) of more tarmac, look out for the turning to the left down the short 4.6-mile (7.4km) gravel Phantom Pass to Knysna which is well worth adding to the route. At the end of Phantom Pass the road meets up with the N2 again, but if you feel like lunch, just under the N2 bridge is the well-known Crabs Creek restaurant on the lagoon water's edge.

Knysna is one of the most visited holiday towns on the Garden Route and some time at the Knysna waterfront is time well spent if you are a first-time visitor. This coastal town is world famous for its oysters, which are cultivated in the lagoon, harvested daily and served in most local restaurants.

Refuel in Knysna and make your way to the Old Cape Road just as you enter Knysna from the George side (GPS: S34 02.191 E23 01.876).

The 15.5-mile (25km) Old Cape Road, known as 'Kom se Pad', winds its way up through the fantastic Knysna forests and is definitely one of the most satisfying roads to ride. It can be very slippery in the wet season, due to the high red clay content on the roads, so take care during the winter months of May, June and July. The road makes a large loop and joins up again with the R339 into Prince Alfred Pass.

← **Entering the Baviaanskloof Wilderne-ss area.**

← **The view from the top of Prince Alfred Pass.**

→ Australian
biker Tom
Gardner rides a
deep water
crossing in
Baviaanskloof.

Prince Alfred Pass

This section of the route is really picturesque and winds its way deeper into the Outeniqua Mountains where you can stop overnight at the Outeniqua Trout Lodge, about 21 miles (33km) along the Prince Alfred Pass just before De Vlugt. The gravel roads are mostly in fantastic condition and easily drivable in a sedan vehicle, but this is the problem for bikers – be cautious of cars in blind corners because they often use the entire road and may be on your (left) side when you come round the corner. Travel slowly and look far ahead on the road for the dust trails of approaching cars. The canyon road is so beautiful that it's more favourable to slow riding in any case. The Trout Lodge is situated in the Middle Keurbooms Conservancy and is frequented by bikers most weekends. It's a fantastic getaway location with tents, log cabins and a historical watermill pub dating back to the 1800s.

Leave the lodge relatively early in the morning as you will need the time later in the day when entering Baviaanskloof. Continue out of Prince Alfred Pass for 11 miles (18km) until you reach Avontuur – where you can refuel again before joining the R62 and turning right towards Jeffreys Bay and Baviaanskloof. The R62 stretch from Avontuur to the N2 crossing near Humansdorp is tarred and in very good condition. Even though we adventure riders dislike the black stuff, this 89-mile (143km) section of road is very scenic and will give you a chance to get some speed after the first day's slow going.

At the end of this stretch, pass under the N2 and continue on to Humansdorp, then north to Hankey and turn left in this small town towards Patensie and Baviaanskloof. Patensie is your last opportunity to refuel.

Baviaanskloof (Valley of Baboons)
GPS: S33 36.225 E24 11.987

The Baviaanskloof Mega Reserve is a protected area that lies between the Baviaanskloof and Kouga mountain ranges, about 62 miles (100km) northwest of the coastal city of Port Elizabeth. The area has an abundance of wildlife, including the elusive Cape leopard, and countless bird species.

The riding level is considered intermediate to advanced riding, so bear this in mind if you're going to tackle the route. Riders on bikes with smaller fuel tanks (less than 15 litres) need to be cautious as the next fuel stop is on the other side of Baviaanskloof, a distance of approximately 126 miles (203km) between Komdomo, at the eastern entrance, to Willowmore in the west. The estimated riding time is six to eight hours.

There are about 60 causeways crossing the rivers throughout the gorge, and although most crossings are concrete, some are low-level drifts of flowing water even during the dry season. In the wet months (May to July) several of the river crossings are very deep (5ft/1.5m) without causeways, such as Smitskraal and Doodsklip, so a little research on local forums may pay off if you intend riding during the winter months.

Some 25 miles (40km) in from Patensie is a great overnight stop called Kudu Kaya, a self-catering lodge (GPS: S33 40.233 E24 34.508) located on the right-hand side of the track; it's well signposted. Ensure that you have already purchased all your food in Patensie for an evening meal and breakfast the next morning.

There is an abundance of accommodation in Baviaanskloof and it's advisable to tackle the route over two days. Although it's easily completed in a single day, you will really want to enjoy this route and spend a second night in the reserve. The Makedaat Caves on the Willowmore side of the reserve are certainly worth a visit. Remember it is slow going, and if some of the river crossings are deep and problematic that will add more time to your journey.

Once you have completed the very memorable Baviaanskloof Gorge, some 87 miles (140km) from one side to the other, you will pass through the steep rock-walled Nuwekloof Pass, 21 miles (34km) from the junction of the N9, where you turn right to Willowmore.

Willowmore is a small settlement used as the final stop before entering the Baviaanskloof Reserve from the western side. The popular Royal Hotel of Willowmore will satisfy your biking hunger with tasty burgers and ice-cold beer. Once you have refuelled at the garage in Willowmore, take the R407 exit on to the gravel directly opposite the filling station. Ride for 58 miles (93km) along the splendid R407 to Klaarstroom, where you will meet the tarred junction of the N12; turn right and travel just 4.4 miles (7.1km) before turning off left on to the R407 again, towards Kredouw Pass and then a further 16 miles (26km) to Prince Albert. A suggestion for great accommodation in Prince Albert is the Karoo Lodge B&B

← **Looking down Swartberg Pass.**

– it's very neat, has a great pool and is well worth a visit.

As a South African biker, being in the small town of Prince Albert can mean only one thing: you have come up or are on your way down the Swartberg Pass, certainly one of the most sought-after and well-ridden gravel mountain passes in adventure motorcycling in Africa. It was constructed by the famous road builder of yesteryear, Thomas Bain, in 1888.

⬇ **Danish adventure bikers Karen Scott (left) and Stig Pehrson (right) on the back roads of Langerberg.**

⬆⬇ **The top of Swartberg Pass.**

The R328 out of Prince Albert descends into the gorge and the 14-mile (23km) Swartberg Pass chisels its way through wonderfully scenic geological rock formations. The Swartberg Pass's vertical rock walls and supporting man-made stonework walls are what makes this route so striking.

Gamkaskloof

Just after the summit of the Swartberg Pass is another spectacular valley – a rider's dream called Gamkaskloof, otherwise known as 'Die Hel'. The route has no exit and takes four hours as a round trip back to the Swartberg Pass. The Elands Pass is deep into Die Hel. It is steep and descends 1,312ft (400m) further into the bottom of the valley. The Gamka River in Die Hel often floods in the rainy season and can become too deep to pass in or out of the valley. If you have time or an extra day it's well worth going into Gamkaskloof for a night.

Once at the bottom of the Swartberg Pass the R328 turns to tarmac again and 1.7 miles (2.8km) after the tar starts is a right turn to Matjiesrivier and Oudtshoorn. The road is only tarred for a further 6.8 miles (11km) and then the glorious gravel meets your tyres again. The 25-mile (41km) route along the Swartberg Mountains to Calitzdorp is spectacularly scenic and takes travellers through Coetzeespoort Pass, Kruisrivierpoort Pass and the lush Groenfontein farming region.

Calitzdorp is a warm and friendly small town and a great place to find lunch and refuel. If you choose to overnight in Calitzdorp, the one place bikers feel at home is the Queens Country Lodge (GPS: S33 32.065 E21 41.192).

Leaving Calitzdorp, travel south on Stasie Road, which turns into gravel shortly outside the town, and after 10 miles (16km) you will begin the climb up Rooiberg Pass,

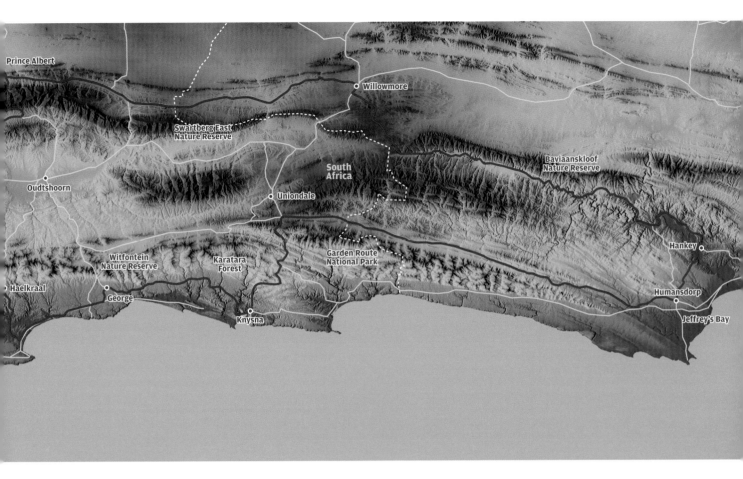

another spectacular gravel mountain pass. Continue on for 12 miles (20km) until a short descent down Assgaaibos Pass and into the flat lands towards the tiny settlement of Van Wyksdorp. Here you join up with the gravel road R327, turn left and travel towards Herbertsdale and after 8 miles (13km) keep to the left fork, again to Herbertsdale. At the next junction turn left again and travel for 12 miles (19km) on hard-packed gravel to the concrete low-level bridge crossing the Gouritz River.

Some 4.2 miles (6.8km) after crossing the Gouritz River is a small gravel road into the Vrederus private farm (GPS: S33 54.373 E21 42.696). This road is actually public access and meanders into the Attakwaskloof for 12 miles (20km) until arriving at biker heaven, the Bonniedale Holiday Farm (GPS: S33 52.430 E21 51.598).

The historical Ox Wagon trail through the Attakwaskloof to Bonniedale Holiday Farm is without doubt one of the best adventure biking roads in the Western Cape. The scenery is remarkable and seems to continue forever. The surface can be a little loose in the summer months, but it's easily ridable for all skill levels of rider. There are four farm gates that you pass through along the trail. Bonniedale (Holiday Farm) is the name of the farm and is not to be confused with the small town in the Overberg called Bonnievale – a common mistake. The farm has plentiful accommodation types ranging from B&B in the farmhouse to permanent caravans with kitchens and separate hot showers. There are also large tents with

double bunks and mattresses and a fully equipped chalet with its own swimming pool, suitable for sleeping up to 16 people. The farm has an abundance of activities including horse riding, hiking, mountain biking and a huge dam with a long zip line into the water.

There's loads of great off-road riding in the area and it's suitable for all skill levels. The route departs the farm at Bonniedale and you need to link up with the main gravel road at the junction. Turn left and travel 4.8 miles (7.8km) to the junction of the tarred R328 at Haelkraal. Fuel is available here if required. Turn right on to the R328 and travel 15.2 miles (24.6km) down towards the coast where you will meet up with the N2 on the Garden Route at Hartenbos, around 26 miles (42km) from George where this fantastic 617-mile (993km) journey began. And what's to stop you from doing it again?

RECOMMENDED MAPS

Cape Town to Port Elizabeth and East London Road Atlas
Publisher: Map Studio
ISBN: 9781770262195
Scale: 1:500,000

Garden Route and Route 62
Publisher: Map Studio
ISBN: 9781868098613
Scale: 1:300,000

Chapter 3

Asia

As the planet's largest continent, Asia covers about 30% of the world's land mass and includes 44 countries. It is an adventure motorcycling paradise, with more and more of the continent proving accessible. Vast tracts remain unexplored, however, and only a limited number of riders have had the opportunity to search out the wonders of Siberia and China.

Asia plays host to a number of outstanding geographic features: the world's tallest mountain – Mount Everest in the Himalayas; the world's most populated countries – China and India; the world's longest coastline; the world's deepest lake – Lake Baykal; and some of the most important rivers on the planet. The scale of the continent is also impressive – Russia alone stretches more than 5,500 miles (8,800km) across.

A great starting introduction to the continent for the adventure biker is the area referred to colloquially as the 'Stans', stretching from the Caspian Sea in the west to China in the east, and from Afghanistan in the south to Russia in the north. This area has historically been closely linked to the Silk Road and has acted as a crossroads for the movement of people, goods and ideas between Europe and Asia for centuries. In more ways than one, today's adventure motorcyclists continue that tradition.

The dramatic mountains of the Hindu Kush form a natural border between Afghanistan and Pakistan, with many snow-capped peaks reaching over 22,000ft (6,700m). This is some of the best riding on the continent, as is the high altitude Pamir Highway which stretches across much of Tajikistan and parts of Afghanistan, China and Pakistan.

You will want to ride the Karakoram Highway – the highest paved international road in the world. It connects China and Pakistan across the Karakoram mountain range through the Khunjerab Pass and extends more than 620 miles (1,000km) at an altitude of 15,397ft (4,693m) – a must on any adventure ride in the region.

To the northeast lie Mongolia and Siberia. The former is the most sparsely populated country in the world, covered by steppes, with mountains to the north and west and the Gobi Desert to the south. The latter is a combination of frozen tundra, rolling hills and plateaus as well as numerous rugged mountain ranges. It plays host to the legendary Road of Bones and BAM Road – some of the most adventurous terrain in the world.

Further east lie the wonders of Nepal and Tibet to contemplate before reaching the off-road riding paradise that is Southeast Asia. Travelling overland between countries is easy and items such as food and accommodation are very well priced. Whatever your destination, adventure motorcycling almost anywhere in Asia will not disappoint. ■

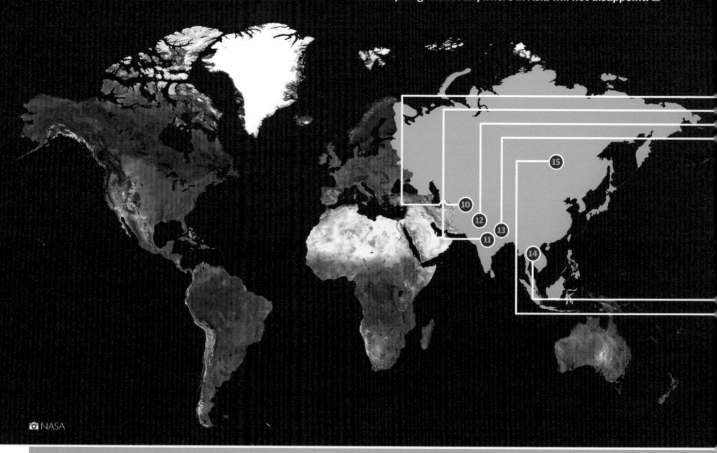

NASA

Central Asia

Adventure riding in the 'Stans'

Krzysztof Samborski

The so-called 'Stans' of Central Asia have become a classic adventure motorcycling destination in recent years. During the era of the former Soviet Union, the areas we know today as Kazakhstan, Uzbekistan, Turkmenistan, Tajikistan and Kyrgyzstan were largely out of reach for adventurers, but the collapse of the USSR in 1991 saw the creation of a number of independent countries, thereby opening up a wealth of new riding opportunities.

Central Asia extends from the Caspian Sea in the west to central China in the east, and from southern Russia in the north to northern India in the south. It is also sometimes known as Middle Asia or Inner Asia, and has historically been closely tied to its nomadic peoples and the Silk Road. As a result, historically the area has acted as a crossroads for the movement of people, goods and ideas between Europe and western, southern and eastern Asia.

An adventure into Central Asia is not to be underestimated, with the sheer scale of the area being the first consideration:

- Kazakhstan is the ninth largest country in the world and is some 11 times bigger than the United Kingdom.
- Uzbekistan is the same size as Sweden.
- Turkmenistan is almost the same size as Spain.
- The combined size of of Kazakhstan, Uzbekistan, Turkmenistan, Tajikistan and Kyrgyzstan is an area equivalent to more than twice the size of Mexico and more than half the size of Australia.

Second, the nature of the terrain, particularly the mountains, is very different from what most adventure riders are accustomed to, while what many people would define as a 'road', a 'border crossing' or a 'procedure' are quite different from other adventure destinations.

Central Asia routes

The typical route for European riders wanting to travel in Central Asia commences at Astrakhan in the south of Russia near the Caspian Sea and ends in the town of Almaty in Kazakhstan near the Chinese border. The return leg is typically further north, returning through Chelyabinsk and the Ural Mountains to Europe. This overall route takes in a little of Kazakhstan, Uzbekistan and Kyrgyzstan but rarely do riders enter Tajikistan.

The most ambitious riders reach Central Asia through the Caucasus countries and the Caspian Sea. This route is generally for adventurers who have lots of time, patience and money.

Kazakhstan is the most 'Soviet' of all Central Asian countries, but in some ways it's also the most 'European' too. From a rider's point of view, it is boring. The steppe provides some excitement during the first day, it's interesting on the second but ultimately boring by the fourth day. In Kazakhstan the most interesting things are to be found to the south and southeast of the country.

The main transit route is also the longest. It leads through Kurgan, Pietropavlovsk and Astana towards Almaty. Another popular option is to enter from the direction of Saratov through Ozinki, heading towards

THE PAMIR HIGHWAY

The Pamir Mountains represent the meeting point of three great mountain ranges: the Tian Shan, the Karakorum/Himalaya and the Hindu Kush. The Pamir Highway, marked as the M41 on most maps, runs through the Pamir Mountains connecting Tajikistan's capital, Dushanbe, with Osh in Kyrgyzstan. From Dushanbe the road leads 325 miles (523km) to Khorog, crossing the Kafirnigan, Vakhsh and Bartang Rivers. From there it continues east for a distance of 193 miles (311km) to Murgab, the highest town in Tajikistan. From here it crosses the Murgab River before turning north. The Pamir Highway reaches 15,200ft (4,650m) at the Ak-Baital Pass, then passes the scenic Lake Karakul (otherwise known as the Black Lake) before crossing into Kyrgyzstan and on to Osh. The Murgab to Osh leg is 261 miles (419km) long.

The Pamir Highway is known as the second highest altitude international highway in the world, and it has been used for hundreds of years as one of the only viable routes through the Pamir Mountains, forming a vital link on the ancient Silk Road trade route.

The route has been off-limits to travellers until recently. This remote highway takes you through wonderful high plateau scenery, but it is sparsely maintained – paved in places, but heavily damaged by erosion, earthquakes, landslides and avalanches. Construction and maintenance levels vary substantially along the way and it is worth talking to riders who have recently ridden the route for up-to-date assessments. The road has several border checkpoints, where you will be required to register. Blue distance posts (marked in kilometres) line the way, with the distance from Khorog marked on one side and from Osh on the other.

← River crossings are a regular occurrence in this part of the world.

⬇ Central Asia is an adventure motorcycling paradise.

↑ Side roads can take you to remote and beautiful places.

→ On the road in the border area between Afghanistan and Tajikistan.

Uralsk and Aktiube. Further on the road goes through the Aralsk and towards Baikonur and Shymkent. Just a few years ago it was quite a challenging route but now the road has been renewed. Another very interesting route to Central Asia is the one leading between the Caspian Sea and the Aral Sea. It leads you through Uzbekistan, though, which has challenges when it comes to visas and border crossings. On this route you will find the most dirt roads and you will have a chance to challenge the semi-desert landscape.

If your goal is not to get through the region in the quickest time possible but instead to take in the best parts, then we are dealing with another world altogether and it is time to think carefully about the mountains of Central Asia.

The Pamir Highway

The best known route is the Pamir Highway between Dushanbe in Tajikistan and Osh in Kyrgyzstan. This is not the most beautiful road, but it is a route which must be travelled when heading through Tajikistan.

In the high mountains – and these cover much of Tajikistan, Kyrgyzstan and even Afghanistan – the road network is poor but the route described cannot be missed. The highest point is the Ak-Baital Pass at 15,272ft (4,655m). It is a more challenging climb from the south side by comparison to the north.

The Pamir Highway is a mainly tarmac road leading through the Pamir Plateau. Most of it runs at 13,123ft (4,000m) or higher. The road is technically quite easy, but look out for debris on the road and large potholes. It's unlikely that you will meet many other vehicles so be prepared to deal with technical breakdowns yourself. A good campsite can be found in the surroundings of Murgab. One can also stop at Kara Kul Lake. Access to the water can be problematic, but it's worth a try to see Lenin's Peak in full view. Keen photographers should wake up at sunrise for some spectacular imagery.

The most problematic part of the whole route can be the Kyzyl-Art Pass at the Kyrgyzstan-Tajikistan border crossing and depends on two key factors – how harsh the preceding winter season has been and how much money has been spent on road renovations. The surface is red clay and travelling on this road after the rains will bring you some 'unforgettable' experiences. Landslides are commonplace and potholes the size of motorcycles lie in wait in the stretch between the border crossings.

From Dushanbe to Khorog fuel is readily available, but from here you need to be prepared as the next fuel station after Khorog is in Sary Tash, some 435 miles (700km) along the route. You will find fuel easily in Murgab by asking for it in the bazaar, failing which fuel can

↑ **Bridge crossing on the Afghanistan/ Tajikistan border.**

be bought in Ali Chur or at Kara Kul Lake. From Sary Tash fuel is available at regular intervals.

Wakhan Corridor

If you have a few days to spare then don't hesitate to head south to the Wakhan Corridor, an area in the far northeastern part of Afghanistan which forms a land link or 'corridor' between Afghanistan and China. The 'Corridor' is a long and slender panhandle 140 miles (220km) long and between 10–40 miles (16–64km) wide. It separates Tajikistan in the north from Pakistan in the south. Many riders describe it as the most beautiful road they have ever seen. It's not necessarily a tough road, but it took the life of my dearest friend in 2010, so be on your guard. There are fuel stations in Khorog and Ishkashim. At times along the route the Afghan border is just 65ft (20m) away.

In most villages on this route you will find shops with basic products and in many you will be able to spend the night. The last place like this towards Murgab is Langar. There are two guesthouses and a hotel managed by the Aga Khan Foundation. It's certainly worth making a one-

day stop to take in a view of the Hindu Kush – the 500-mile (800km) mountain range that stretches between central Afghanistan and northern Pakistan. It is the westernmost extension of the Pamir Mountains.

For a good hot shower, head towards Garm-Chashma and Vrang. While you are in the area take a look at the old fortress ruins, the remains of the Buddhists' influence and the stone paintings. Try to plan your route to be in Ishkashima on a Saturday to visit a bazaar alongside the border crossing, situated on the island on the Panj River. It's populated by inhabitants from both the Afghanistan and Tajikistan sides of the river and you can cross over without needing a visa to pick up a few Afghan souvenirs.

Murgab to Zorkul

This is a route that requires good preparation. First of all you'll need a permit that will allow you access to visit Zorkul. It's not only a natural reserve but also a lake that borders Afghanistan. Get a permit from the border police in Khorog, as information about securing the permit in Murgab is sketchy at best. The route leads through a

↑ **En route from Jalalabad to Kazarman.**

high mountain wilderness and the road is good up to Jarty Gumbez. Further on it is less obvious and quite demanding. In Jarty Gumbez there is a hunter's hut and one can sleep over in it. On this road you will probably meet no one else, and from the exit off the M41 the roads are only dirt. The highest pass is at 14,271ft (4,350m) and there are little or no supplies available. A light adventure bike is best and it pays to have a reasonable level of off-road riding experience. Completing the route on one of the larger adventure bikes is possible, though not advised.

Bartang Valley

The stark Bartang Valley with its barren rock walls lies in the western Pamirs. It is a breathtaking landscape and a real adventure playground. The road into the valley branches off the main road to Dushanbe, just before the village of Rushan, some 38 miles (61km) from Khorog. The valley is a very rarely accessed short cut leading from Rushan towards Kara Kul Lake. The inhabitants of Bartang have the well-deserved title as the most

→ **You will undoubtedly attract interest from the locals.**

hospitable in the whole of Tajikistan. Research this route carefully before attempting it – it's vulnerable to landslides which can keep the road blocked for weeks. Once again, the likelihood of meeting other vehicles is minimal. The downside of this route is that you are likely to miss out on the Wakhan Corridor. Solo journeys are discouraged, given the remoteness, and it's imperative to take all provisions as well as additional fuel.

Kyrgyzstan – Sary Mogul – Lenin's Peak base camp

Should you have a day or two to spare, an option is to divert off the main road and through the Alay Valley, heading west towards the city of Sary Mogul.

Poor quality tarmac covers much of the route from Sary Tash to Sary Mogul. There you turn left and pass the first and only bridge in the area. The road to Onion Fields – the location where alpinists from different countries pitch their tents before attempting to climb Lenin's Peak at 23,405ft (7,134m) – and base camp is about 25 miles (40km) and you must cross a couple of shallow streams. The proximity of the mountains is remarkable in this area and they are not to be underestimated – in 1990 an earthquake moved a massive rock, which rolled on to a camp, killing 43 climbers.

Be sure to refuel in Sary Tash and leave any unnecessary kit there as you must return back through the village. Sary Tash is a minor village and major crossroads in the Alay Valley of Osh Province, Kyrgyzstan. In addition to the petrol station, this remote village has a few small shops and two guesthouses. To the north, the M41 goes over the Taldyk Pass to Gulcha and Osh in the Ferghana Valley. One travel guide describes this as 'spectacular' and 'one of the most beautiful drives in Kyrgyzstan'. To the south, after leaving the Alay Valley, the M41 deteriorates quickly and rises to the 14,041ft (4,280m) Kyzyl-Art Pass into Tajikistan. This route requires considerable preparation and paperwork. The route is not used regularly and there are few services between Sary Tash and Murgab. Approximately 50 miles (80km) to the east on the A371 is the Irkeshtam Pass into Xinjiang, China. To the west, the A372 leads down the Alay Valley. The pass at the western end is closed to foreigners.

Jalalabad – Kazarman – Ak Tal

This is a good route to follow if you need to make up time on the Osh-Bishkek road to the Lake Song Kul region. The most challenging part of the route is the Kaldama Pass between Jalalabad and Kazarman. It's particularly steep in places but the views are wonderful, the most scenic of which is near the Kara Koo Pass on the last 37-mile (60km) stretch before reaching Ak Tal. Fuel is available in Jalalabad, Kazarman, Ak Tal and Baetov, if you turn right past Kazarman heading for Tash Rabat.

Lake Song Kul region

Lake Song Kul is a true paradise for off-road amateurs. It's a nature reserve and safely accessible with your own

THE STANS

Kazakhstan
Population:	15 million
Capital:	Astana
Currency:	Tenge (KZT)
Total area:	1,052,089 square miles (2,724,900km2)
Terrain:	Vast flat steppe extending from the Volga in the west to the Altai Mountains in the east, and from the plains of western Siberia in the north to the oases and deserts of Central Asia in the south.
Fast fact:	Kazakhstan is the ninth largest country in the world and in 1961 Yuryi Gagarin, the Russian cosmonaut, made the first manned space flight from the Baykonur Cosmodrome in Kazakhstan.

Kyrgyzstan
Population:	5.5 million
Capital:	Bishkek
Currency:	Som (KGS)
Total area:	77,201 square miles (199,951km2)
Terrain:	Peaks of the Tien Shan Mountains and associated valleys and basins encompass the entire nation.
Fast fact:	A country of incredible natural beauty and proud nomadic traditions, most of Kyrgyzstan was formally annexed to Russia in 1876. The Kyrgyz staged a major revolt against the Tsarist Empire in 1916, in which almost one-sixth of the Kyrgyz population was killed.

Tajikistan
Population:	7.5 million
Capital:	Dushanbe
Currency:	Somoni (TJS)
Total area:	55,251 square miles (143,100km2)
Terrain:	The Pamir and Alay Mountains dominate the landscape; the western Fergana Valley lies in the north, Kofarnihon and Vakhsh Valleys are in the southwest.
Fast fact:	More than 90% of the country is mountainous, with Ismoili Somoni the highest point at 24,589ft (7,495m).

Uzbekistan
Population:	28 million
Capital:	Tashkent
Currency:	Sum (UZS)
Total area:	172,742 square miles (447,400km2)
Terrain:	Mostly flat to rolling sandy desert with dunes; broad, flat, intensely irrigated river valleys along the courses of Amu Darya, Syr Darya (Sirdaryo) and Zarafshon; Fergana Valley in the east is surrounded by mountainous Tajikistan and Kyrgyzstan; the shrinking Aral Sea lies in the west.
Fast fact:	During the Soviet era, intensive production of 'white gold' (cotton) and grain led to overuse of agrochemicals and the depletion of water supplies, which have left the land poisoned and the Aral Sea and certain rivers half dry.

Turkmenistan
Population:	5 million
Capital:	Ashgabat
Currency:	Manat (TMM)
Total area:	188,456 square miles (488,100km2)
Terrain:	Flat to rolling sandy desert with dunes rising to mountains in the south; low mountains along the border with Iran; borders the Caspian Sea in the west.
Fast fact:	Eastern Turkmenistan for centuries formed part of the Persian province of Khurasan; in medieval times Merv (today known as Mary) was one of the great cities of the Islamic world and an important stop on the Silk Road.

Nomadic villages such as this are a common sight.

Central Asia's lakes make for a spectacular backdrop.

motorcycle from May to September. During this time, shepherds from Kyrgyzstan camp in the area with their animals. Thousands of horses and sheep grazing on green meadows near the blue lake and surrounded by snowy mountains make an enormous impression. The lake measures 11 miles (18km) by 18 miles (29km) and is 42 feet (13m) deep, making it the second largest lake in Kyrgyzstan.

The most popular road to the lake (and the one in the best condition) is that leading from Sary Bulak. You must turn right off the main road towards Naryn and after 25 miles (40km) you will get to the Kalmak Ashuu Pass at 11,305ft (3,446m), from which you will see the lake. Other roads lead from the city of Kurtka (en route from Kazarman to Ak Tal) and provide a beautiful climb through a valley resembling the Alps, with spectacular views. A similar route exists from Kochkor towards Naryn – you head through the Dolon Pass at 9,960ft (3,038m) and turn right after the city of Kara Ungkur. The final climb up to the lake is challenging – a real test of your bike's clutch and brakes (depending on whether you're headed up or down)

– but you'll finally be rewarded with spectacular views. The hardest road to Song Kul leads from Susamyr through the Kara Keche mines. It's not worth taking this route unless you're specifically on your way from Susamyr.

It's certainly worth spending a few days at the lake, whichever route you take. You will not find any fuel here, or electricity for that matter – just the basics on which shepherds exist – but there's an authentic 'simple life' to be experienced here. Accommodation is offered in yurts (portable, felt-covered, wooden lattice-framed structures, traditionally used by nomads in the steppes of Central Asia). It's best to stay on the north side of the lake, close to a concrete monument with the inscription 'Save Song Kul' (in this location there is some mobile phone coverage). The shepherds and yurta owners there are very hospitable towards bikers – you can borrow horses from them or order a fish dinner. If you travel with a bigger group you can ask for a dinner of a whole lamb; the ritual of its killing is an interesting photo opportunity. Just remember that at the culmination of the dinner you are likely to be offered the lamb's eye to eat. You should not refuse it. And what does a lamb's eye taste like? Like an eye…! Culinary delights aside, you should ride the 75 miles (120km) around the lake, leaving all unnecessary belongings in your yurta. Bear in mind there is no fuel at the lake, so head to Sary Bulak or Ak Tal to fill up.

Lake Issyk Kul region

About 60 miles (100km) northeast of Lake Song Kul lies Lake Issyk Kul in the northern Tian Shan Mountains in eastern Kyrgyzstan. With a shoreline of 427 miles (688km), it is the tenth largest lake in the world by volume and the second largest saline lake after the Caspian Sea, surrounded by numerous 16,400ft (5,000m) snow-capped peaks.

The lake is an ideal spot for a few days' rest. If you need some amenities you should choose the northern route,

↟ On the Pamir
Highway.

around the top of the lake, where you will find some hotels and cafés. The rich folk of Almaty holiday here. If you are looking for some peace, then you should choose the wilder southern side of the lake; the beaches around the cities of Tamga and Barskoon are worth a visit. The route around the lake is about 240 miles (400km) and can be ridden in two days. Look for your own paths around the lake – you're almost guaranteed some great adventure riding in any of the valleys. A spectacular road leads to Barskoon Pass from the city of the same name. The road is in great condition and within an hour you can climb to a height of 13,123ft (4,000m).

When to go?

It is best to travel through the 'Stans' from the end of May through to the end of September. The climate is predominantly dry and only the higher mountains will still have snow. The permanent snow line in Tien Shan and Pamir sits at around 16,400ft (5,000m), and the routes described in this section reach up to 15,300ft (4,655m) above sea level, but snow has been known to fall at any time both in Pamir and Tien Shan. Fresh snow does not usually exceed a depth of 4in (10cm) and melts within a few hours. When travelling through the 'Stans' it is commonplace to experience quite dramatic temperature swings: from Murgab in Turkmenistan to Osh the distance is approximately 250 miles (400km) and can be ridden in a single day, but the route can see an extreme swing of 40°C.

Which motorcycle to ride?

Most of the routes described can be ridden on most adventure motorcycles. The distances involved place the emphasis on the bike's range, as well as the necessity to replace tyres and carry out an oil change. The long straight sections leading through Russia or Kazakhstan will be tiring for singles and their vibrations will deter some riders. For those who want to travel quickly, see a lot and not go off the main roads, a twin cylinder dual sport machine is more than capable. For those who have more time and prefer exploring secondary roads, a simple single cylinder bike is the way to go.

Fuel

Key questions for adventure bikers heading to the 'Stans' relate to fuel, the distances between fuel stations and a bike's behaviour at high altitudes. Each year the quality of the petrol is better, but if you intend to cross the Pamir Highway then it's best to leave your catalytic converter at home. Above 10,000ft (3,050m) all motorcycles will lose some power but a properly adjusted engine should make riding relatively comfortable to 14,750ft (4,495m). The distances between fuel stations can be significant. Even recently, in some places it could stretch to 620 miles (1,000km), but fortunately it's possible to purchase a limited quantity of fuel in most villages.

Health

Unsurprisingly, healthcare facilities are often very basic, especially in remote parts of the region. A trip to Central Asia does not require any specific vaccinations. Be conscious of the local food you eat and try to limit the inclusion of new items on your menu. Snakes, scorpions and some poisonous spiders are fairly commonplace, so be aware when camping. Again, given the distances involved, it can be at least a day if not more before you might find a doctor.

Be wary of medicines such as Diamox and Diuramid which are designed to reduce the impact of Acute Mountain Sickness (AMS), something of which you need to be aware given the altitude in the region. If you have symptoms such as a dry cough, weakness, consciousness disorder, headaches, nausea and drowsiness, then it is highly likely that the altitude is affecting you. The best remedy is to ride down to below 10,000ft (3,050m). In the Pamir Mountains, for example, this is not exactly an easy task and can mean a good few hundreds miles before you reach a safe altitude. Local doctors are very helpful, but poor diagnostic equipment can limit their capabilities. Hospitals in Central Asia, even those in large cities, are a 'significant experience' for a western European citizen.

Currency and cash machines

Each year there are more and more ATM machines, but outside the larger cities they are scarce and not everyone will eagerly co-operate with a credit card. When travelling the best advice is to take US dollars; the Euro is still an 'exotic currency' and in many parts of Central Asia it is, in fact, totally unknown. Dollars should be taken in bills not smaller than US$20 and issued after the year 2000, otherwise one should expect the transaction to attract an unfavourable exchange rate.

Insurance

In most of the 'Stans' there are no specific insurance obligations (Kazakhstan is the exception). It is worth noting that in the event of an accident, by default you will bear the responsibility of damages to the other vehicle(s). Also note that the traffic regulations in Asian cities are not necessarily obvious for a newcomer from the West.

Visas, registrations, permits and documents

Travel through countries in Central Asia requires those from the European Union to hold a visa. These cannot generally be obtained at the border and it is best to have them organised in advance. Despite this frustration, the regulations are easing and visitors no longer need a special invitation to visit. It remains difficult to obtain a visa for Turkmenistan and Uzbekistan, so it may be worth considering transit visas and shortening your stay in these countries. Most of the countries mentioned have done away with the obligation for foreign travellers to register with the OVIR (Office of Visas and Registrations); however, that rule still applies in Uzbekistan (to be done within three days of arrival) and in Kazakhstan (within five days). If you stop at a hotel then this can generally be done by the receptionist. You should receive specific confirmation of your registration, as you can be asked for this by any policeman. These rules are quite strictly followed in Uzbekistan and not following them can cause issues and attract a fine.

Be advised that entry into the Pamir region requires a special permit. The so-called Gorno-Badakhshan Autonomous Oblast (GBAO) area starts at Kalaikhum and ends at the Kyrgyz border at Kyzyl-Art Pass. This region of Tajikistan is a special border zone and an additional permit is required to travel there. When applying for the visa you should indicate a wish to visit the Pamir. In addition to the visa in your passport there will be a large stamp allowing you to travel through the GBAO.

A carnet de passage is not required to travel through the 'Stans' – a vehicle registration document, passport with all the relevant visas and international driver's licence will suffice. When entering Tajikistan via some of the border crossings you will have to pay a 'tax' of around 40 Somoni (£5.00) per bike. Don't let the authorities persuade you that it's more than this!

Language

Russian is still the lingua franca in the region. It is worthwhile acquainting yourself with a few of the most useful words.

English is increasingly popular with young people, but outside the cities it will be hard to communicate without some basic Russian phrases.

Safety, bribes and tricks

In all the countries and routes described, travellers can feel safe and generally travel without concerns. I travelled there in 2010 right after the ethnic riots between the Kyrgyz and Uzbeks in Osh. There was no sign of any hostility or dislike towards foreigners. Bribery is common, but if you don't wish to engage in this then you don't have to pay. It is enough to say that you don't understand anything. Always write down a badge number of a policeman confronting you. Withholding of a passport or a driver's licence has been known to happen, and in such cases you should call your embassy to inform them and to request their intervention, which more often than not has the desired effect. If for some reason you have transgressed, then it is not uncommon to bargain on the level of penalty levied. Always remember to complete any declarations thoroughly, but refuse if there are no documents in English. Customs officers will soon identify inexperienced travellers who don't know the 'local procedures'.

RECOMMENDED MAPS

Turkmenistan, Tajikistan and Kyrgyzstan
Publisher: International Travel Maps
ISBN: 9781553412854
Scale: 1:1,350,000 / 1:1,000,000

Kazakhstan
Publisher: International Travel Maps
ISBN: 9781553412694
Scale: 1:2,300,000

Silk Road Countries
Publisher: Gizi Maps
ISBN: 9789633041384
Scale: 1:3,000,000

Central Asia (road edition)
Publisher: Gizi Maps
ISBN: 9789630372381
Scale: 1:1,750,000

The Pamirs
Publisher: Gecko Maps
ISBN: 9783906593357
Scale: 1:500,000

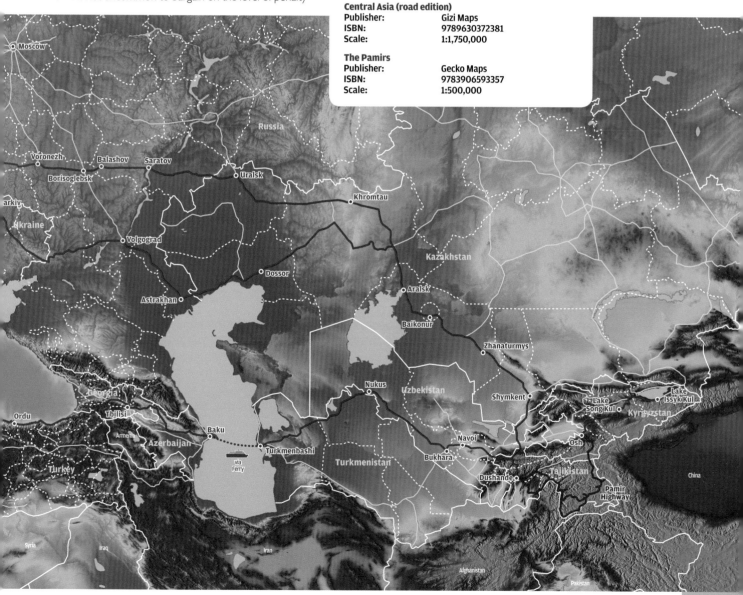

India's Golden Triangle

Sights of wonder on the subcontinent

Sam Manicom

India. It's a land that entices and teases at the same time, yet it's also the country most likely to give you a full-on culture shock. It's a huge subcontinent which has the ability to surprise even the most hard-core overlander. With more than 44,000 asphalted miles (71,000km) of National Highway, plus minor roads and countless sand and gravel roads, it holds a complex weave of delights that easily tempt you to spend far more time than perhaps your visa and budget allow for. And yes, some of the off-road trails are the best in the world, but none of those routes give the traveller such an enormous taste of this varied, exotic and mysterious land as the 'Golden Triangle'.

To my mind, adventure should be a mix of every challenge that can possibly assault your senses. And I mean all your senses. Your sense of sight should be astounded. Your sense of smell should be tantalised. Your sense of touch should come not only from the feel through your handlebar grips, but you should be able to take in the texture of luxurious silks and the tastes of strange foods. There's no doubt that your sense of hearing will be hammered in India, but this trail will also allow you to appreciate the sound of silence.

As for your sixth sense, the traffic alone will make you very happy that you possess even the smallest dash of that. Indeed, there are times when you'll be wishing that this one was the most enhanced sense you possess. Why? Well, in the on-the-road pecking order, as a motorcyclist you are one of the lowest of the low. Only pedestrians and bicycle riders are lower down the food chain than you are. And the rules of the road are guaranteed to challenge every thought you have about the rights and wrongs of road travel. The rules of your homeland simply don't apply here.

If you start your ride with a sense of machismo, then you'll soon find that the rough edge of this thought process is quickly knocked off. You'll equally rapidly find yourself becoming a believer of fate ruling all. If it's your time, then it's your time, and nothing you can do will affect what's going to happen. But common sense will have you fighting hard against letting yourself fall fully into the arms of fate!

Does this all sound far too dramatic? Well, the rules of the road are as follows: (1) I'm bigger than you are, so I go first; (2) I was here first, so I go first; (3) my horn is louder than yours, so I go first. And the kings of the road? They are the buses, whose drivers definitely believe in fate. Many of the glittering posters and signs in their bus windows ensure that you have no doubt about this – not that their driving styles could leave any element of doubt in your mind. The vehicles that stand at their 'royal' shoulders are the trucks. Truck drivers are the James Bonds of India. Leastways, they think they are, and that this gives them the right to dispose of anyone in their path. I'm led to believe that many have bribed their way into possession of that licence…

Hardly a day will go past without your seeing an accident involving one or the other of these two vehicles, and the only thing that will protect you from them is that paranormal sixth sense and an ability to get out of the

ROAD STATISTICS IN INDIA

- India has around 44,000 miles (71,000km) of National Highways, of which 372 miles (600km) are classified as expressways.
- In 2000, around 40% of villages in India lacked access to all-weather roads and remained isolated during the monsoon season.
- A 2009 estimate put the total road length in India at 2,063,210 miles (3,320,410km), making it the third largest network in the world.
- The roads carry almost 90% of the country's passenger traffic and 65% of its freight.

way faster than they can get to you. Expect to be literally run off the road! Oh, and overtaking on blind bends is the norm. Ponder this for a moment: it's reported that in 2009 180,000 people were killed on India's roads. That figure was only 80,000 back in 1994.

So are trucks and buses the only hazards? No! Taxi drivers often happily spend more time looking over their shoulders as they chat to their passengers than they do looking where they are going. Those who do concentrate put all of their energy into ensuring that the one foot of space around their vehicle is OK, while the rest of the traffic can go sing. Small children seem to have a belief in fate bred into them from birth, and the goats are too stupid to know any better. Dogs? Sometimes I think that all they want to do is to end their miserable lives as quickly as they can, under your wheels … but seriously, most of the dogs are feral and few have owners. Scavenging a daily meal in a hungry land like India can't be an easy task. When I see a weakened, heat-baffled bag of bones on four legs heading out into the road in front of me, I know it's going to be unpredictable. But hey, the biggest four-legged surprises are the cows. They are esteemed

← **In the cool of the dawn.**

⬇ **Tempo Taxi – Delhi.**

It's 6.30am – and it's rush hour already.

as holy creatures by Hindus, which means they can go anywhere and do anything they want. If a cow wants to cause a traffic jam on the motorway by stopping for a nap, everyone lets them. If they feel like congregating for a cud-chewing session in the middle of the high street, so be it. And, of course, there is that story of Benetton in Mumbai being closed for three weeks because a cow had taken up residence in the entranceway…

Does this all sound far too dire or bizarre to entice you to attempt this wonderful journey? Well, let me tell you this. Put all of these elements of colourful, potential doom and gloom into one great big mix and the result is a huge adrenalin buzz. And when you can thread that buzz through a weave of ancient and modern history,

then there is no better trip to be had. The route through the Golden Triangle is excellent. You can also consider this triangular route as the centre of a spider's web of roads that will lead you to some of India's most amazing sights.

You'll be setting off from Delhi, the capital of India, and taking in Agra and Jaipur. The Golden Triangle hosts many of India's great cultural gems as well as a wonderful selection of the country's different landscapes. It is so called because of the triangular shape formed by the locations of New Delhi, Agra and Rajasthan on a map.

The older quarters of Delhi will take you riding through alleyways bordered with stalls, and past tiny shops that are tucked away into walls little changed since the times of the Moguls. The flip side of the city is the spread of elegantly laid out squares, boulevards and imposing buildings that were built in the time of the Raj. Dotted into this mix of the centuries are neck-achingly tall, skinny-sided skyscrapers. You'll be riding this seemingly endless city amid a cacophony of noises that are layered one upon another. The buzzing sounds of fume-belching auto rickshaws and the urgent horns of bright yellow Ambassador taxis are an assault that will make you happy you are wearing a crash helmet. Horn-blasting buses and trucks blend with the sounds of vendors touting their wares, and the eclectic mash of noise that is always there when you have several million people living their lives in close proximity.

Before leaving Delhi, make time to explore the Red Fort, Jama Masjid, Chandni Chowk, Rajghat, Qutub Minar, Old Fort, Lodhi Garden, President House, Parliament House, Humayun's Tomb, the Lotus Temple and the Akshardham Temple. Then it's on with the ride on a set of roads that, over the coming days, will give you a taste of virtually every road surface which India has to challenge you with. You'll be rolling your wheels along immaculate asphalt, potholed nightmares which will have you wishing you were slaloming the cool of Europe's ski slopes, cobblestones that will rattle

Pleasing the eye for centuries.

your teeth as they take you skirting steep hillsides and earth tracks that you'll be sharing with timeless ox carts.

You start by heading out along the relative peace of 127 miles (204km) of smooth, flat, open road that crosses the fertile lands of Uttar Pradesh, to the city of Agra. This city is the showcase of the Mughal Empire and is the home of Shah Jahan's magical Taj Mahal; one of the Seven Wonders of the World. Be warned, though, this is no two-hour journey. You need at least double that time to allow for all the eventualities that any Indian road is going to offer you. You'll want to make stops, too.

From there you'll head south and west on a five-hour ride, more or less, to the edge of the dramatic deserts of Rajasthan and the Rajput's royal pink city of Jaipur. On your way there you'll often find wheat on the road, as villagers use the passing vehicles to thrash it. This can be a slippery surprise! After you've sampled the delights of this city, including the Birla Temple, the architecturally brilliant Amber Fort, the City Palace, the Hawa Mahal (the Palace of Winds) and, of course, the street bazaars, you are faced with a choice. Head further west into the Thar Desert and

the magnificent fortress city of Jaisalmer, or continue back through an ever-changing landscape, sharing the roads with camel-drawn vehicles, towards Delhi again.

The 430-mile (692km) Golden Triangle route shows you the dramatic changes that are India, and this is one of its main attractions. Over at least a week, this magical route will allow you to travel back and forth in time from the brash modernity of cosmopolitan Delhi to the side roads where life remains much as it has for hundreds of years.

Central Delhi to Agra Fort

Start off from the Connaught Circus in central Delhi. Leaving in a southeasterly direction, ride along Kasturba Gandhi Marg, past the Embassy of Malta, keeping straight as the road name changes to Curzon Street.

Keep straight on until you get to India Gate Hexagon Road. As the name suggests, this hexagonal road skirts the India Gate. Head southeast from India Gate along Shershah Road. Turn right at the T-junction on to Mathura Road and head south, continuing on over the Mahatma Gandhi Mark Ring Road (the NH2). This is the 'Raja Garden' junction.

↑ 'Hey Misters, you want to swop?'

TIPS FOR RIDING IN INDIA

- Fit a very loud horn to your bike!
- Drive on the left or right of the road? Actually both. Technically you should drive on the left, unless it is occupied. If that's the case, go to the right, unless that is also occupied. Then proceed by occupying the next available gap. Really!
- At road tolls ask to see the receipt before you pay. The prices are often doubled for foreigners.
- There are many unofficial tolls. If there isn't an official receipt, drive on.
- Early starts are the best way to avoid traffic when leaving cities. You need to be thinking about a 6am start to avoid the main traffic rush. It's often cooler at that time of day anyway, which is an added bonus.
- Pay auto rickshaw drivers to guide you to your hotels in big cities; 50 rupees is about right for this – but don't pay them until you get to your destination.
- There are a few road signs around. Those that are there are often in English and Hindi, sometimes just the latter. Many junctions don't have any signs. Ask if you get lost, but ask someone well dressed because they are more likely to speak English and to know something about anything beyond the place where you are. If you are really stuck, ask in a pharmacy: you'll get very level-headed answers there, more often than not.
- If you have to ask the way, never ask a leading question such as 'Is this the road for Delhi?' You'll often get a 'Yes', but it may well be meaningless, because people often don't know the answer but they don't want to disappoint you. Sometimes 'Yes' is the only English they know. It's much better simply to ask 'Delhi?', of several people where possible, and take note of the most answers for one direction. If you do get lost, though, no worries – it's just the start of a new adventure.
- Night-time riding in India? Unless you have no choice, don't do it. It's a bit like playing Russian roulette, because you don't know who among the drivers is loaded with illicit arrack. It's also a fact that truck drivers have to drive a ridiculous number of hours to make a living and many of them are half asleep from the strain of doing this. Many of the roads, even the main roads, don't have hard shoulders. Some have a foot drop off the asphalt on to a sandy, boulder-strewn surface. Trucks and buses often don't use their headlights! Those that do often have them at a mismatched but still dazzling full beam, which they will use at the last minute. Many only have one light working, so don't assume it's a motorcycle heading towards you.

↑ A roadside truck stop.

Continue on along the Mathura Road, which has now rather oddly turned itself into the NH2. (You'll find this sudden and somewhat illogical change of road numbers quite common in India.) Keep going straight in a southeasterly direction, and you'll start to see signs for Faridabad and Agra.

Ride straight through the sprawling town of Faridabad, still on the NH2. If you've made an early start to get out of Delhi, the roadside truck stops here are great places to grab chai, 'aigs' and 'tost'. You might even be lucky enough to find 'Corn Flaks'.

The NH2 takes a looping left hook through the town of Palwal and then skirts the town after which it is named, Mathura.

Once into Agra, just before the river, take a right turn on to the Charan Tiwari Road and head for the Jama Masjid Road and the Agra Fort.

Further south from this point is the Taj Ganj, which is the main small hotel and backpacker-type accommodation area. Several of the hotels have off-road parking for bikes or will allow you to put your bike in their reception area. Some of these hotels have great rooftop views out over the Taj Mahal.

Agra Fort to Jaipur

From the Jama Masjid Road, ride straight over the multiple road junction on to the Mantola Road and head west. After two minor crossroads take the fork right on to the Ghalibpura Road.

At the major crossroads with the Mahatma Gandhi Road, take the (staggered) straight-over option on to the Syed Ali Nabi Road, which is NH11. Keeping straight and heading southwest, this road changes its name to the Fatehpur Sikri Road, but it remains the NH11.

After a while you'll find yourself riding through the middle of the Kheria airport! You'll also be getting glimpses of the mainline railway. It's well worth stopping to watch these trains. India still has the largest rail network in the world and the trains are living history.

Your next stop is Fatehpur Sikri, which will take you roughly an hour. As you approach the town the NH11 swings to the right, to loop around the top of the built-up area. The Fatehpur Sikri Fort is well worth spending several hours exploring.

Head back out along the same road and rejoin the NH11, turning left as you do so. Your next stop is Bharatpur, which will also take you around an hour's ride. From Bharatpur you could do a side trip into the Keoladeo National Park, if you have time. It is worth making time as this park has a huge variety of wildlife, both native and migratory.

The NH11 snakes through the southern side of Bharatpur, which is also worth exploring. You'll find many market areas, including several great spots to get a motorcycle cover made. These covers act as invisibility cloaks for your bike in India. You could, at this junction, take a turning off and head down the 180-mile (288km) road to the Ranthambhore National Park. The park is famous for its large population of tigers and it's considered to be one of the best places in India to see

↑ Gravel road fun.

the Royal Bengal tigers in their natural habitat. It's also the site of one of the largest banyan trees in India. Follow NH11 west out of town and then head south along State Highway 43. At the Ucchan junction head off southwest along State Highway 1. You'll see signs for the park when you get to the town of Sawai Madhopur, which is at the junction of NH116 and MDR111.

If you are heading for Jaipur, though, stay on the NH11, passing through the towns of Bamanpura, Dausa and Kanauta. You cross over NH8 on the outskirts of Jaipur. Be warned, if you ask to be guided by a rickshaw driver in this city, you'll get taken to a hotel of the driver's choice! Unless, that is, your target hotel is on the list of 30% commission hotels for that particular driver. You need to be insistent, but this city is far easier to find your way around than Delhi, so you probably won't need help. I tend to head for the Jaipur Inn, as you have a choice of

↓ Straight to the Thar Desert.

ABOUT THE AUTHOR

Over a period of eight years, Sam Manicom rode 200,000 miles (322,000km) through 55 countries around the world. He is the author of four adventure motorcycle travel books: *Into Africa, Under Asian Skies, Distant Suns* and *Tortillas to Totems*. Sam has been a freelance travel writer for magazines and newspapers around the world since 1996. See www.sam-manicom.com for media reviews, reader feedback, excerpts and photographs from his books.

camping and rooms, so that's where my route is going to take you. I also like this spot because it's within walking distance of the old town and there's plenty of off-road parking for your bike.

From the NH8 crossroads, continue straight along the Agra Road (or Marg). This is pretty much due west, with some jiggling, and plenty of juggling with the traffic. It's simply not worth entering this city in the dusk or at night time! Two junctions past the Agrawal Campus (on your left) take a right turn on to the Johari Bazaar Road. You are back – amazingly – on the NH11. Take a left turn on to Shiva Marg. Head down to the first roundabout and you'll find the Jaipur Inn on your left.

If you want to head out to Jaisalmer, follow the NH8 out of Jaipur and then the NH112 to Jodhpur. From there follow the NH114 to Jaisalmer. This route is approximately 665 miles (1,070km) and will take you at least 15 hours, so expect to stay in Jodhpur. Don't miss out on the chance to go out and play with your bike in the endless sand dunes near Jaisalmer; a camel ride too if you fancy a change of steed.

You can do an interesting 650-mile (1,046km) loop back to Jaipur following the NH114, then the NH15 to Bikaner (eight hours). From there follow the NH11 back to Jaipur (also eight hours).

Jaipur to Delhi

You have two choices here. Head back to Delhi, covering just over 360 miles (580km) on the main route, the NH8 – this will take you approximately eight hours – or start off on the NH8 but then scoot off on semi-parallel roads. I'd recommend the latter, although you do need to be aware of the lack of road signs, and you'll need a very early start unless you plan to find a spot to camp along the way. You'll be adding roughly 100 miles to your route and it's much slower going, so expect to add at least another five hours to your ride time. And that's not taking into account getting happily lost, or spending time to stop and look at things. There are no official campsites but locals will show you suitable spots. You'll not have to mind an audience if you choose this option!

At Manoharpur, turn left off the NH8 and head northwest. This junction is approximately two miles after the junction with NH11A – a right turn which would take you south.

→ **The bazaar in Jaipur.**

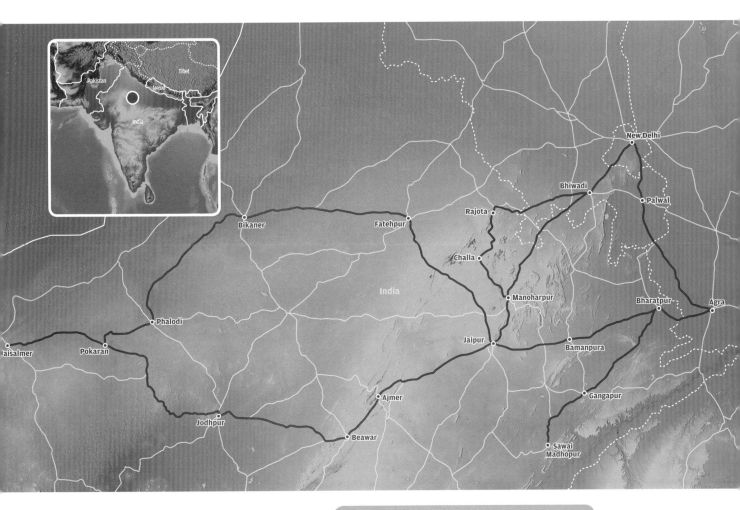

The road swings you north through the villages of Bishangar, Peeplod Narayan and Devipura until it meets State Highway 13. Turn left at this T-junction, taking SH13 on through Ajeetgarh, Thoi and Challa. This whole area is veined with small back streets and earthen tracks which are well worth exploring if you want a real taste of the rural patchwork of agricultural India. There are few signposts if you do that, but it is relatively straightforward to navigate by using a compass.

At Challa turn right on to SH37B towards Neem Ka Thana. When you reach there turn left on to SH13 and head towards Babai and Rajota, then on to Singhana where you turn right on to SH26, riding east towards Narnul which, though only a couple of miles across, is the first town of any size on this route. Keep on the SH26 as it loops through the northern part of the town and then carries on to Rewari.

State Highway 26 takes you right into the centre of Rewari which, if you have the time to visit, has an interesting brass market. I've not seen another like it in the region. More unusually, it also has a model town. Just after the Rao Tula Ram Park turn right on to NH71, which will take you past the brass market and the bus stand. At the first corner of the bus stand, on your left, the NH71 turns right and heads south. You need to continue straight on the NH71B and then on towards

the small towns of Hansaka and Dungarwas.

Shortly after Dungarwas the NH71B intersects the NH8, which you turn left on to and then follow north into Delhi. This is approximately 50 miles (80km) and it's a bit of a shock to ride after the sleepy back roads you've been on for the past couple of days. The NH8 takes you right back into the city centre and leaves you where you began, on Delhi's Connaught Circus.

RECOMMENDED MAPS

Western India
Publisher: Nelles Verlag
ISBN: 9783865742339
Scale: 1:1,500,000

Fancy buying a bike in India?
- You can legally do this.
- The paperwork takes 7–10 days.
- A signed affidavit from a magistrate is required, which a dealer should arrange for you.
- Be sure to check the regulations about selling the vehicle.
- Buy-back schemes are a good idea if you are returning to your start point.

Blue Ladakh Expedition

Exploring India's high-altitude lakes

Sumit Tyagi and Harish Daita

In June 2008 four friends – Sumit, Pankaj, Harry and KK – attempted to ride their Royal Enfields across the Chagarchan La ('La' stands for pass in Ladakhi) in the Ladakh region of northern India at a height of 16,732ft (5,100m), taking in the three famous High Altitude Lakes (HAL) – Pangong Tso, Tso Moriri and Tso Kar ('Tso' means lake). Their route covered the Himalayan border villages of Spangmik, Merak, Takung, Chushul, crossing Tsaka La and on to Rhongo, Hanle, crossing Lenak La at 18,077ft (5,510m) to Chumur along the Pare Chu River and finally from Chumur and Ungti, crossing the Chagarchan La to Peldo, Korzok, Puga and Tso Kar.

There were no roads, limited maps, certainly no guides and the only signs were the dirt tracks of jeep trolleys used by the locals to fetch raw materials like stones to construct their homes. Apart from these locals, the Indian Army and Indo-Tibetan Border Force (ITBF) are the only others in this area, given that it borders the disputed Kashmir region.

Ladakh (or 'land of high passes') is a region of Jammu and Kashmir, the northernmost state in India. It lies between the Kunlun mountain range in the north and the main Great Himalayas to the south, inhabited largely by people of Indo-Aryan and Tibetan origin. It is renowned for its remote mountain beauty and culture, and is sometimes called 'Little Tibet' as the area has been strongly influenced by Tibetan culture.

There is a traditional, commercial route taken by many riders around the Himalayan border villages, but we decided to find an alternate route to Tso Moriri from Pangong Tso, covering Tsokar and all the lakes in the High Ladakh district, most importantly, without any backtracking.

We ventured into the unknown and uninhabited land of the Changtang Plateau, made famous by Gaurav Jani and his award-winning solo documentary, *Riding Solo on the Top of the World*. We planned to go beyond the village of Chumur. It was at this point that Gaurav Jani turned back,

RIDING TIPS

If you are going to attempt this ride, make sure of a few things:

- ▨ **Motorcycle reliability** – there are no repair shops in the area.
- ▨ **Food** – bread and cheese spread work best. So do chocolates!
- ▨ **Fuel** – depending on the route, you're looking at having fuel available for 620–870 miles (1,000–1,400km).
- ▨ **Environment** – treat it with respect and avoid driving on grass which, at these altitudes, will take a full season to grow back.
- ▨ Try to park your bike where it will catch the morning sun – even in summer some parts can see –5°C in the early morning.
- ▨ **Overheating** – be aware of overheating your engine. At high altitude the air is much thinner and constantly running in a low gear at medium to high revs can do some damage.

having completed a study of the Changpa people. What we gathered from the locals was that there was a route, taken rarely by the most adventurous trekkers. Naïve and insignificant as it may seem, we were quite adamant about trying this out, creating a niche for ourselves of riding on non-motorable roads, covering the Himalayan border villages and all the blue-green lakes of Ladakh.

We reached Pangong Tso after a four-day ride from home. One of the first things we managed to achieve was to source a basic hand-made map from one of the old-time trekkers in the area. This was an original trekking route map, a route which we ended up covering on our motorcycles. From here we began our off-road journey to Chushul, riding alongside Pangong Tso for 28 miles (45km) of its 37-mile (60km) boundary in India, the remaining 56 miles (90km) being in Tibet. This is one of the most beautiful stretches of riding in the world and

← **The south-eastern point of Tso Moriri, descending from Chagarchan La (altitude 5,100m).**

↓ **Heading from Chumur Gompa towards the ITBF (Indo-Tibetan Border Force) camp.**

⬆ **Stopping at Pang for chai and food.**

⬆ **Crossing one of the many streams before ascending for Baralacha La.**

⬆ **Taking a breather on the banks of Pangong Tso.**

⬆ **Riding along Pangong Tso, through sinking tracks towards Merek village.**

a photographer's paradise, with the lake sparkling in its display of most vivid and natural colours. The crystal-clear water reflects the sunlight with a magical effect, giving an impression of an illusionist at work.

The next leg took us from Chushul to Hanle and this stretch was a little more revealing in terms of what we could expect from the terrain ahead. Right after passing the villages of Tsaga and Rhongo, we encountered the famous Changtang Desert, complete with sand dunes and the Indus River flowing nearby. Picturesque as it was, we soon found it tough going trying to manoeuvre the bikes in the sand for more than 28 miles (45km).

We reached Hanle with just enough time to enjoy the sunset close to the Indian Astronomical Observatory. The location of both the village of Hanle and the observatory are highly sensitive due to the close proximity of the Tibetan/Chinese border and special permission is needed from the Indian government to visit either. The fatigue from the ride disappeared within minutes of reaching this beautiful valley, surrounded by mountains on three sides and the only opening covered by the desert. The desert riding had been

tough and had taken its toll on man and machine, but we decided to press on, not knowing what lay ahead. We took a rest day in Hanle as we needed time to fix our bikes and give them some rest after the last few days of tough riding.

Our group was reduced to three riders from Hanle onwards as we headed over the little-known Lenak Pass at 15,000ft (4,572m). This stretch featured a remarkable array of fauna and flora, with wild asses and yaks offering us a welcome reception. Coming down the sandy roads into the Chumur Valley offered some respite, only for us to realise that in a short while we were into marshlands. Overnight was spent at the Chumur ITBF camp.

Starting the bikes very early in the morning is always a problem at such altitudes, with temperatures dropping below zero. After sweating it out for about ten minutes, and bidding adieu to the ITBF folk, we headed off again into the wilderness.

For much of the journey we were completely on our own. Getting lost was something that became part of our daily routine and we had to rely on the help of the few local people we encountered to retrace our steps and get back on track. On one stretch we discovered a jeep track with army markings along it. We assumed this would take us to our destination, and followed it blindly. We made various river crossings, we passed over sandy and marshy stretches, rocks, gravel, loose stones and grass tracks but there was certainly no road to speak of. Eventually we came across a village that looked quite self-sufficient and prosperous but for some reason the place was completely deserted, as if plagued by some disease. There was not a single living soul in sight and all the houses were locked or just simply abandoned. The village had this bizarre silence all around.

The area to the east of Lake Moriri features a number of Changpa settlements, serving as a summer home for the Changpas because of the availability of pasture and snowmelt streams. We stopped at an abandoned settlement called Ungti to quench our thirst at the stream.

The Changpas take about three days to dig trenches for laying out their Rebos (yak-hair tents) and build pens for their livestock (herds of yak, goats, sheep and horses). They stay for a few months, until the nearby grasslands are depleted, before heading off in search of new lands. They leave behind the stones they have used, intricate designs, and a few of their worldly possessions for people like us to gaze at in wonder.

Beyond Ungti we finally reached the base of a hill and lost the jeep track altogether. It was as if it were a runway and the plane had taken off. On closer inspection we determined that jeeps had been on this track, up and over the hill, thanks to their 4WD ability. We sat for about 15 minutes and contemplated a return, but in the end we gathered our courage and took to the climb. According to the locals, we were the first riders they knew of who'd tackled this pass, together with a subsequent one further on. Sitting proudly at the top, we christened it 'Ungti Pass'.

On the descent we caught our first glimpses of Tso Moriri but all hell broke loose as we headed down. We were scattered all over the hill, trying to find the shortest way possible to the lake. We found ourselves riding on horse tracks that led nowhere, and we even reached the end of a cliff that invited nothing but a drop into the blue waters of the lake.

Once we had come to our senses we started making a plan to get back on track. The only way out seemed to be a long, steep, jeep track. Harry, on a 500cc Bullet, took on the hill and scaled it, and about 45 minutes later, and after much sweat and tears, we managed to get both 350cc Bullets to the top. We promptly named this 'Trolley Pass' (for the trolley tracks we saw on our way up) and later realised it was Chagarchan La from our maps. Another hillock and we were riding right beside the lake. We stopped for a break by the water – the lake had its own charm and poise, with the snow-covered mountains as a backdrop. A few water crossings and some challenging terrain under our belts and we met a Changpa coming back with his sheep – he was the first human being we had seen in more than 12 hours. It was quite a relief in some ways.

As we headed towards the main road that would lead us to the village of Korzok, with the throttles being wrenched like the ear of a little schoolboy who is punished for not getting to school on time, the headmistress stood before us in the form of a raging river. Flowing with its full capacity of icy water, taking the complete day's load of melted snow, it did give us a while to think if the next step would be suicidal or an act of bravery. But since there is a very thin line between bravery and stupidity, we decided to cross both the line and the stream. Step one – to remain warm one needs to get rid of warm clothes down to the basics to brave the chill. Step two – get your limbs frozen so that there is no more realisation of the cold. Steps three, four, five and so on follow underwater, when you are half-immersed in the river and pushing the bikes.

⇩ **Finally on motorable road after riding for 60km towards Peldo, Korzok.**

ABOUT THE AUTHORS

Sumit Tyagi started adventure motorcycling in 1999 with a trip to the Himalayan border villages. The attraction to the mountains was so strong that he decided to quit his corporate career and spend a substantial part of his life in the mountains. Today he lives with his wife, Jasmine, and young daughter, Rubani, in the village of Ghyagi, in the remote Himachal area where he runs a Mountain Nature Camp www.camphimalayan.com.

'Look for faults in the Enfield Bullet, and you can find hundreds! But they have heritage and class and there is a certain charm to them,' says Sumit. 'Once you get used to the comfort and joy of thumping along through the most out of the way places in the Himalayas, you're well and truly hooked,' he added.

Harish 'Harry' Daita works for American Express in New Delhi and is a gifted writer and enthusiastic motorcyclist. Harry spent time in the military and previously had the opportunity of exploring the remote border villages of the country. 'If I had the chance I would quit my corporate career and settle down in the Himalayas,' he says.

Repeat this exercise about three times and when you are half-blue, half-brown, you have achieved nirvana.

Don't let the body relax, just start the bikes and find a shelter, as we did at Korzok, the village that is the tourist destination for Tso Moriri.

After a night of recovery we started off on good roads towards the last of our watering holes, that of Tso Kar. This was a different place altogether – at first glance it seemed to be an icy lake, but it turned out instead to be salt deposits, giving the icy illusion. A very secluded village with just one family welcomed us for a cup of tea. And after spending a few minutes of questioning (and cross-

questioning) the villagers about the roads out, we left with a great sense of achievement and also a feeling that I cannot explain in words about the places we visited. This was a mixture of the senses that someone experiences when witnessing something beautiful, huge, magnificent, natural, and which oozes with an aura of something unachievable.

Julley! (Ladakhi greetings.)

Pangong Tso

A lake in the Himalayas situated at a height of about 14,270ft (4,350m). It is 83 miles (134km) long and extends from India to Tibet. More than half of the lake lies in Tibet. It is 3.1 miles (5km) wide at its broadest point. During winter the lake freezes completely, despite being saline water.

Tso Moriri

Lake Moriri is a wetland conservation reserve situated at an altitude of 15,075ft (4,595m) in Ladakh. It is the largest of the High Altitude Lakes (HAL) in the Trans-Himalayan bio-geographic region.

Tso Kar

This lake is approximately 28 miles (45km) northwest of Tso Moriri, at a height of 14,714ft (4,485m). It is also called the 'White Lake' because of the salt deposited around it. The water here is so saline that salt is taken from its banks and sold all over Ladakh and Kashmir by the local nomads.

The Changpas

The Changpas live on the desolate Changtang Plateau in Ladakh, of which Rupshu is the highest inhabited part. The region has an extremely dry climate, living conditions are extremely difficult and population density is very low. Animal husbandry is the main source of income for the Changpas. Members of this community also collect salt from the impure deposits on the northern shores of Tso Kar. The Changpas are known, too, for acting as porters for the defence forces and various mountaineering expeditions.

Harry and Sumit at Lenak La, altitude 5,510m.

Pankaj and Sumit near Takung, south of Pangong Tso, on the way to Chushu.

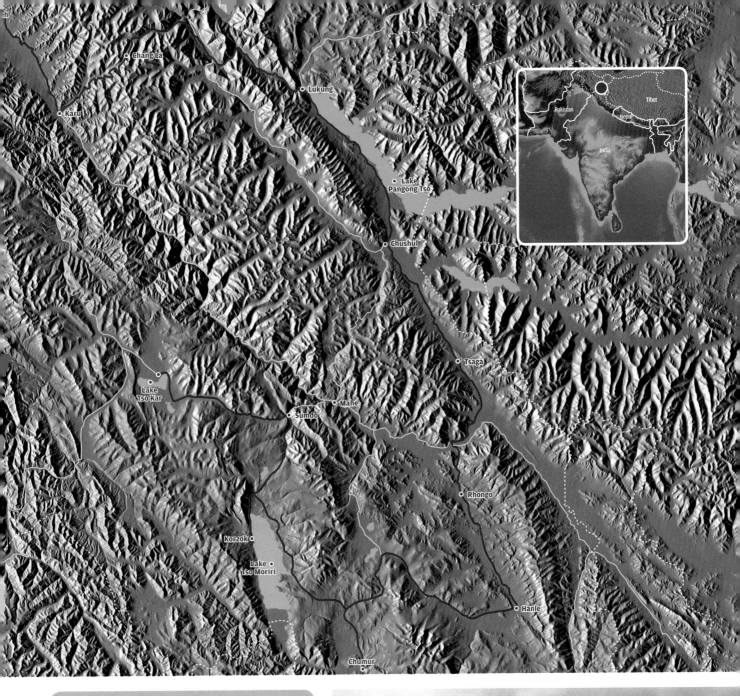

RECOMMENDED MAPS

**India Himalaya Map 3: Jammu and Kashmir
(Nubra Valley, Leh, Markha)**
Publisher: Leomann Maps
ISBN: 0906227755
Scale: 1:200,000

**India Himalaya Map 9: Jammu and Kashmir
(Rupshu, Tso Moriri, Mahe, Chumar)**
Publisher: Leomann Maps
ISBN: 0906227763
Scale: 1:200,000

India: North
Publisher: Nelles Verlag GmbH
ISBN: 9783865742308

Tibet

A motorcycle expedition to the top of the world

Joe Pichler

Tibet, the 'Roof of the World', is a vast and remote country that has been cut off from the rest of the world for centuries, its formidable geographical barriers contributing significantly to its isolation. It is this combination of isolation, altitude and mystery that gives the area significant appeal for adventure motorcyclists, and the route from Kathmandu to Lhasa along the Friendship Highway is one of the world's great overland journeys, with thrilling and exciting sections featuring steep cliffs and waterfalls.

The highway, on the Tibetan Plateau, starts from Lhasa – the capital of the Tibet Autonomous Region – and passes the turquoise Yamdrok Lake before connecting to Shigatse (the second largest city in Tibet and the home of the Panchen Lama) via Gyantse. The road forks after this, with one branch heading west to the city of Ali. The other branch continues south, past Tingri, New Tingri and on to the renowned Rongphu Monastery near Everest Base Camp. From here the road continues on to the Nepali border at Zhangmu, traverses the Sino-Nepal Friendship Bridge and continues on to Kathmandu in Nepal.

Sights along the route include various important cultural monuments, the upper valley of the Yarlung Zangbo River, vast grasslands on the plateau, and mountain vistas including five of the world's highest peaks: Everest, Lhotse, Makalu, Cho Oyu and Shishapangma.The highway is used by pilgrims making their way from all corners of Tibet to the spiritual centre in Lhasa.

On my adventure in Tibet the monsoon rains had left the route badly affected. If this wasn't enough, there was the altitude to be conscious of (slow, steady acclimatisation is vital) as well as the innumerable twists and turns as we passed through dense tropical vegetation, cascading waterfalls and the barren rocky

TIBET

- Tibet sits on a plateau in Asia, north of the Himalayas, and is the highest region on earth, with an average elevation of more than 15,000ft (4,570m).
- From plateaus and mountain ranges to hills and valleys, Tibet has a diverse, rugged landscape. The terrain also includes desert, glaciers and forests, as well as springs and waterfalls.
- Between 1949 and 1951 the Chinese illegally annexed and invaded the formerly autonomous region of Tibet. The natural wealth of the area was plundered and Tibetans were turned into virtual aliens in their own land.
- The region measures about 1,200 miles (1,900km) from east to west and about half that distance from north to south, giving an area of around 470,000 square miles (1,220,000km2).
- The dominant religion in Tibet is Tibetan Buddhism, although there are also Muslim and Christian minorities.
- In the Himalayas, which mark Tibet's southern border, is the world's highest peak – Mount Everest, at 29,029ft (8,848m).
- Several major rivers have their source in the Tibetan plateau, including the Yangtze, Yellow River, Indus, Mekong and Ganges.
- The Yarlung Zangbo Grand Canyon, which runs along the Yarlung Zangbo River, is among the deepest and longest canyons in the world.
- The atmosphere is very dry for nine months of the year, and average annual snowfall is only 18in (45cm). Western passes receive small amounts of fresh snow each year but remain traversable all year round.
- Northern Tibet is subject to high temperatures in the summer and intense cold in the winter.
- Lhasa is Tibet's traditional capital and the capital of the Tibet Autonomous Region. It contains two World Heritage Sites – the Potala Palace and Norbulingka, which were the residences of the Dalai Lama. Lhasa also contains a number of significant temples and monasteries, including Jokhang Temple and Ramoche Temple.

← ← Riding the KTM up to the Everest Base Camp at 5,200m was something special.

← Yaks are used to carrying loads in the Tibetan highlands.

landscape of the ice giants. The view from the summit of
the pass at Lalung La (16,574ft/5,052m) was breathtaking –
a chain of six- and seven-thousand metre peaks (19,685ft–
22,965ft) – only topped by the 26,318ft (8,022m) of
Shishapangma.

From Lalung La we left the monsoon rains behind
us and headed across the highlands of Tibet. The route
followed a good gravel road and we passed small villages,
with farmers harvesting crops at over 14,763ft (4,500m).
Yaks were grazing in the meadows, with some of the
world's highest mountains as the backdrop.

A visit to the Tashi Lhunpo Monastery was the first
cultural highlight of the trip. This is the seat of the Panchen
Lama, the second most important spiritual leader of Tibet.

The monastery was founded in 1447 and is one of the four great monasteries of Central Tibet. At one time more than 3,000 monks lived in this impressive facility. Today there are 800 monks practising Buddhist teachings again. When visiting the midday sacrifice ceremony I felt transported back in time, receiving a real impression of the former richness of these monasteries.

In Nagchu, the last major town on the road, just to the east, the annual equestrian festival was in progress. Over 5,000 nomads ride from all corners of Tibet to partake in and celebrate horse racing and traditional pastimes such as archery, horsemanship, stone-lifting and tug-of-war competitions. I felt like I fitted right in on my KTM from Salzburg! As well as the horse racing there was a real festival, with numerous food stalls selling the full range of Tibetan and Chinese cuisine. Chang, the traditional Tibetan barley beer, was undoubtedly responsible for my headache the next morning and I decided to postpone my departure by a day to recover.

From Nagchu the road led to Shagchu, but I came across an impassable section where a massive landslide had swept away the entire road. After hours of deliberation we resolved to carry our panniers and other luggage over the rocks and to take the bikes cross-country over the mountains on the other side. It was a good decision as later that day the road was closed and declared impassable for days.

The next stop was Chamdo, a major town in the historical region of Kham. It is Tibet's third largest city after Lhasa and Shigatse; as the crow flies it's about 300 miles (480km) from Lhasa, but it is about 695 miles (1,120km) by the road, which was in a terrible state. Muddy sections alternated with torrential river crossings and icy passes. Progress was slow and certainly no more than 125 miles (200km) in a day.

The nomads' tents provided a warm break from the cold and we were regularly treated to a cup of 'butter tea' — a speciality of Tibet, consisting of black tea, yak butter and soda. Normally I'm not a fan of this but with temperatures around freezing and icy winds I was grateful for the brew.

Pastures and farms lined the route towards Riwoche

↑ Once a year, for the Shötun festival, the huge Tanka is unveiled close to the Dreprung monastery.

TRAVEL TIPS

- The route from Lhasa to Kathmandu is approximately 730 miles (1,175km), including the excursion to Everest Base Camp.
- Be sure to check on the latest visa requirements, which changed most recently in 2008. Independent travel is not always the easiest and the Chinese government simply regard Tibet as just another autonomous province. Be prepared for lots of paperwork and other 'manufactured hassles'.
- The best time to travel is between April and May as well as October to mid-November thereby avoiding the rainy season (July to September) and the snow that falls from December to March.
- Local accommodation on the route will be very basic and a hot shower should be considered a luxury.
- Look out for signs of altitude sickness and know how to deal with them.
- Try to use local Tibetan dialect when communicating.
- Road conditions vary according to the weather.
- Be conscious of the political situation and associated sensitivities.
- Respect local customs and beliefs – for example, always walk around Tibetan Buddhist religious sites in a clockwise direction, and when in a monastery do not wear a hat, smoke or touch frescoes. Refrain from climbing on to statues, or other sacred objects.
- Don't photograph people without their permission, and be aware that some locations prohibit photography without a fee.
- Give donations directly to individual monks and nuns – in this way the money will be used to maintain and support the local religious infrastructure.
- Help protect Tibet for future generations by not purchasing products made from wild animals, as many items are made from endangered species.
- Be conscious of litter, as the ecosystem in the Himalayas is very fragile.
- Stay on designated tracks to minimise erosion.

and brought back memories of riding in the Alps. We stopped at a small restaurant and of course I could not read the menu, but I was able to find familiar dishes such as pork ribs and fried mushrooms. In the remote monastery at Riwoche a monk showed us various treasures with much pride. For over 700 years statues have survived, despite the turbulent times in Tibet.

After a long, dusty day's riding we reached our destination – Lake Rawok – in the late afternoon. This was a truly breathtaking sight. The lake has an area of 8,494 square miles (22,000km²). It is some 16 miles (26km) long and sits at an altitude of 12,631ft (3,850m). The waters of the lake appear as different colours during the different seasons, ranging from aquamarine to turquoise.

The southern route between Lhasa and Bayi is considered the most dangerous road in Tibet. Construction by the Chinese military began in 1955, for strategic reasons, and they built the road through moist subtropical forests and over icy mountain passes. Thousands of workers are constantly busy on this vital road link to make it passable as it suffers regularly from landslides.

The 'Forbidden City' of Lhasa showed little Tibetan influence. Only in the centre of the old town did we find the Lhasa we had imagined. Here we discovered the Jokhang which, for most Tibetans, is the most sacred and important temple in Tibet and the ultimate goal of a long journey – all year round many Tibetan Buddhists go on a pilgrimage to Lhasa, from all over Tibet and other provinces like Qinghai, Gansu and Inner Mongolia, and their destination is the Jokhang Temple. We were sure to enjoy the pleasures of Lhasa – for the first time in a week there was a hot shower and the yak steak was delicious. The remaining dust in our throats was washed down with several bottles of Lhasa beer.

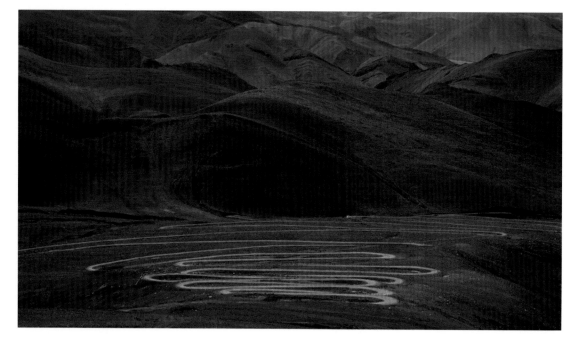

→ It's a long and winding road over the Pang La Pass to the Mount Everest Base Camp.

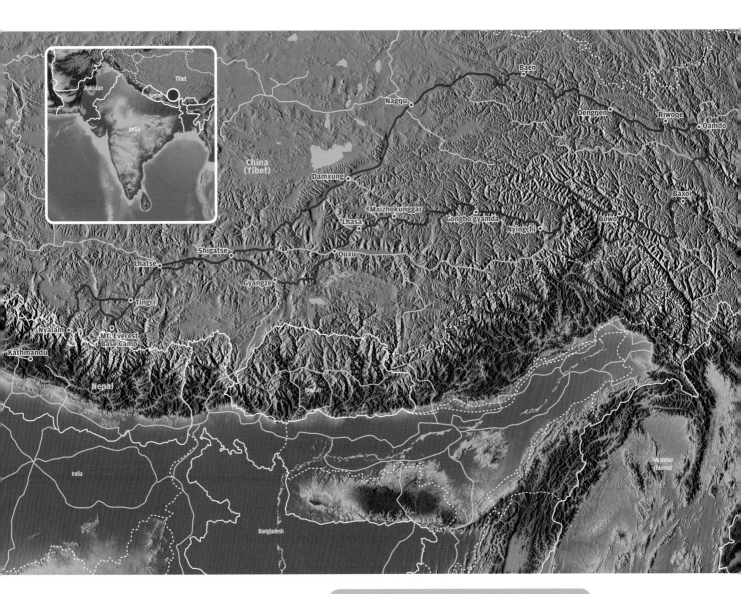

Our time in Tibet would not have been complete without a visit to Mount Everest Base Camp. The route took us over the Pang La Pass and the view from there was unique: like pearls on a string, the highest mountains in the world sit on the horizon. From Makalu in the east to Everest and Cho Oyu in the west, the view was spectacular. Sharing the view were road workers doing hard manual labour at 16,404ft (5,000m) – for me that was unthinkable; I was out of breath just walking about!

We passed the Rongphu Monastery en route. At an altitude of 16,728ft (5,100m), this is the highest monastery on earth. There is a hostel in Rongphu with a hundred beds, a dining room, a post office and a store, where food is available. Just 6 miles (10km) away was Everest Base Camp.

As our adventure came to an end there was not much to see of Qomolangma, as the Tibetans call Mount Everest – the 29,029ft (8,848m) peak was covered in thick cloud. The night in the tent was icy cold, but the first rays of the sun the following morning broke up the last remaining clouds to reveal the daunting north face rising before us.

RECOMMENDED MAPS

Tibet (road edition)
Publisher:	Gizi Map
Stanfords catalogue no:	115650
Scale:	1:2,000,000

Himalaya Tibet Road Map
Publisher:	Gecko Maps
ISBN	9783906593418
Scale:	1:1,600,000

Tibet Travel Map
Publisher:	Reise Know-How
ISBN	9783831770854
Scale:	1:1,500,000

Note: www.tibetmap.com has a free downloadable set of maps covering much of the country, with good levels of detail.

South-east Asia
Adventure riding in the Orient

Adam Lewis

Southeast Asia is a wonderful region for adventure motorcycling – border crossings are easy (with the exception of Myanmar (Burma), which remains a stumbling block to the overland route from Europe), routes are plentiful and offer great variety, there is great value for money, people are friendly and there are so many sights to see – from ancient temples to sandy white beaches.

Malaysia or Thailand make arguably the best starting points as they are far more western than any of their neighbours (I'm not including Singapore in this) and so not only are spare parts, tyres and maps readily available but they also act as a stepping stone into the likes of Cambodia, Laos and Indonesia. All the main roads in Thailand and Malaysia are tarmac and it's only when you get to Cambodia and Laos that you will find main routes that are still dirt. Of course, with a good map and a lightweight set-up there are plenty of dirt-road options for those looking for life off the beaten track.

Our route through Southeast Asia went from Thailand to Cambodia, on to Laos and back to Thailand before finishing in Malaysia.

After spending the best part of two days running around the various departments and agencies at Bangkok's International Air Cargo Centre, we finally rode out into the evening traffic. Having heard many stories of the poor driving in Bangkok we were shocked to see vehicles with not only all of their lights working, but being used for their intended purpose! Cars maintained lane discipline and stopped at red lights. It was a far cry from our experiences in Iran, Pakistan and India where we'd spent the past six months – just another lesson in everything being relative.

Thailand

Boasting arguably the world's best cuisine, some of the world's best beaches, world-class diving and snorkelling, plus trekking, hill tribes, elephant sanctuaries and, of course, its Buddhist culture, there's a lot more to Thailand than you might imagine.

If you're travelling through as part of a bigger trip, then you have little choice but to carry what you already have (make the most of your camping gear on some secluded beaches). If, however, you're just going to tour Southeast Asia then you really need to carry very little – a day sack would suffice. Apart from any overnight excursions into the hills, choose the right time of year and you'll spend all your time off the bike in flip-flops and shorts. If you do head into the hills, though, be aware that temperatures can drop to zero in December and January. Accommodation prices literally go from one end of the scale (under U$5) to the other, and with roadside food being so good you'll always be spoilt for choice on both accounts. I don't recall ever eating in a 'proper' restaurant in Thailand. There's simply no need, the street food is that good.

Heading southeast away from Bangkok our first stop was Pattaya. Some love it, some hate it; we fell into the latter category and it became the only place in the world I've walked away from a paid hotel room. We took the ferry to the island of Koh Chang where we spent Christmas and New Year. The evening tide receded almost out of sight so the plentiful restaurants arranged their tables on the beach. Fresh fish carts were packed with ice where you chose your own fish from the 'when it's gone, it's gone' menu.

← Rice paddies near Moni, Flores, Indonesia.

← Thong Pha Phum on the road to Kanchanaburi, Thailand. The Africa Twin in the background was owned by Dutch couple Maarten and Ilse Duijvestijn, who spent two years riding to Malaysia and back. Danny nicknamed the bike 'BOB' – Beast of Burden!

Vehicle conditions and driving standards in Cambodia are well below those of Thailand and Malaysia, so you'd do well to step up your levels of alertness. It's worth avoiding Phnom Penh during the busier times of day, especially if you don't know your way around, as the driving can often get rather aggressive. Although we had no trouble, I have read several accounts of foreign motorcyclists being stopped for fictitious traffic infringements ('I know there's no sign, but I say you can't turn right there').

⬆ **Banteay Sray, Angkor Wat complex, Cambodia.**

⬈ **Bayon, Angkor Wat complex, Cambodia.**

Cambodia

We entered Cambodia at Koh Kong to explore the coast. We struggled to get permission to ride the bikes in Cambodia and so we followed a guy to the customs office in Koh Kong where we were told they could only grant permission for us to ride in that province and that only in the capital, Phnom Penh, could we be granted permission for riding across the country. We elected to ride on without permission.

Next stop was Sihanoukville (also known as Kampong Som), a popular and relaxed seaside area and, bizarrely enough, the location of the last official battle of the United States army in the Vietnam War. It was nice to get off the tarmac again and kick up some dust on route NR48 as we hopped our way across the four river ferries that were necessary to catch along the way, given the numbers of bridges under construction at the time.

From Sihanoukville we rode to Kampot – best known for its black pepper – stopping along the way at Kep. We used Kampot as a base to visit the Bokor Hill Station, accessed via a 21-mile (33km) rough track that ascends 3,280ft (1,000m). Stunning panoramic views over Cambodia and Vietnam can be enjoyed from the mountaintops. The little island of Koh Tonsay can be visited from Kampot by boat and there are long stretches of golden sand and tasty local crab curry to savour.

Phnom Penh

An easy 93-mile (150km) ride took us to Phnom Penh. Like most people my age I recall listening to Kim Wilde's 'Cambodia' and seeing the 1984 movie *The Killing Fields*. Nine miles (15km) south of Phnom Penh is the memorial to the killing fields while in the capital itself you'll find Tuol Sleng Museum (otherwise known as S-21), the notorious prison and interrogation centre where incomprehensible atrocities were committed by the Khmer Rouge in the late 1970s.

Some months earlier, at the Thai Embassy in Kathmandu, we'd met Andrew, a British aid worker and his Cambodian wife on holiday from Phnom Penh and he told us he had a Suzuki DRZ400. By complete coincidence, as we stopped at traffic lights riding into the city, a DRZ400 appeared from our left – it was Andrew! A great coincidence and an opportunity to catch up.

Angkor Wat

From Phnom Penh we headed for Siem Reap via Battambang and Sisophon. Siem Reap is where you'll base yourself for visiting what would easily be included in a rewritten 'Seven Wonders of the World' – Angkor Wat. You can't rent a motorcycle in the town of Siem Reap and some will try to tell you that you can't ride your own to the temples (they want you to take a guide and local transport), but the roads are public and you can use them. This not only gives you the opportunity to avoid the crowds but also the heat of the day. Having your own bike here is a real winner.

The temple complex at Angkor Wat was built in the early twelfth century and is regarded as the world's largest religious building. It has become a symbol of Cambodia, appearing on its national flag, and it is the country's prime attraction for visitors.

While the Angkor Wat complex is the most famous, it isn't the only one. A good graded gravel road heads northeast to the Thai border and the disputed region around the 1,000-year-old hilltop temple of Preah Vihear. Since 2008 disputes between Cambodia and Thailand over ownership have made this area potentially dangerous, which is a shame as it receives a fraction of the visitors to Angkor Wat.

Leaving the temples behind us we headed east, following directions given to us by Andrew back in the capital. Unfortunately, while the route did take us to where he said it would, it wasn't the route he'd had in mind – and before we knew it we were axle-deep in sand. Now while tall blokes can slow down and 'paddle' we short blokes can't and that means resorting to the only other technique: speed! This tends to work reasonably well when the track is straight and there's plenty of space, but it's a disaster waiting to happen when the track twists, turns and is lined with trees. It wasn't long before my riding partner, Danny, went missing from my mirrors and I backtracked to find a very unhappy short bloke lying on the floor, cursing a damaged pannier.

It soon became apparent we weren't going to make it to Thala Bariyat (and the Mekong River) that day and so, with the help of the local police, we spent the night in Chhaeb.

The following morning it was my turn to crash. I failed to notice a fallen tree cut off flush with the trackside undergrowth and hit it with my left pannier. I was in third gear at the time and the next I knew I was flying through the air, my bike flipping over as it came to a standstill. The pannier was pretty well smashed in and a mirror was broken. Our decision to continue wearing our riding suits despite the heat had been validated – I didn't have a scratch on me.

Eventually we made it to Thala Bariyat and manhandled the bikes on to a boat across the Mekong River to Stung Treng where we paid a panel beater U$15 to repair all four boxes. Once repaired, we took another boat to Laos, passing a new bridge under construction across the Mekong River. That bridge has since been completed and it is now possible to obtain a Laos visa at the Dom Kralor/Voeung Kam border north of Stung Treng (at the bridge).

⬆ **Boats moored at Nong Khaiw. Laos.**

Laos

This is the most heavily bombed country in the history of warfare (apparently 500kg per capita) and, as a result, you'll find huge signs out in the countryside warning people about the dangers of handling ordnance. You don't have to go far off the beaten track to find limbless locals and cattle troughs made from shell casings.

⬅ **In Laos Danny chats with Swede Soren and his wife, who were travelling from Vietnam to Bangkok with their three-year-old son three-up on a 125cc Minsk!**

by Gordon Hirst

My most recommend routes are:

- Highway 12 from Phitsanulok to Khon Kaen – a very memorable route through the national park where there is a real chance you will come head to head with an elephant.
- The road through the Golden Triangle following the banks of the Mekong is worth a look. The road surface is not the best and there are some serious potholes.
- The 1095/108 which heads northwest from the city of Chiang Mai into the mountainous region that borders Burma (Myanmar) before heading south through Hong Son and looping back round and returning to Chiang Mai from the southwest.
- On the whole Thais are a gregarious and friendly people and their welcome is warm and generous, but their practical navigation, sense of direction and geographical awareness are not great. This may sound somewhat condescending but make sure you have a good map to hand. Oddly enough, in Laos I found the opposite to be true – the locals were only too happy to draw a map on any scrap of paper to get me to my destination.
- Thailand surpassed all my expectations of a 'motorcycling adventure' – great roads, breathtaking scenery and great weather, remarkably cheap, with friendly and welcoming people.
- You don't have to ship your bike from your home country – you can buy or hire a motorcycle on your arrival. Bear in mind that crossing international borders on a hired bike comes with a set of bureaucratic headaches so research loads and choose wisely.
- Border crossings across most of the region are pretty straightforward but it is extremely difficult to get a motorcycle into Laos from Thailand and vice versa. It is essential to do your homework first. Contact the Laos 'Department of Tourism Control' (yes, for that is what it is called) well before you intend to cross the border and have your official documentation available. Thai-registered motorcycles are not allowed to cross into Laos (and vice versa).
- 'Officially' no motorcycles larger than 250cc are allowed on Laotian roads. Of course as soon as you get there you find this is not quite true.
- Buying a motorcycle in Laos is a real headache. Again 'officially', foreigners are not allowed to own vehicles but as always there are loopholes in almost every law; perhaps that's why Laos is known sometimes as the 'land of a thousand answers'.
- Both in Thailand and Laos there are no self-service petrol stations. It is wise to ask for a given amount of fuel as the petrol pump attendants do not really have a concept of 'fill' and on numerous occasions they overfilled the tank, spilling fuel all over the bike.
- The best advice I can give is 'when in Rome'. Accept that things don't happen the way you're used to. In Thailand don't bother with a watch, in Laos don't bother with a calendar – things happen at their own pace so get used to it, taking it as part of the experience.

Major centres like Vientiane, Vang Vieng and Luang Prabang see a lot of tourists but they soon thin out once you get away from the Mekong. A few options include the northeast, where you can visit the caves used by the Pathet Laos during the 'Secret War' in the region surrounding Xam Neua, and the dirt road to Phongsali in the far north.

The border with Thailand at Houay Xai/Chiang Khong involves crossing the Mekong River. The vehicle ferry does not operate on Sundays.

Thailand

The most 'famous' route in Thailand is undoubtedly the 370-mile (600km) 'Mae Hong Son' loop, a well-surfaced route of 1,184 bends that heads northwest from Chiang Mai, through Pai, Mae Hong Son and Mae Sariang and back to Chiang Mai. It's not just great motorcycling but also provides an opportunity to visit Doi Inthanon National Park with the country's highest mountain, temples, caves, waterfalls and hill tribe villages. It can be ridden in two days but you could easily spend at least twice that long.

At Tek we turned south, leaving the loop to head south to Kanchanaburi, home of the 'Bridge over the River Kwai' and the horrors of the Burma Railway before continuing further south to the Andaman Island of Koh Lanta for diving and snorkelling.

Our final week in Thailand was spent camping on the beach at Hat Yao. Thanks to the 29°C (84°F) seawater, as well as the fresh squid and tuna from the local fish market, it was a tough place to leave!

We weren't sure if the small border crossing at Wang Prachan was classified as 'International' but we gave it a try and crossed without a problem. It saved us a long ride to Padang Besar.

Malaysia

Home of the Petronas Twin Towers and a Moto GP circuit, it's not hard to conclude that Malaysia sits a little closer to Singapore in terms of development by comparison with its neighbours. You'll find several BMW dealers there, all of whom are extremely helpful and will have club members keen to meet foreign motorcyclists. Whether you ride a BMW or not, they're a great source of local and regional knowledge. Islands, beaches and diving off the east coast, colonial towns in the west and the Cameron Highlands in the middle are just a few of the highlights to string together on a motorcycle tour.

Indonesia

Indonesia is a huge place with a low average speed and whether you're planning to return to Malaysia or ride through to East Timor (to ship to Australia), you would do well to apply for a 60-day visa rather than the standard 30-day version. Extensions are available in the capital, Jakarta, but travelling from the east you're likely to have already exceeded 30 days by the time you arrive there.

Indonesia itself is hard to describe as each island on the main Australia to Southeast Asia route (Timor – Flores – Sumbawa – Lombok – Bali – Java – Sumatra) has its

⬆ Awaiting a 'ferry' along the west coast of Sumatra. In 2007 many bridges had still not been rebuilt following the 2004 tsunami.

⬅The Petronas Twin Towers in Kuala Lumpur.

⬅⬅ Tea stall in Georgetown, Malaysia.

ABOUT THE AUTHOR

Adam got his first bike (a Yamaha DT50MX) to ride to college aged 16. Two years later he started road racing, and by the time he was 20 Adam was racing in the British Supersport Championship. He has also raced in the USA, Northern Ireland and Austria. His racing career came to an end in 1997 and two years later he bought a Yamaha R1 on which he toured Spain, France and Germany. 'I was paranoid about losing my licence on it so I traded it for a new Suzuki DRZ400, went trail riding and entered a few enduros,' he recalls. Soon he was hooked on enduro riding and then the idea of a round-the-world trip took hold. Adam has spent almost six years on the road, travelling more than 125,000 miles (200,000km). He has been a regular contributor to the Haynes *Adventure Motorcycling* series of books and hails from Andover in Hampshire.

For more information visit www.shortwayround.co.uk.

⬇ **Gunnung Bromo rises out of the early-morning mist on Java, Indonesia.**

own culture, religion(s), food, geography and, of course, traffic. From the volcanoes of Flores to Bali's beaches and Sumatra's rainforests, you'll be squeezing every day out of your visa. There are volcanoes to climb, wrecks to dive, beaches to relax on, Hindu and Buddhist temples to visit and certainly no visit would be complete without seeing the Komodo dragons. The list just goes on and on.

The inter-island ferries are another experience and

you won't be the first to breathe a sigh of relief each time you roll off one. When northern Europeans finish with a ferry they sell it for use in the Greek Islands, and when the Greeks finish with it they sell it to the Indonesians. It's no surprise, then, that a ferry sinking is not, shall we say, 'as unusual' as it would be in the Western world. The shortest crossing is about two hours and the longest (Flores to Timor) is around 13 hours, so be sure to stock up on supplies before departure as there's nothing once you set sail – and unless you've developed an ear for Indonesian teen pop music a pair of earplugs may just stop you jumping overboard.

The traffic was quiet until I reached Java (about half the size of the UK) – it's home to 140 million people (and you'd swear every one of them rides a motorcycle). Passing Jakarta and Bandung was a lesson in patience, because motorcycles aren't allowed on the Bandung ring road.

I managed to arrive in Sumatra during Ramadan and so often found myself hungry. Every time I descended into a town or village I would look for the church or mosque tower. A cross indicated a Christian region and I would find food; a crescent moon and star meant I wouldn't! And eating wasn't the only problem. At 3.30am the mosques would announce over their loudspeaker systems that it was time to wake up and start cooking. At 5.00am they would announce that it was time to commence fasting, and when I was *really* unlucky they wouldn't stop talking in between. At 6.00pm they would announce sunset and with it came a mad rush to any and every food vendor.

The 'unknown' part of the Indonesian route is the Sumatra to Malaysia leg. With no vehicular ferry (bikes are

Cambodia
Publisher: Gecko Maps
ISBN: 9783906593319
Scale: 1:750,000

Laos
Publisher: Gecko Maps
ISBN: 9783906593296
Scale: 1:750,000

Thailand
Publisher: New Holland
ISBN: 9781843307556
Scales: Various (Road atlas)

Malaysia
Publisher: Reise Know-How
ISBN: 9783831712472
Scale: 1:800,000/1:1,100,000

Vietnam (North and South)
Publisher: Reise Know-How
ISBN: 9783831770915 (North)
     9783831771837 (South)
Scale: 1:600,000

Indonesia
Publisher: Reise Know-How
ISBN: 9783831771264
Scales: Various

One of the best sources of information on border crossings and maps for the region can be found at www.gt-rider.com, including:
- The Golden Triangle Map
- Mae Sa Valley to Samoeng Loop Map
- Laos Guide Map

not allowed on the passenger ferry) it's a case of finding a shipping agent/fixer and a cargo boat to carry your bike.

Singapore

The only *real* reason to take your motorcycle to Singapore is for shipping/collection. Before entering Singapore (from Malaysia) you must first purchase insurance. Take your carnet to the AA office in Singapore (using public transport as you can't take your bike in yet) where you hand it over along with your insurance document. They will 'authenticate' it by stamping the back of what will become your Singapore page. They will also charge you a road tax and issue a receipt. Back in Malaysia you can then present your 'authenticated' carnet and road tax receipt at customs where they will charge you an additional road toll fee before finally granting you entry.

Note: Burma has been excluded as one is not able to gain access to the territory. The other problem area is Vietnam – until a few years ago access was granted if you were travelling on a motorcycle of less than 225cc but now, apparently, no foreign vehicles are allowed access to this country.

Siberia

Riding across Asia's 'sleeping land'

Walter Colebatch

Siberia, the great sleeping land, is the largest part of the largest country on earth. The name conjures up images of hardship and suffering, of exile and misery. Yet for today's motorcycle traveller, it also represents some of the greatest adventures to be had on two wheels. The Trans-Siberian Highway, the Road of Bones, the Chuisky Trakt, the BAM Road, the Pole of Cold, Lake Baikal, and legendary cities like Vladivostok, Magadan and Yakutsk have all found their way on to the adventure motorcyclist's fantasy list.

I first moto-travelled in Siberia in 1994 and was stunned by the beauty of the land and touched by the warmth of the people. Since then I have returned many times to explore this rarely travelled region further and to encourage other motorcycle adventurers to venture beyond the main highway.

Siberia, for our purposes, is all of the Russian Federation east of the Ural Mountains. The land was conquered for the Russian Empire by the Cossacks in the late 1500s and early 1600s. The western section is flat and low, notable for extensive farmlands. Further east, from Novosibirsk to the Pacific, Siberia is dominated by the world's largest forest – the Taiga. In this eastern half of Siberia, the population clings tightly to the Trans-Siberian Railway. The railway, built in the late 1800s, is one of the busiest in the world and has been so successful in transporting goods and people across Russia that it significantly delayed the construction of roads across the country.

Trans-Siberian Highway

Prior to 2004 there was no 'main road' across Russia. Earlier motorcycle journeys across the Trans-Siberian route relied on the train between Chernyshevsk in the west and Shimanovsk in the east, as there was no all-season road in that section. This gap in the cross-country highway was nicknamed the 'Zilov Gap' by the 2001 Terra Circa expedition that became the first to cross the gap on lightweight motorcycles in the summer of that year. The extraordinary paraplegic rider Dave Barr had ridden the route in winter a few years earlier, with a bike and sidecar, over frozen swamps and rivers.

Less than three years later, in early 2004, President Putin declared the Trans-Siberian Highway open. A gravel road had been cut through the Taiga forest linking up the eastern and western ends of the highway. With the opening of the gravel link, Trans-Siberian motorcycling was able to take off. In the late summer of 2010 the Russian government completed paving the Trans-Siberian Highway, meaning riders can now cross Siberia from the Ural Mountains to Vladivostok on asphalt.

The Trans-Siberian route begins at Chelyabinsk in the Ural foothills, and heads across the plains through Kurgan, Ishim and Omsk to Novosibirsk. Novosibirsk is the largest city in Siberia, with around 2.5 million people. It is also the turn-off for highways to western Mongolia and northeastern Kazakhstan.

From Novosibirsk, the highway continues through Krasnoyarsk, Taishet and Tulun, where the BAM Road joins

SIBERIA BY JOE PICHLER

- ▨ River crossings are common in Siberia. Know the height of your bike's air intake. Some rivers are too risky to consider on a bike and it's best to try and get your bike on the back of a truck if you're suitably concerned or if the river level is higher than your bike's air intake. Even some 4WD vehicles rely on a tow from the big trucks to get across.
- ▨ A glass of vodka and a shashlik (skewer with meat) are often the best way to seal a new friendship.
- ▨ Corrugations on the road can make riding rough and really punish the bike. Ideally try to find a speed where your suspension 'floats' over the corrugations. At low speed the bike will bounce around and vibrate like mad. Try to accelerate through this and the pounding will smooth out. Moderate your speed on the dirt and consider lowering your tyre pressures.
- ▨ Beware of the mosquitoes – they don't care how expensive your mosquito cream is! Russian mosquito repellent tends to work better than weaker imports.
- ▨ Trucks on the road often leave deep ruts, especially in softer sand, so be cautious, especially on a heavy adventure bike.
- ▨ Siberia is a land of temperature extremes – in the late summer Yakutsk can be 34ºC (93.2ºF), but it is also one of the coldest cities in the world, built entirely on permafrost, which starts 3ft (1m) deep.
- ▨ Heavy rains and flooding can certainly affect your route planning, so be prepared to be flexible.
- ▨ Riding in Siberia is indeed remote. For example, from Khandiga to Ust Nera there are over 310 miles (500km) through a largely untouched landscape and there is only one gas station en route.
- ▨ Old, dilapidated wooden bridges are very common, although many of these are being repaired or replaced with new concrete bridges.
- ▨ Fuel quality and octane levels vary dramatically. In Kyubeme, for example, there is no village, only a neglected gas station; 92 octane is occasionally out of stock, so we had to use 76 octane instead to make our way to Ust Nera.
- ▨ Siberia is a region famous for gold mining and huge excavators beside the road are a common sight. The prospect of earning a lot of money attracts adventurers from all parts of the country to work in remote northeastern Russia. New towns pop up directly next to the mines and, once exploited, the industry moves on and ghost towns come into existence. The government simply turns off the power so if people want to survive they have no choice but to move on too.

the Trans-Siberian Highway, and on to Irkutsk, before skirting Lake Baikal and reaching the capital of the Buryat Republic, Ulan Ude. At Ulan Ude there is a turn-off for the main road into Mongolia. The Trans-Siberian Highway continues eastwards, through Chita. Soon after Chita the new road of immaculate asphalt begins and heads towards Skovorodino. At Skovorodino the Lena Highway heading north to Yakutsk branches off and the Trans-Siberian Highway continues on to Birobidzhan and Khabarovsk before turning south to Vladivostok and the end of the road.

← **Bridge over the Indigirka River, near Tomtor, Road of Bones – Old Summer Road.**

⬆ Road of Bones, near Razvilka.

➡ Old dilapidated convict-built wooden bridges are a feature of remote Siberian roads, though many are now being replaced with more modern concrete bridges.

It is close to 6,200 miles (10,000km) from Moscow to Vladivostok, much of which is asphalt the whole way. Being a major highway, you should expect significant truck transport, a police presence, and no shortage of roadside cafés. Fuel stations are very common west of Irkutsk (every 6–12 miles/10–20km), less common east of Irkutsk (every 30 miles/50km) and in the newly built section between Chita and Birobidzhan fuel stations are rare (every 60 miles/100km) but expect that to change over the next few years. Fuel en route will be 92 octane in all stations, while 95 and even 98 octane will be available in more modern stations.

For travellers to Mongolia, visas are available at Mongolian consulates in Ulan Ude and Irkutsk. A nice side trip from Irkutsk is to ride to Khuzhir on Olkhon Island, in Lake Baikal, for a couple of days of serene rest in a beautiful natural setting. Olkhon Island is ideal for exploring on an off-road capable motorcycle.

The larger cities en route have many motorcyclists, bike clubs and bike shops. You will be able to find staples such as high quality motorcycle oil in towns like Chelyabinsk, Omsk, Novosibirsk, Krasnoyarsk, Irkutsk, Khabarovsk and Vladivostok. Oil filters and other bike-specific spares are less likely to be available. Siberians in general are a resourceful lot and will typically be able to manufacture or repair almost anything mechanical that goes wrong with your bike. There is a BMW Motorrad dealer in Krasnoyarsk and a KTM dealer in Barnaul, two hours south of Novosibirsk.

The Road of Bones

One of the most romantic of adventure motorcycling routes anywhere in the world, the Road of Bones is high on the wish list of many riders. Popularised by the challenging, difficult and ultimately unsuccessful attempt to ride it during the 2004 *Long Way Round* journey, the Road of Bones became a byword for toughness and adventure,

THE ROAD OF BONES

- The road was built by prisoners during the time of Stalin to supply labour camps in the most inhospitable part of the then Soviet Union.
- The gulags that supplied the project with a seemingly endless source of disposable labour were camps to which the Soviet regime banished any 'undesirables' – political prisoners, radicals, criminals, or people who spoke out about the government.
- Any worker who died during construction of the road was 'buried' where he fell – survivors' reports indicate that bodies were as common a sight as fallen logs.
- After the fall of the Soviet government the road was first travelled by Western motorcyclists in summer 1995 – Austin Vince's Mondo Enduro team (from west to east) and Norwegian adventurer Helge Pedersen (east to west).
- Simon Milward completed the journey in 2001 on his 'home-made' motorcycle.
- Rapid bridge building and highway construction are under way and it will not be too long before this iconic ride risks fading into adventure biking history.

just for taking it on. Despite its infamy, the remoteness of the Road of Bones means it is only ridden by about 20–25 people each year, though numbers have been growing again in recent years. It lies in far northeastern Russia and is sometimes confused with the Kolyma Road that goes all the way from Yakutsk to Magadan. The Road of Bones, however, begins at Khandyga, as the river port was the western end of the gulag-built road network.

The Kolymsky Trakt, or Kolyma Road, is the official Federal Route from Yakutsk to Magadan. It begins with a new road between Yakutsk and Khandyga, then follows

← **Yakutian hunters take a tracked GAZ 71 down the Vilyuisky Trakt.**

Fires cause visibility problems on the good gravel road between Susuman and Magadan.

the Road of Bones to Magadan, taking the northern variation both times the Road of Bones splits.

'Road of Bones' (*Doroga na Kostyakh*) is a term given to roads built by gulag labour between Khandyga, a former major river port before the road to Yakutsk was built in the last ten years, and Magadan. As most people know, the term 'road of bones' was used for the gulag prisoners who died during its construction, and reports are of hundreds of thousands of them who had their bones and bodies used as landfill for the next section of road; quite literally the corpses were bulldozed into the road. As a point of interest, the Russians don't really use the term at all, and it's heavily discouraged by local governments who want

to move on from reliving unpleasant histories. It is only in the Western imagination that the term 'Road of Bones' conjures up all sorts of images of harshness and misery, and of course, adventure. Note that just as there is no one route for the Silk Road, there is also no one route for the Road of Bones. All parts of the network of roads built under the gulag system were termed a 'road of bones'.

The original summer through-route began in Khandyga and ran via Kyubeme (now deserted), Tomtor (these days accessible by motorcycle only in August and early September), Kadykchan (now a ghost town) and then south to Magadan via Ust Omchug. There was also an all-weather spur up to the gold mining town (and major gulag centre)

➔ Water crossings are frequent on the Old Summer Road.

of Ust Nera from Kadykchan, connected to a *zimnik* (winter road) from Kyubeme to Ust Nera. There was an additional road up from Magadan to Susuman and Kadykchan via Atka and Orutokan. The whole lot was originally built in the 1930s and 1940s by Stalin's gulag system.

The *zimnik* from Kyubeme to Ust Nera, once the roughest and toughest part of the network, has now been upgraded to all-weather road status and forms part of the new Federal Route.

The section from Magadan to Susuman via Atka, when combined with the original road from Susuman down through Ust Omchug to Magadan, is known as the 'Kolyma Ring' and is the heart and soul of the 'Gulag Archipelago', made famous by Aleksandr Solzhenitsyn. It was on or near this ring that dozens of Stalin-era gulags existed in the 1930s, '40s and early '50s, only to be abandoned after the deaths of deputy prime minister Lavrenty Beria and Stalin in 1953.

Due to significant investment and roadworks on the Federal Route, the Road of Bones is now very much rideable by anyone capable enough to get there in the first place. It's around 1,370 miles (2,200km) from Yakutsk to Magadan, and a fuel range of 280 miles (450km) will be sufficient for the easier route via Ust Nera. The road is all unpaved, apart from the last 60 miles (100km) or so into Magadan. Due to the short summer season at that far north a latitude, it's recommended the road be attempted only between mid-June and mid-September. Food, accommodation and fuel are not at all common on the route and must be taken when available.

For the more adventurous, looking for a real challenge, the Old Summer Road, an unmaintained section of 270 miles (430km) in the middle of the route from Yakutsk to Magadan, can be a real highlight. The Old Summer Road branches off the main route at the abandoned village of Kyubeme, requiring a significant crossing of the Kyubeme River, and travels 93 miles (150km) to Tomtor, the first and only town on the Old Summer Road. Tomtor and the neighbouring village of Oimyakon are known as 'The Pole of Cold', for being the coldest permanently inhabited settlements on earth. A temperature of −71.2°C (−96°F) has been recorded there. There are limited shops and fuel in Tomtor. After Tomtor, the road deteriorates rapidly. By 37 miles (60km) out of Tomtor, it is to all intents and purposes abandoned and unused. There are many smaller water crossings. Often fallen trees may block the track. Bear prints will be visible on muddy sections.

Expect five to six long days of riding between Yakutsk and Magadan, with an extra day or two budgeted if taking the Old Summer Road. Fuel available en route will be 92 octane.

Vilyuisky Trakt

A new route between Irkutsk and Magadan that has opened up recently is the Vilyuisky Trakt. This is a route that will take you through the heart of Yakutia, and along a couple of enormous Siberian rivers – the Lena and the Vilyui.

The route goes from Irkutsk to Ust Kut, via either Tulun

and Bratsk (mostly asphalt), or via Kachug and Magistralny (mostly dirt) for the more adventurous. From Ust Kut it is first necessary to board a barge to go 620 miles (1,000km) downstream on the River Lena to Lensk. The road goes north from Lensk to the outskirts of Mirny where it turns east through Suntar, Nyurba, Vilyuisk and eventually Yakutsk. From Irkutsk to Ust Kut is around 620 miles (1,000km). From Lensk to Yakutsk is 930 miles (1,500km) of gravel road. A fuel range of 220 miles (350km) should be sufficient, and 92 octane will be the most common fuel en route.

Chuisky Trakt

The M52 highway from Barnaul to the Mongolian border is one of the most scenic in Russia, and is known as the Chuisky Trakt. The all-asphalt road begins in the plains and climbs through the mountains after meeting the Katun River, into the Altai Republic. From Gorno Altaisk onwards, the Katun River is a popular holiday region for Russians and the highway is lined with restaurants and hotels. Kosh Agach near the Mongolian border is a good place to stock up on fuel and supplies before heading into Mongolia.

⬆ **Stunning scenery on the Road of Bones.**

MAGADAN

- Magadan is located 4,197 miles (6,755km) from Moscow (straight-line distance) and there is a +8 hour time difference between Magadan and the Russian capital.
- The co-ordinates for the town are GPS: N59 33.00 E150 48.0.
- The history of Magadan and the surrounding area started in the 1920s when geological survey expeditions arrived and within a matter of years had discovered significant gold deposits.
- During the Stalin era, Magadan was a major transit centre for prisoners being sent to labour camps.
- The operations of Dalstroy, a vast and brutal forced labour gold-mining concern, were the main economic driver of the city for many decades during Soviet times.
- Anchorage in Alaska is a sister city to Magadan.

→ Olkhon Island, Lake Baikal.

The BAM Road

The BAM – Baikal-Amur Magistral – is a transcontinental railway line built in the 1930s under Stalin and completed almost 70 years later, in 2003, under Putin (the track was finished in 1991, but tunnels were not finished until 2003). The Russians already had the Trans-Siberian, but it hugs the Chinese border. Having a vital 'one and only' railway line next to them for thousands of miles was, therefore, strategically risky, even back in the 1930s, so they began building the BAM Railway, a second route across Siberia, but this time at least several hundred kilometres from the Chinese border.

So what of the BAM Road? At one time, in the 1980s, it was theoretically the first and only road across the Soviet Union. It was never more than a railway service track for the BAM Railway, but the authorities promoted it as a major road – despite it never having anything in the way of traffic, never being passable by anything less than a 4WD, and missing dozens of vital bridges that have never been built over rivers. There was a purpose to talking up the road; by pretending they had a good road across the country, the Soviets were trying to bluff the Chinese and the Americans into thinking their transport infrastructure was better than it actually was.

Following the collapse of the Soviet Union back in 1991, there was no further interest in the road from the authorities, and under Boris Yeltsin the road went the same way as the rest of the former Soviet Union – it disintegrated without so much as a hint of maintenance. When Vladimir Putin came to power, a new strategy was developed. It was recognised that a transcontinental road was needed to supplement the railways, but the BAM wasn't the place to have it. The BAM went through empty country. The entire population across Siberia was near the Trans-Siberian Railway, so any major road across the country had to be built following that – and so it was. In February 2004 Putin went on TV to proclaim the Trans-Siberian Highway open.

What of the BAM Road now, a road that was once the only route across the country? Most parts haven't seen maintenance since the days of the Soviet Union and the eastern half is so overgrown and eroded that only 6WD trucks can drive it... and then only without loads; it's impassable to normal 4WDs. It is so sparsely populated that some stretches include a ride of three to four days just to get to a settlement of 300 people. The 2,670 miles (4,300km) of the BAM Road are unsealed, except for a few short stretches.

The BAM Road begins in Taishet and heads to Bratsk, home of one of the world's largest hydro-electric plants. There is a simpler way to Bratsk, via Tulun and on an asphalted road. From Bratsk the BAM Road passes through the key river port of Ust Kut before touching the northern tip of Lake Baikal at Severobaikalsk. The road continues

→ **Expect to do some gardening on the BAM or Old Summer Roads.**

on to Novy Uoyan, beyond which it is no longer regularly maintained. Taksimo is the last major town on the BAM Road – beyond is serious adventure country, and riders should be prepared for long days, hard riding conditions and fuel and food stops a long way apart. Leaving Taksimo, the road passes through Chara, Hani, Olyokma and Yuktali before continuing on to the main city on the BAM, Tynda, halfway along its length.

Tynda is a small oasis of civilisation on the BAM, and it is also on the main road north to Yakutsk and the Road of Bones.

Leaving Tynda on the BAM, the increasingly deteriorating road passes through Verkhnezeisk, Fevralsk, Novy Urgal and Beryozovy before reaching the city of Komsomolsk. From Komsomolsk to the coast is via a good road through Lidoga and on to the port city of Vanino on the Pacific Ocean.

Fuel on the BAM Road will sometimes be less than 92 octane, and again a range of 280 miles (450km) is recommended. The length of the road, its remoteness and the very low population density along the route mean it should not be underestimated. Significant planning and preparation should go into any attempt on the BAM Road. A lightweight single cylinder motorcycle would be considerably more appropriate for this route than a large adventure bike.

Mongolia – main routes

In many ways, Mongolia is an adventure biker's paradise. Vast expanses of fence-free grasslands and semi-desert mean a rider with good navigation skills can simply head across country, away from any prepared routes. For international motorcycle travellers, there are four road border crossings into and out of Mongolia: Tsagaannuur in the west, Altanbulag in the north, Ereentsay in the east and Zamyn Uud in the south. The most common routes through Mongolia take in Tsagaannuur and Altanbulag. Apart from the major roads within 185–250 miles (300–400km) from Ulaanbaatar, Mongolia has very little asphalt, but that is changing rapidly.

There are two well-travelled routes from Tsagaannuur to the capital, Ulaanbaatar. Both are just over 1,240 miles (2,000km) long. The northern route is largely through more hilly and occasionally mountainous terrain, while the busier southern route skirts the Gobi Desert.

The southern route begins in Tsagaannuur, the first town in Mongolia, just 18 miles (30km) after the Russian border, and heads, appropriately enough, southwards through the regional capital of Olgiy, then Hovd, Altai City, Bayanhongor and Arayvaheer before reaching Ulaanbaatar. This route, being flatter and with straighter sections of road, is a little quicker than the northern route which tends to be more challenging and scenic.

The northern route heads northeast from Tsagaannuur, and it passes several mountain ranges on its way through Ulaangom, Baruunturuun, Mörön, Erdenet and then into Ulaanbaatar.

Both routes require a fuel range of 185 miles (300km), and it is rare to find better than 92 octane fuel on either. An interesting variation on the northern or southern routes is to take the 'middle route' – available from Altai

⬆ **Crashed aircraft, Verkhnevilyuisk, Vilyuisky Trakt.**

City on the southern route, and Tsetserleg on the northern route. From Altai City, head north through Uliastay to Tosontsengel (Zavhaan Province), then east through Terhiyn Tsaagaan Nuur (Great White Lake), Tsetserleg (Arkhangai Province), Kharkhorin and into Ulaanbaatar.

From Ulaanbaatar to the Russian border at Altanbulag is 223 asphalt-covered miles (360km), and this can be done in a morning.

Mongolia – other routes

Many riders to Mongolia take the opportunity to head directly down into the Gobi Desert to test their sand riding skills. This can be done by heading south through Mandalgovi to Dalanzadgad – the desert regions around Dalanzadgad are full of desert opportunities for adventurous bikers.

The road to the Chinese border town of Zamiin Uud from Ulaanbaatar is taking on increasing significance for the Mongolian economy and is being upgraded and paved rapidly. The route goes through Nalaykh, Choyr and Saynshand on the way to the Chinese border. The Chinese border road is 466 miles (750km) long. Note that you will not be able to enter China on a foreign-registered motorcycle unless you have a Chinese tour guide waiting for you on the other side to escort you through the country.

East of Ulaanbaatar is a rarely visited part of Mongolia, but there is a border crossing with Russia in the far eastern corner. An asphalt road leads through Nalaykh, past a huge silver statue of Genghis Khan on his horse, to Ondoorkhaan. From Ondoorkhaan onwards it's off-road riding to the eastern city of Choibalsan, from where a series of tracks across the grasslands head northeast to the twin border villages of Ereentsav/Chuluunhooroot and the Russian border.

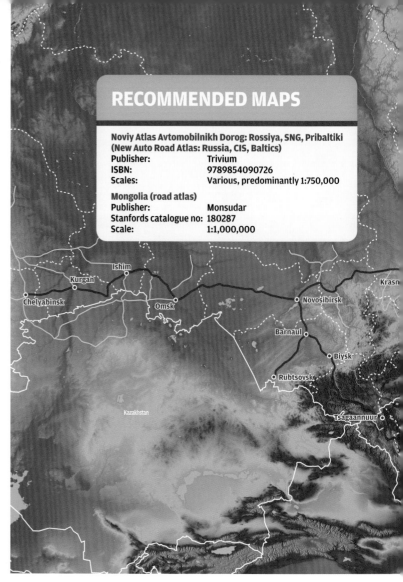

RECOMMENDED MAPS

Noviy Atlas Avtomobilnikh Dorog: Rossiya, SNG, Pribaltiki (New Auto Road Atlas: Russia, CIS, Baltics)
Publisher: Trivium
ISBN: 9789854090726
Scales: Various, predominantly 1:750,000

Mongolia (road atlas)
Publisher: Monsudar
Stanfords catalogue no: 180287
Scale: 1:1,000,000

ABOUT THE AUTHOR

Originally from Australia, now based in London, Walter Colebatch's motorcycling adventures began in 1994 with the 'Tokyo to London Project', a commercially sponsored crossing of Eurasia. That trip, which included a unique unescorted motorcycle crossing of China, was followed by motorcycle adventures in Australia, North America, South America and Africa. However, it is Siberia and Mongolia where Walter has found his niche with a series of uniquely challenging journeys throughout the region, culminating in the recent 'Sibirsky Extreme Project'. Walter holds a commercial pilot's licence and a ski instructor's certificate; he enjoys history, photography and cocktails, and speaks Russian. His travel writing and photography have been published in many motorcycle magazines, Lonely Planet travel guides and other motorcycling books, including *Building the Ultimate Adventure Motorcycle*, an earlier book in the Haynes series.

⬅ **Khovd Valley, near Tsengel, Mongolian Altai.**

⬇ **The Northern Route, Mongolia.**

Chapter 4

Australia & New Zealand

Australia is an extremely dry continent, with more than a third of the country receiving very little, if any, rain. It's not surprising, therefore, that much of the region is some form of desert and presents some challenging adventure riding. The sheer scale of the continent – Australia is almost as large as all of Europe put together – means distances between major centres are always going to be substantial and an extended trip around the continent can easily cover more than 12,500 miles (20,000km).

The Great Sandy Desert is some 150,000 square miles (388,498km2) in size and has very few inhabitants. At about a third of the size is the Simpson Desert where the summer heat is brutal – temperatures can exceed 49°C (120°F) in summer and travelling here in the winter months is advised. The Great Victoria, Gibson and Tanami are other notable deserts, typified by their red dunes, scrub vegetation and isolation. This is some of the most adventurous riding on the planet, but bear in mind that distances are significant, fuel is limited and conditions are challenging when it comes to riding in Australia's deserts.

The Great Dividing Range runs along the eastern and southeastern edge of the country and separates the dry interior from the coastal areas. A few days in the Blue Mountains (about two hours' ride from Sydney) is a worthy addition to any itinerary. At the northern extremity of the range lies the Great Barrier Reef – 1,250 miles (2,000km) of the world's largest deposit of coral and a World Heritage Site. Get out of your crash helmet and don some goggles and a snorkel for an unforgettable experience here.

Situated in the centre of Australia is Ayers Rock (Uluru) – the largest solitary rock on the planet. To the north, roads are few and far between for riders wanting to access the Kimberley Plateau west of Darwin. Regular tourists typically only gain access to the area by boat and much of the region remains unexplored.

Use the Eyre Highway to cross the Nullarbor Plain – a sparsely populated slice of southwestern Australia. The route is named after the famed explorer Edward John Eyre, who was the first person to survive an east to west crossing of Australia in the mid-1800s. Visit the enormous stretches of pure white sand in the Bilbunya Dunes; the Baxter Cliffs, found along the Bight, are absolutely stunning.

Secondary roads in the outback and in central Australia are almost all unsealed and heavy rainfall, when it happens, can make travel on unsurfaced roads hazardous. Avoid riding between sunset and sunrise, particularly at twilight, given the likelihood of animals on the road.

New Zealand is more easily accessible but also offers some of the most exceptional riding anywhere in the world, as the routes presented by Mike Hyde in his chapter clearly demonstrate. ■

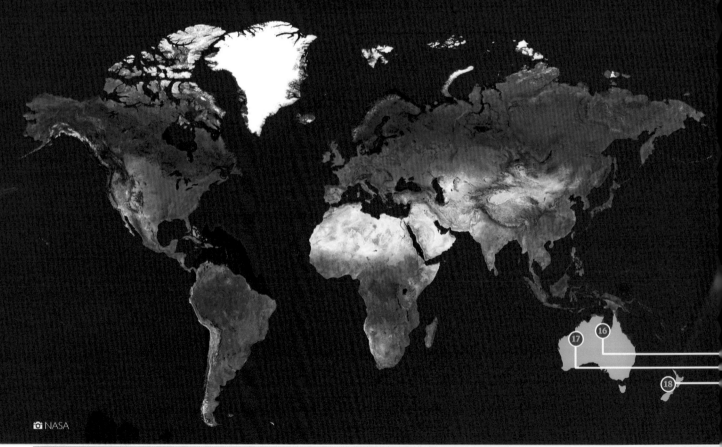

NASA

The Big Red

Adventure riding in Australia's outback

Rob and Pete West

'G'day mate. Adventure riding in the Red Centre of Oz? Bonzer, ripper, grouse.' If you understand that down-under slang you are well on your way to an appreciation of the culture that exists in the Australian outback. Rather, there isn't any. In fact, there is practically no civilisation in which to detect any elements of culture. But that's not what you're there for as an adventure motorcyclist. Thousands of miles of barren, lifeless, unforgiving, monotonous landscape are there to be tackled, full of unrelenting sunshine, big skies, shimmering mirages, endless red dusty tracks and silence. Yet a brief rain deluge can render your creek crossing an impassable obstacle. 'Sport, you've got Buckley's chance of carrying on unless you're some kind of dingbat.' In northern Queensland you are keeping an eye out for freshwater crocs during river crossings. In the Simpson Desert your enemy is hydration and the red bulldust. Australia offers adventure riding nirvana, with kangaroos.

Australia is the world's smallest continent and the world's largest island. The sixth largest country on earth, it is also the flattest. With fewer than three (2.8) inhabitants per square kilometre and most of those living on the east coast, there is a whole lot of semi-arid nothing in which to ride. In short, ship your bike to Australia and lose yourself.

The tracks showcased here have been chosen as a cross-section of what may be termed typical Aussie adventure riding. We have stitched together a route commencing in Broken Hill, NSW and ending at the tip of Cape York. The tracks are presented in the order of a rider completing the entire 6,200-mile (10,000km) route from south to north.

Track 1: Red Centre's Three Corners Four Tracks

From: Broken Hill
To: Alice Springs
Length: 2,223 miles (3,578km)

Leg 1

From: Broken Hill (GPS: S31 57.00 E141 27.00)
To: Cameron Corner (GPS: S28 29.56 E141 00.02)
Length: 265 miles (427km)
Route: Broken Hill – Silver City Highway – Tibooburra – Cameron Corner Road – Cameron Corner

⬆ Adventure riders' mild annoyance number 16: road trains and their swirling vortexes of gritty blinding dust.
📷 R. West

⬅⬅ Endless, dusty and red. The Peninsula Developmental Road towards Cape York (Track 7).
📷 R. West

⬅ Alice Springs: fuel, clean sheets, oil change, tyres, internet, cold beer and laundered T-shirts. A true oasis (Track 1).
📷 R. West

Dusk at Ayers Rock, also known as Uluru (Track 1).
📷 J. Townsend

Leg 2
From: Cameron Corner (GPS: S28 29.56 E141 00.02)
To: Birdsville (GPS: S25 53.56 E139 21.06)
Length: 469 miles (756km)
Route: Cameron Corner – Bore Track – Innamincka
          – Haddon Corner – Birdsville Developmental
          Road – Birdsville

Leg 3
From: Birdsville (GPS: S25 53.56 E139 21.06)
To: Marree (GPS: S29 38.00 E138 03.00)
Length: 426 miles (686km)
Route: Birdsville – Poeppel Corner – K1 Line
          – Warburton Track – Birdsville Track –
          Mungerannie – Marree

Leg 4
From: Marree (GPS: S29 38.00 E138 03.00)
To: Marla (GPS: S27 18.00 E133 37.00)
Length: 445 miles (717km)
Route: Marree – Oodnadatta Track – William Creek –
          Oodnadatta – Marla

Leg 5
From: Marla (GPS: S27 18.00 E133 37.00)
To: Alice Springs (GPS: S23 7.00 E 133 87.00)
Length: 616 miles (992km)
Route: Marla – Stuart Highway – Erldunda – Lasseter
          Highway – Uluru (Ayers Rock) – Luritja Road –
          Ernest Giles Road – Kings Canyon – Mereenie Road
          – Hermannsburg – Larapinta Drive – Alice Springs

Services

The Three Corners Four Tracks route mixes tarmac with popular 4WD tracks, but remember that as soon as you head off road in the desert, there are significant risks. Long stretches without fuel are common and even bikes with extra-large tanks will be pushed to the limit of their capacity. The entire region, covering thousands of square miles, is highly weather-dependent in terms of the impact of heavy rain. In many areas described here it is mandatory to register with the police, and the time of year you are riding is crucial, as is advance research into the conditions of the tracks. Roadhouses are the best source of information before setting out on the next leg.

Features

Reaching the three corners, where state lines and time zones intersect, is a well-known goal of many local Australian adventure riders. The fourth corner, Surveyor General's Corner, much further west, is basically unattainable outside of being in a guided group, and is not worth the extra effort. This route takes in the iconic outback tracks of Birdsville, Bore and Oodnadatta. Sand lovers will face their nemesis in the Nappanerica Big Red Dune as they cross part of the Simpson Desert to reach Poeppel Corner and south on the often closed tortuous Warburton Track to intersect with the Birdsville. However, there is a bypass if it doesn't work out. Water, fuel and a satellite phone will be your friends on this route. Seeing the sunset shades of Uluru and gazing on the first green trees for a week in Alice Springs will be among the moments to remember.

Track 2: Tanami Road aka Tanami Track

From: Alice Springs (GPS: S23 7.00 E133 87.00)
To: Halls Creek (GPS: S18 13.37 E127 40.05)
Length: 653 miles (1,051km)

Services

The longest stretch without fuel is from Billuna to Yuendumu – a distance of 371 miles (597km). The infamous Rabbit Flat roadhouse is now closed. Camping under the stars is the way to go for this track, although some haphazard donga (cabin) accommodation may be available at the few roadhouses on a hit and miss basis.

Features

Most of the route travels across the Tanami Desert, flat, lifeless and home to spinifex grass and saltbrush plants. The track is prone to bulldust and sand and there are numerous creek bed crossings – all good news to the adventure rider. The Tanami is widely used by adventure motorcyclists to link with the well-known tracks over in the west such as the Canning Stock Route (which intersects with the Tanami at Billiluna) and further north the Gibb River Road, Buchanan Highway and Barkly Stock Route leading back to northern Queensland.

Track 3: Gibb River Road

From: Halls Creek (GPS: S18 13.37 E127 40.05)
To: Kununurra (GPS: S15 46.25 E128 44.19)
Length: 646 miles (1,041km)
Route: Halls Creek – Fitzroy Crossing – Windjana Gorge
         – Gibb River Road – Kununurra

Features

This is an easy, 410-mile (660km) partially sealed two-lane gravel track through the Kimberley, with plentiful

The ability to travel most outback tracks is critically dependent on whether it has rained recently. Rainfall in the region is low all year round, but a sudden deluge may render a track impassable to bikes for the rest of the year. Dry creek beds turn into torrents and sandy creek bed bases make for instant sludge. The protocol is to check for conditions ahead at each point of civilisation, whether roadhouses or a small town's police station. Day to night temperature extremes see most adventure riding in the 'comfortable' seasons of spring (September to November) or more typically in the autumn (from March to May).

services. Well known for its mini national parks, gorges and accommodation options at cattle stations, the Gibb is an adventure riding antidote to the other remote and lifeless tracks in that it has greenery, water and bends.

Track 4: Buchanan and Carpentaria Highways

From: Kununurra (GPS: S15 46.25 E128 44.19)
To: Borroloola (GPS: S16 04.224 E136 18.436)
Length: 631 miles (1,016km)
Route: Kununurra – Timber Creek – Buchanan Highway
         – Top Springs – Daley Waters – Carpentaria
         Highway – Cape Crawford – Borroloola

Features

These two routes are included as they connect the Gibb with the Savannah. Otherwise it's fairly featureless and just 'another day at the office' for the adventure rider. All roads are unsealed, with attention required for potential fuel range issues.

◀ Want to know what the **XXXX** stands for? Ask these riders when they come out. Aussie outback pubs are beacons in the wilderness.
📷 R. West

⬆ The QAA Line, from Birdsville to Poeppel Corner in the Simpson Desert (Track 1).
📷 R. West

Track 5: The Savannah Way

From:	Borroloola (GPS: S16 04.224 E136 18.436)
To:	Normanton (GPS: S17 40.00 E141 04.00)
Length:	435 miles (700km)
Route:	Borroloola – Hells Gate – Burketown – Normanton

WHERE TO GO

The ideal itinerary is to link the various tracks in a looping fashion. Most bikes will ship into Sydney, Melbourne or Brisbane, any of which make suitable start/finish places for a looping ride connecting the tracks. Our view of the ultimate adventure itinerary, which would span 3–4 weeks, would see a Sydney to Brisbane loop in a counter-clockwise direction. Using the track references in this section we would ride Sydney to Track 3, to Track 4, to Track 1, to Track 2 and end up back in Brisbane. Most international riders will continue on to New Zealand for the sheer contrast in adventure riding on offer. Shipping from Brisbane or Sydney to Christchurch either by air or sea is straightforward and relatively quick.

Features

The Savannah Way is the 'brand name' given to the 2,175-mile (3,500km) route from Cairns to Broome, promoted as a 'self-drive' itinerary. Of interest to the adventure motorcyclist is the 435-mile (700km) unsealed and remote portion with some challenging terrain as it parallels the coastline of the Gulf of Carpentaria.

Track 6: Burke Developmental Road

From:	Normanton (GPS: S17 40.00 E141 04.00)
To:	Dimbulah (GPS: S17 08.56 E145 06.38)
Length:	397 miles (640km)

Services

Practically none. Fuel and services are only at each end – Normanton and Chillagoe – so it's a 335-mile (540km) stretch away from any civilisation. Breakdowns are reliant on any passing 4WD traffic which will be eventual, but sparse. It's essential you carry spare fuel, water and a satellite phone.

Features

Wide open outback at the base of the Cape York

⬆ On tracks like the Birdsville, you grab fuel whenever it is on offer. Mungerannie Hotel (Track 1).
📷 R. West

⬇ Croc country on the way to the Telegraph Track, Cape York (Track 7).
📷 R. West

➡ Lengthening shadows at dusk in the outback near Burketown (Track 5).
📷 R. West

Peninsula is traversed by this relatively little travelled gravel and sand road; it is prone to closure in heavy rain, which will also make river fords, otherwise dry, impassable. Much of the track surface is the notorious fine bulldust, making this route appealing to adventure riders who relish this type of masochism.

Track 7: Cape York (also known as the Telegraph Track at the northern end)

From: Dimbulah (GPS: S17 08.56 E145 06.38)
To: Cape York tip (GPS: S10 41.00 E142 32.00)
Length: 696 miles (1,121km)
Route: Dimbulah – Cairns – Port Douglas – Bloomfield Track – Cooktown – Peninsula Developmental Road – Telegraph Road – Bramwell Junction – Telegraph Track – Jardine River – Bamaga – Cape York

Services

Readily available fuel and supplies can be found at roadhouses handily spaced along the route. This route lends itself to camping, although roadhouses have some cabins or 'dongas' for rent.

Features

This is one of the most popular adventure rides, to the northern tip of Australia. Cairns to Cape Tribulation is a touristic sealed road along the palm-fringed Queensland coast. Cape Trib to Cooktown is an easy adventure ride over the Bloomfield Track, with straightforward river

WHAT TO RIDE

The range of tracks and their individual 'dynamics' will drive the best type of bike. The larger adventure bikes, such as BMW GS machines and KTMs, will have the fuel capacity to tackle the long stretches with perhaps a small 5-litre auxiliary supply for safety. The exception is the Simpson, where a light bike is the only way to go. The lighter weight bikes will be more manageable in adverse conditions such as creeks, sand and bulldust, and for those bone-jarring corrugations and outpacing emus! However, the overriding criteria will be fuel capacity and the amount of support gear (such as camping items and water) required to be carried in panniers.

ABOUT THE AUTHORS

The father and son team of Rob and Pete West make annual forays into the 'Big Red' and opt for lighter bikes such as DRZs. Rob West hails from Nottingham, England, where he started his riding career from the minute he was old enough. Countless weekends were spent riding in Europe and many holidays involved travelling around the USA. Rob moved to Dubai in 1990 where his passion for off-road riding started to develop, with early morning rides in the desert. Rob was a scrutineer for the Desert Challenge, rode from Dubai back to England, and then spent the best part of a year riding 39,000 miles (63,000km) from Tierra del Fuego to Alaska. Moving to New Zealand in 2004, Rob's love of adventure riding has paid dividends as he has explored and enjoyed his adopted home and, of course, the vast expanse of Australian tracks 'over the ditch'.

⬇ **The bike's fuel range is 450km. Man or mouse? The Barkly Stock Route, Northern Territory.**
📷 M. Hyde

crossings. From Lakeland the Peninsula Developmental Road is a gravel 'motorway'. Some 31 miles (50km) after your last fuel top-up at Archer River roadhouse, you turn off on to Telegraph Road for a continuation of the gravel and this somewhat well-travelled 4WD route. The excitement starts at Bramwell Junction roadhouse where your bike type, riding skills and capacity for risk-taking will drive you either to continue along the Telegraph Road as it bypasses a series of rivers descending from the Great Dividing Range or, to justify the very reason you are probably riding in this part of the tropical north, branch off on to the Telegraph Track. 'The Track' is 81 miles (131km) from Bramwell Junction to the obligatory Aborigine-operated ferry across the Jardine River, and entails countless river crossings with names like Gunshot, Cockatoo and Cannibal Creeks, with risks of crocs, bush bashing and other obstacles. This section is highly weather-dependent in terms of your ability to get through without reverting back to the bypass road. Once over the Jardine River you are at the tip of Cape York and only 93 miles (150km) from Papua New Guinea across the Torres Strait.

RECOMMENDED MAPS

Australian Motorcycle Atlas
Publisher: HEMA
ISBN: 9781865005188

Australia's Great Desert Tracks (map pack)
Publisher: Hema Maps
ISBN: 978-1-86500-552-2
Scale: 1 : 1,250,000
Purchase online: www.exploreoz.com

Australia Road and 4WD Atlas
Publisher: Hema Maps
ISBN: 978-1-86500-570-6

Purchase online: www.hemamaps.com.au

WARNING NO FUEL FOR 500km

Tablelands Hwy 228

AUSTRALIAN DESERTS

Desert	State/Territory	Size (km²)	Size (square miles)	Proportion of Australian landmass
Great Victoria Desert	Western Australia, South Australia	348,750km²	134,650 square miles	4%
Great Sandy Desert	Western Australia	267,250km²	103,190 square miles	3.5%
Tanami Desert	Western Australia, Northern Territory	184,500km²	71,200 square miles	2.4%
Simpson Desert	Northern Territory, Queensland, South Australia	176,500km²	68,100 square miles	2.3%
Gibson Desert	Western Australia	156,000km²	60,000 square miles	2.0%
Little Sandy Desert	Western Australia	111,500km²	43,100 square miles	1.5%
Strzelecki Desert	South Australia, Queensland, New South Wales	80,250km²	30,980 square miles	1.0%
Sturt Stony Desert	South Australia, Queensland, New South Wales	29,750km²	11,490 square miles	0.3%
Tirari Desert	South Australia	15,250km²	5,890 square miles	0.2%
Pedirka Desert	South Australia	1,250km²	480 square miles	0.1%

The Big Red

Canning Stock Route

1,000 miles across the Australian outback

Andreas Hülsmann

A report in the *Kalgoorlie Western Argus* on Tuesday 12 September 1911 reads as follows:

'Mr A. W. Canning, district surveyor of Perth, yesterday received a telegram from Mr Urquhart, of Wiluna, stating that Tom Cole, who has just arrived at Wiluna with the first mob of cattle to come down by the Canning stock route, reported that the cattle had evidently gained in condition on the journey and he was highly pleased with the route.' If only the same could be said about adventurers who take on what remains one of the toughest and most remote tracks in the world.

The Canning Stock Route (or CSR) runs from Wiluna to Halls Creek in Western Australia, a distance of over 1,000 miles (1,600km). A former stock driving route, the CSR was established 100 years ago in order to get cattle from the green farmland in the north of Western Australia to the goldfields round the town of Kalgoorlie. It remains the longest historic stock route in the world.

One of the early explorers was David Carnegie, who had lost men during his expedition in the area and advised against continuing the search for such a route. 'We have demonstrated the uselessness of any persons wasting their time and money in further investigations of that desolate region,' Carnegie wrote.

After a number of other failed expeditions, surveyor Alfred Canning was contracted to find a way from Wiluna to Halls Creek in the north. Canning started off in May 1906 with eight men, 23 camels, two horses and provisions for a nine-month journey from Wiluna. They returned 13 months later. In 1908 Canning left Wiluna again, this time followed by 35 men, 70 camels, 267 goats, four wagons and tons of building materials to set up the wells along the

route. Working in temperatures of around 50°C (122°F) for weeks at a time, his crew completed 51 wells, averaging one every 18 days. Canning's party constructed the wells with the forced help of Aboriginal people whose land the route traversed. The deepest was Well 5, at more than 30m; the shallowest, Well 42, was just 1.4m. A year later the first cattle drive started through the desert.

OUR BIKES

It took a long time to decide on a suitable bike for this trip but in the end we decided to use the BMW F650GS (single cylinder). One main reason for this was that it had a good balance between weight and power – 190kg to 50hp. But the main reason was the fact that aftermarket suppliers, Touratech, had a 22-litre tank which enabled us to carry a total of 39 litres of fuel in three tanks (the main tank under the seat and two tanks up the front of the bike). In addition to this we carried two 12-litre plastic canisters, embedded in a special aluminum casing, giving us each a total fuel capacity of 63 litres.

The bikes had a starting weight in Wiluna of 340kg, without the rider. This included 63 litres of petrol, 26 litres of water, food for three weeks, tools, spares, camping gear and photographic equipment. We switched the rear suspension to Whitepower and changed the forks into an 'upside-down' version, also from Whitepower.

Whatever bike you choose must be light but with sufficient power and capable of carrying enough fuel and water. Possible choices are a modified BMW G650 X-Challenge or Yamaha XT660. On the CSR the fuel consumption varies a lot and can be three times higher compared to normal riding conditions.

⇐ **Nearly 1,000 run-ups must be done to cross the Canning Stock Route – the sand dunes are not very high, but the way to the top can be very long.**

⇐ **The entrance to the CSR in Wiluna is just an ordinary road sign. Anyone wishing to pass this point should be well prepared.**

↑ In total 63
litres of fuel – an
additional
22-litre tank
mounted on the
bike plus two
12-litre plastic
canisters under
each aluminium
box.

Between 1911 and 1931 only eight cattle herds were driven along the CSR as a result of disputes with the local Aborigines, who claimed the CSR passed through holy land and was an unnecessary drain on precious water resources. Records show the last cattle drive along the CSR started in 1958; in total only 31 cattle drives were ever successfully completed along the CSR.

It took until 1968 for the CSR to be covered in a car. Two surveyors completed the journey, sometimes taking days to find a well.

Adventure riding on the CSR route

Water and petrol weighed the BMW F650s down. Each bike carried 63 litres of petrol and 26 litres of water, plus the rest of the gear – tools, spare parts, photo equipment, food, camping gear and a first aid kit, along with other essentials. In total, each bike weighed 750lb (340kg), without the rider.

We left Wiluna – it was surprisingly not nearly as emotional or as serious as I'd feared it might be. Behind us was more than a year of preparation, but as we rode out

of town my thoughts were on the equipment. Had we packed everything? Did we forget something? If yes, it was too late anyway, because we were on the run. More than 1,200 miles (2,000km) of the outback lay in wait, more than 1,000 sand dunes to cross. And the water? What about the water? Would there be enough out there? Water would ultimately decide our fate.

The first days were not too bad. The CSR led through farmland. The ground was solid. There were only a few sand dunes to cross. But soon we faced the first challenge. We had to climb the first big sand hill. To get more grip, we deflated our tyres. We knew that speed was the only way to drive through sand, but that wasn't possible. In the middle of the climb a sharp turn robbed us of all momentum, but there was no alternative – we had to go up. The only other option was back, so it was first gear and go. The motor yelled, but there was only a little progress. I was working my whole body to push my bike forward. Jörg, on the other bike, was pushing his bike hard too. If we had to stop we'd have to dig the bikes out. The climb seemed endless, the F650 becoming slower and slower. Finally we reached the top. The first serious sand dune was exhausting; then our minds began to think about what lay ahead.

As demoralising as those initial thoughts were, we improved our riding technique every day. However, to climb to the top of dunes with the bikes remained an exhausting job, and that wasn't the only problem: we were travelling too slowly, on average covering just 44 miles (70km) per day. The plan had been to cover between 60 and 75 miles (100–120km) per day. That meant we had to ration the food and conserve our water. Breakfast consisted of one cup of cereal, dried milk, water and a vitamin pill; lunch was one cereal bar and for dinner we had a pack of '2-minute noodles' and two cups of tea. How could one make savings from that, I asked myself.

Another problem was the vegetation. Bushes and branches hung across the track and were impossible to avoid. Barely a day would go by without having a pannier knocked off by a protruding branch. Add to that the strain my knees were taking from regular falls in the sand and I was feeling pretty beaten up. It was more 'stumbling' than driving through the desert. Then there was the heat, and the flies, and the sand that got everywhere, and the fear of breaking down, and the worry of being stranded hundreds of miles from anywhere and anyone in the middle of the desert.

Why were we doing this? Because the CSR is a true adventure track, isolated, far from civilisation. It's not often that one can find this kind of place. Then there was the landscape of the desert, which is simply breathtaking, not to mention the history of the trail. Few of the wells dug along the route now hold any water, which made us nervous, but equally we were enjoying the excitement of adventuring in such a remote landscape. It's a strange but good feeling to be in the wild on your own.

At Well 23, after 454 miles (730km) of sand dunes,

CANNING STOCK ROUTE

- The nearest capital city to the Wiluna start point is Perth, 625 miles (1,000km) southwest of Wiluna.
- Wally Dowling, a drover who had made nine runs along the stock route, took what were probably the last horses northwards along the route in September 1951.
- In 1964 Henry Ward became the first person to travel by vehicle up the stock route as far as the Durba Hills and Well 18. 'We went up in a four-cylinder Land Rover. We set up a fuel dump out near Well 11 and followed cattle pads between the wells,' he said.
- In 1968 the entire length of the track was driven for the first time.
- During the 1980s fuel dumps were created and adventurous travellers became interested in the history of the track and the challenge of riding or driving it.
- In 1994 long-distance walker Drew Kettle walked the route.
- In 2004 Kate Leeming completed the route by bicycle.
- In 2005, Jakub Postrzygacz became the first person to traverse the entire track without back-up, travelling alone by bicycle for 33 days. Using large tyres and a single-wheel trailer, he carried all his food with him, stocking up on water at the periodic wells.

we located the drum of petrol we'd arranged to be waiting for us. An access road to this point on the CSR had allowed it to be brought in from a roadhouse some 370 miles (600km) away. We organised this way in advance, from our home in Germany. Without this drop-off arrangement the route would be almost impossible. In recent years Kunawarritji, an Aboriginal community 155 miles (250km) further along the trail, has opened up to 'outsiders'. Here it's now possible to replenish fuel and stock up with more food. This community marks the halfway point; beyond it, the CSR

← The Great Sandy Desert isn't just sand; the desert is also full of vegetation, which hampers progress.

Michael Tobin was one of Alfred Canning's men, killed by Aborigines in the survey expedition of 1907.

Then it was on to the highest dune of them all, between Wells 41 and 42; 55ft (17 metres) doesn't sound very high, but the run up it was horrible. The track ascended steeply and on the other side we found a 4WD jeep buried deep in the sand. Its occupants had made progress in digging it out and our assistance wasn't required, so we pressed on, sensing there wasn't much of the track left to ride.

The end of the desert is marked by the Breaden Hills, a scenic highlight of the CSR, and an important landmark for explorers in former times. Then, finally, after two weeks of sand and wilderness we reached farmland again, though still with another 220 miles (350km) to go. We were in the territory of the Halls Creek community, but it was still another four days before we saw any signs of civilisation. The first spot after that lone track was Billuna, an Aboriginal community, where we stopped to fill up our tanks and to fill up ourselves with food. We had a couple of beef pasties from the shelf. They tasted awful, but after all the deprivation we'd endured on the CSR those pasties felt like a full gourmet dinner!

Route facts

To ride the CSR requires substantial planning and is only practical during the cooler months. The track crosses four deserts – the Gibson Desert, Little Sandy Desert, Great Sandy Desert and the Tanami Desert, taking you through some of the most remote areas in Australia. The route requires you to scale more than 1,000 sand dunes, heavy corrugations and even thick mud patches. An additional challenge is the vegetation – bushes and branches often stick out into the track and catch on your panniers as you ride by. Exiting the track is nearly impossible as the vegetation on the sides is so dense.

↑ Camp set up right beside the track. The space between the bushes was just big enough for the tent.

becomes more demanding. We faced higher dunes and deeper sand. We passed Well 37, the 'ghost well' where the stockmen Shoesmith and Thompson were killed by Aborigines in 1911. Legend says these guys still hang around Well 37, so we chose an alternative campsite further down the track!

After all the sand dunes it was a relief when we finally reached Lake Tobin, a salt lake, with solid ground and smooth surfaces. Here we pushed the bikes up to 62mph (100km/h) – our speed record on the CSR. After the lake we visited Tobin's Grave at Well 40.

➡ The CSR claims its victims. There is no way to get broken vehicles back to civilisation.

Distance

The CSR is more than 1,325 miles (2,130km), taking into account all 51 wells, but not every one of these is situated directly on the track. It is unlikely that this route is achievable by motorcycle without a support vehicle. The shortest version of the CSR is 1,131 miles (1,820km), passing only the wells directly along the track and taking in no extra detours.

Duration

The minimum time needed is 16 days. Andreas and riding partner Jörg Becker needed 22 days for the trip. Cars can complete the track in 14 days, although most need at least 18 days.

Season

The only time to attempt this trip is in winter (dry season), from May to August. In the wet season (November–March) there can be localised flooding and it is simply too hot, with temperatures in excess of 40°C (104°F).

Food supply

Between Wiluna and Halls Creek there is only one possibility to fill up with food – at the thriving modern Aboriginal community of Kunawarritji, some 620 miles (1,000km) from Wiluna and 515 miles (830km) from Halls Creek. The store is stocked with supplies including a variety of frozen meats, fresh fruit, vegetables and the usual assortment of tins, packets and frozen bread.

Fuel supply

There is a fuel dump at Well 23, some 440 miles (712km) from Wiluna. Fuel drops typically need to be organised up to two months in advance; your fuel is then made available in 200-litre drums. The order can be made at the Capricorn Roadhouse. Fuel is also available at the Kunawarritji community.

↟ Fuel is delivered in 200-litre drums to the fuel dump at Well 23. The Aboriginal community at Kunawarritji, 180 miles further north, also provides a fuel supply for the CSR.

↡ Solid ground and a smooth surface have turned Tobin Lake into something of a highway on the CSR, but only for a few miles.

Andreas Hülsmann is a well-known German motorcycle and travel journalist. He has been riding motorcycles the world over for more than 25 years. His travels have taken him through Australia, North and South America, Arabia, Siberia, Mongolia, Central Asia and across Europe. He has written more than 100 stories for the German motorcycle press and four books about his journeys. His illustrated book entitled *Heading East* has been published in German and English and is available for sale through aftermarket specialists Touratech.

In memory of Jörg Becker

Jörg Becker rode with Andreas along the Canning Stock Route in Australia. He was an enthusiastic motorcycle rider, always ready for an adventure. Jörg had previously explored North Africa, South America, Canada and the USA. He was a firefighter by profession and took time out to support Andreas on motorcycle tests or travel documentaries. Jörg sadly lost his life in May 2009 at the age of 39 in a motorcycle accident in Germany.

Water supply

The series of wells, originally constructed to water stock, are now in various stages of disrepair or restoration, but they do offer points of interest and welcome shade. Many of them, however, are now little more than depressions in the ground and some have their water tainted with the corpses of rotting animals. According to recent reports, drinking water is generally available from Wells 6, 12, 15, Georgia Bore, Well 26, the tank at 33 and at Well 49. Other wells may be found flooded at any time or have suspicious water. Well water quality is poor at many wells and you will need to be able to take on large amounts (100 litres plus) at wells where water is good. A good water filter is an essential piece of kit. You will also need to take a strong bucket to draw water up from most wells, plus a length of either metal or nylon rope of approximately 60ft (20m).

⬇ **The restored Well 46 is located in a broad plain and is surrounded by eucalyptus trees. After 180 miles, this is the first spot to replenish your water.**

Water road book

Start	0000.0km	Start in Wiluna
	⬇ 235.1km	
P1	0235.1km	Well 6 GPS: S25 14.27 E121 05.58
	⬇ 62.3km	
P2	0297.4km	Well 9 GPS: S25 01.06 E121 35.12
	⬇ 142.5km	
P3	0439.9km	Well 15 GPS: S24 08.27 E122 12.08
	⬇ 63.4km	
P4	0503.3km	Biella Spring
	⬇ 12.7km	
P5	0516.0km	Durba Springs
	⬇ 29.7km	
P6	0545.7km	Well 18 GPS: S23 33.48 E122 13.44
	⬇ 144.2km	
P7	0689.9km	Georgia Bore, 750ft (250m) left of the track GPS: S23 03.309 E123 01.023
	0712.3km	Fuel dump GPS: S23 04.45 E122 13.13
	⬇ 82.5km	
W8	0772.4km	Well 26 GPS: S22 54.58 E123 30.21
	⬇ 134.9km	
W9	0907.3km	Mujingarra Cave GPS: S22 31.40 E124 09.86
	0975.1km	Well 32 GPS: S22 24.22 E124 35.08 Nyarruri: Water available in case of emergency, 2km on the left-hand side Mallowa Native Soak: water available, but you have to dig 6ft (2m) deep
	⬇ 10.4km	
W10	0985.5km	Well 33 GPS: S22 20.294 E124 46.308 Near Kunawarritji community
	⬇ 74.2km	
W11	1059.7km	Well 36 GPS: S22 08.23 E125 16.59
	⬇ 22.5km	
W12	1082.2km	Well 37 GPS: S22 09.16 E125 27.31
	⬇ 59.5km	
	1141.7km	Well 39 GPS: S21 46.02 E125 39.06 Water available in case of emergency
	⬇ 232.2km	
W13	1373.9km	Well 46 GPS: S20 38.31 E126 17.15
	⬇ 101.0km	
W14	1474.9km	Well 49 GPS: S20 09.51 E126 40.52
	⬇ 344.6km	
Finish	1819.5km	Halls Creek – end of the Canning Stock Route

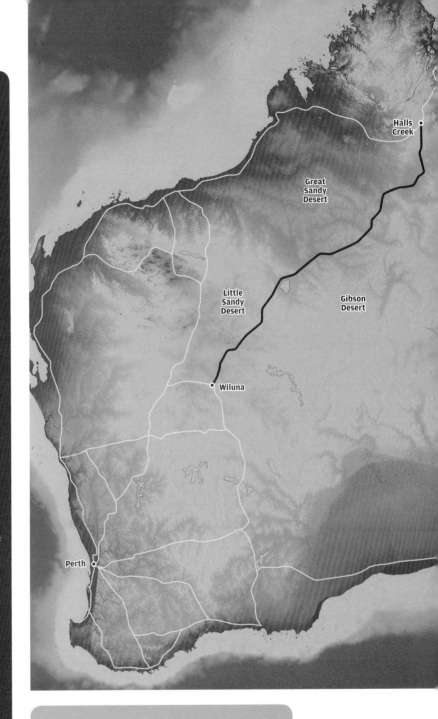

RECOMMENDED MAPS

Canning Stock Route (4th edition)
Publisher:	**Westprint Heritage Maps**
ISBN:	**9780646182230**
Scale:	**1:1,000,000**

This map contains notes on the history of the surveying and building of the CSR by Alfred Canning. The map is clear, with symbols referring to textual information provided on the back of the map explaining each point of interest, and the surrounding flora and fauna. Westprint Heritage Maps are highly regarded maps for desert areas. The maps are very clear to read and have road distances, rest areas and fuel outlets noted.

Australian Motorcycle Atlas
Publisher:	**HEMA**
ISBN:	**9781865005188**

📷 All photographs courtesy of Andreas Hülsmann

Canning Stock Route   **151**

New Zealand

Latitude 45° south: adventure riding in Middle Earth

Mike Hyde

New Zealand. Middle Earth. Aotearoa. Land of the Long White Cloud. The country is tucked away at the bottom of the world and is closer to Antarctica than any other land mass, barring its close neighbour down under, Australia. If Frodo had ridden a GS this would have been his backyard.

New Zealand consists of two islands, innovatively named the North and South Islands. Of the country's population of 4.3 million, just one million live in the South Island, an area the size of England and Wales. What this means for adventure riders is wide open spaces, often deserted roads and purist off-road riding in a safe and clean, green environment. No dangerous animals, plenty of fuel, meat pies and no borders.

After riding in Australia and America a returning Kiwi like me tends to find New Zealand somewhat claustrophobic due to its size. Yet this is arguably its greatest motorcycling feature – in one day you might ride through rainforest, alpine beech forest, barren tussock lands, green rolling farmland and craggy coastal scenery. Many movies, from the *Lord of the Rings* trilogy to *The Chronicles of Narnia* and *The Lost World*, used locations which were less than a three-hour ride from my front door in Christchurch. An all-day ride to Queenstown sees no traffic lights, motorways or toll roads. My favourite full-duration adventure ride on the South Island is, in fact, a back-to-back series of 19 individual tracks linked by some spectacular sealed road riding.

Many of these 'off the beaten tracks' you would not find yourself as a tourist. The route known as 'Latitude 45° South' after the 45th parallel which bisects the island (and as described in this chapter) takes no less than two weeks, allowing for one non-riding day and a leisurely pace

WHEN TO GO

The best riding is in late summer to early autumn, namely February–April, a period known as New Zealand's 'Indian summer'. This avoids the peak tourist season, school vacations and holidaying New Zealanders. Roads are uncongested, high country stations are free of lambing and mustering, and accommodation is easy to find on the go. Rivers that you will ford are at their lowest. Daylight saving means you are riding in the light until 9pm. The South Island's mean annual temperature is 8°C (46°F), making it desirable to ride in summer. Off-road tracks are at their rideable best during this window.

averaging 155 miles (250km) per day. At around 2,175 miles (3,500km), the route comprises 40% unsealed legal roads, called shingle tracks, 4WD routes crossing high country farms, known as stations, and gravel roads built to access the power pylons servicing the country's hydro-electric network grid.

Due to New Zealand's comparative isolation in terms of the effort of getting there and back, most visiting motorcyclists make a proper trip of it and spend anywhere between a fortnight and a month to make their time worthwhile.

Latitude 45° South starts in the South Island's main city, Christchurch, the place where you are likely to fly into from overseas. Here you prepare yourself and your bike and gear for the fortnight's ride ahead. As a stunning introductory couple of days of tarmac riding in New Zealand, perhaps re-orientating yourself to travelling on the left-hand side of the road, my route takes you across

← **Old Dunstan Trail (Track 6).**
📷 M. Hyde

← **Mt White Road, Waimakariri River, Arthur's Pass.**
📷 G. Sargent

WHICH BIKE?

The route is entirely suitable for larger adventure bikes as well as mid-range machines. The most common adventure bikes ridden by locals are the BMW 1150/1200GS, KTM 990 Adventure, Kawasaki KLR650, Yamaha Super Tenere or XT660, and also the Suzuki DR650. Riders will find ready supplies of servicing and spares, the fuel ranges of these bikes are adequate, and they will be at home on all the listed routes.

the Southern Alps through Arthur's Pass to the West Coast. Your first fuel and meat pie stop in the middle of the mountains may see you having to guard your bike seat from being savaged by the cheeky local mountain parrot, the Kea.

The West Coast is a narrow strip of land on the Tasman Sea side of the island, well known for its rainforests and glaciers. Finally you ride back across the Alps through the southernmost route called Haast Pass. Your destination is Queenstown, an idyllic paradise nestled among mountains and a glacial lake. It is from Queenstown that the series of 19 adventure mini-rides, that will span the next 10–11 days, commences.

⬆ **Riding on the South Island's empty sealed roads between the off-road tracks is a welcome break from gravel. The scenery is no less stunning. Lake Pukaki and Aoraki Mt Cook.**
📷 O. Pflug

⬇ **Old Dunstan Trail (Track 6).**
📷 M. Hyde

↑ **Nevis Road
(Track 5).**
📷 M. Hyde

← **Rainbow Road
(Track 16).**
📷 G. Sargent

NEW ZEALAND ROUTES

TRACK 1: SKIPPERS CANYON

From: Queenstown (GPS: S45 01.957 E168 39.582)
To: The Branches station (GPS: S44 44.298 E168 43.539)
Length: 54 miles (87km) return
Features: A narrow gravel road (closed to rental vehicles) through remote gold mining country to a high country sheep station and return to Queenstown. Steep drop-offs, fords and sandy tracks.

TRACK 2: GLENORCHY 'ISENGARD'

From: Queenstown (GPS: S45 01.957 E168 39.582)
To: Greenstone Track car park (GPS: S44 55.657 E168 20.615)
Length: 101 miles (164km) return
Features: Arguably the most scenic track on the route, into jaw-dropping *Lord of the Rings* locations such as Isengard; 30% gravel.

TRACK 3: VON RIVER VALLEY AND MAVORA LAKES

From: Walter Peak station (GPS: S45 06.717 E168 32.73)
To: Milford Highway (GPS: S45 32.333 E167 57.897)
Length: 51 miles (82km)
Features: Transport your bike on the SS *Earnslaw* steamer which crosses Lake Wakatipu and offloads at Walter Peak station. Remote back country gravel road with fords take you through to the main highway to Milford Sound.

TRACK 4: BORLAND ROAD

From: Lake Monowai turn-off (GPS: S45 46.857 E167 40.141)
To: South arm of Lake Manapouri (GPS: S45 35.122 E167 22.373)
Length: 55 miles (90km) return
Features: Invest 1-2 days riding to Milford Sound through mountains and a tunnel on the way to the start of the Borland Road, following pylons into a remote arm of Lake Manapouri. 4WD track prone to washouts. Summer only.

TRACK 5: NEVIS ROAD

From: Garston (GPS: S45 27.337 E168 41.622)
To: Clyde (GPS: S45 11.144 E169 18.927)
Length: 61 miles (98km)
Features: Dry-weather shingle track famous for its 27 fords of variable depth. Very remote, yet a favourite with locals.

TRACK 6: OLD DUNSTAN TRAIL

From: Lawrence (GPS: S45 54.753 E169 41.236)
To: Bendigo (GPS: S44 53.667 E169 19.943)
Length: 133 miles (214km)
Features: A detailed map is essential to manage your route in the remote series of tracks high up on an exposed range, with moonscapes and tussock reminiscent of the moors.

TRACK 7: OMARAMA SADDLE

From: Omarama (GPS: S44 29.271 E169 58.004)
To: St Bathans (GPS: S44 52.316 E169 48.683)
Length: 45 miles (73km)
Features: A dry-weather farm track across rolling tussock hills.

TRACK 8: DANSEYS PASS

From: Naseby (GPS: S45 01.814 E170 08.497)
To: Duntroon (GPS: S44 51.323 E170 41.159)
Length: 40 miles (64km)
Features: Legal gravel road through gold mining hills. A must-stop pub halfway serves refreshing local brews.

TRACK 9: BLACK FOREST ROAD

From: Benmore Hydro Dam (GPS: S44 34.256 E170 11.934)
To: Haldon arm, Lake Benmore (GPS: S44 20.556 E170 13.657)
Length: 28 miles (45km)
Features: Steep and scenic gravel track across two private stations, Te Akatarawa and Black Forest, for which access permission and a fee are required.

TRACK 10: TEKAPO RIVER

From: Haldon arm, Lake Benmore (GPS: S44 20.556 E170 13.657)
To: Tekapo Power Station (GPS: S44 00.966 E170 27.339)
Length: 25 miles (41km)
Features: Rutted and stony track which follows the Tekapo River, including a slimy weir and old iron bridge crossing.

TRACK 11: LILYBANK

From:	Tekapo (GPS: S44 00.518 E170 29.727)
To:	Lilybank station (GPS: S43 43.498 E170 34.706)
Length:	52 miles (84km) return
Features:	Gravel road alongside scenic Lake Tekapo as far as the impassable Macaulay River at Lilybank.

TRACK 16: RAINBOW ROAD

From:	Hanmer Springs (GPS: S42 31.292 E172 49.777)
To:	St Arnaud (GPS: S41 46.208 E172 56.574)
Length:	55 miles (89km)
Features:	This memorably tortuous track with fords is a must-do, although be aware that it is often closed.

TRACK 12: MACKENZIE PASS

From:	Dog Kennel Corner (GPS: S44 05.822 E170 34.043)
To:	Geraldine (GPS: S44 07.170 E171 11.918)
Length:	76 miles (123km)
Features:	Rural back roads descending from the high country towards the coast and into rolling farmland.

TRACK 17: FRENCH PASS

From:	Rai Valley (GPS: S41 13.090 E173 35.163)
To:	French Pass (GPS: S40 55.484 E173 50.472)
Length:	76 miles (123km) return
Features:	A twisting gravel road through subtropical native 'bush' and via secluded coves.

TRACK 13: EDORAS

From:	Hakatere Gorge (GPS: S43 36.865 E171 10.121)
To:	Jumped Up Downs, Erewhon Station (GPS: S43 30.299 E170 51.276)
Length:	39 miles (62km) return
Features:	Erewhon is 'nowhere' all but spelled backwards and there is a reason for that. Ride to Mount Sunday, site of Edoras, in the *Lord of the Rings* movie. Look out for Orcs.

TRACK 18: MOLESWORTH STATION

From:	Blenheim (GPS: S41 31.023 E173 57.168)
To:	Hanmer Springs (GPS: S42 31.292 E172 49.777)
Length:	130 miles (209km)
Features:	Easily rideable long gravel road through a remote high country sheep and cattle station, open over a short summer window.

TRACK 14: LAKE HERON/GLENFALLOCH

From:	Hakatere Gorge (GPS: S43 36.865 E171 10.121)
To:	Sheffield (GPS: S43 23.440 E172 01.333)
Length:	88 miles (142km)
Features:	A 4WD gravel track crossing stunning back country on two private high country stations for which access permission and a fee are required. Superb accommodation possibilities plus a unique way of having a day off the bike in a typically pure New Zealand setting. Glenfalloch's paper bag 'musterer's lunch' is legendary.

TRACK 19: MOTUNAU

From:	Hurunui Mouth (GPS: S42 54.529 E173 16.644)
To:	Omihi (GPS: S43 01.203 E172 51.101)
Length:	39 miles (61km)
Features:	Rural country shingle roads through rolling hills and coastal scenery.

TRACK 15: LEES VALLEY

From:	Oxford (GPS: S43 17.837 E172 11.303)
To:	Macdonald Downs Station (GPS: S43 00.343 E172 30.734)
Length:	43 miles (69km)
Features:	A gravel road through a picturesque farming valley. Ford the Okuku River using discretion.

Arriving back in Christchurch you will be in need of a major overhaul, clean and battery recharge. Your bike will need one as well. Having completed the Latitude 45° South adventure ride there is only one way to mark the occasion, like a true South Islander, and that involves a handle of ice-cold Speights. I'm afraid you'll have to research that a little more to find out why.

Bring your own or buy one?

There are essentially three options for getting a bike in New Zealand.

Ship your own bike

Unless you intend making your New Zealand trip into an extended ride incorporating the North Island, or this is just another stop on your round the world ride, shipping to New Zealand will not be an economical option for most.

Rent a bike

Rental companies in New Zealand do not allow their bikes on gravel and will monitor this strictly due to insurance constraints. You can only rent a bike for road riding. There are some rental companies who run off-road tours according to a set itinerary in a localised area and on lower spec bikes. This is probably not an ideal option for you, unless your time is short and you are content to stick to sealed roads.

Buy-back

My full recommendation is to consider buying a bike under a guaranteed buy-back arrangement wherein a dealer in Christchurch, your typical start and finish location, sells you a ready-to-ride bike, such as a DR650, usually new with the first 600 miles (1,000km) and service tucked away, kitted out with soft luggage, bash-plate and GPS. You simply arrange this, and pay, in advance, then fly in and ride out on the same day.

On your return the dealer will purchase the bike back from you at what amounts to a reasonable trade-in price, except that you walk away with cash (thus avoiding the pitfalls of attempting to sell a bike in a fairly saturated small and second-hand market) less any damage you may have incurred during your ownership. The resulting cost for you is roughly equivalent to renting a bike, but as the bike is yours you are free to ride where you wish, unconstrained by rental limitations.

ABOUT THE AUTHOR

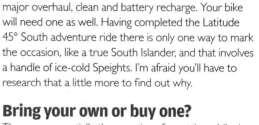

Mike Hyde is a New Zealander who, like many of his fellow-Kiwis, looks to spread his motorcycling wings in foreign lands to get in some real distances. In Mike's case he rode around the 10,500-mile (17,000km) edge of Australia followed by a '50 states in 60 days' ride in America, both on a Suzuki DL1000 V-Strom. A trip to Antarctica resulted in helmeted photos with penguins but zero riding. His rides are documented in an unorthodox fashion in the *Twisting Throttle* series of books. Visit Mike's website at: www.twistingthrottle.com

↖ Molesworth
Station (Track 18).
📷 D. Britten

➡ If you puncture out on one of the South Island's remote tracks it's better to be in a group.
Tekapo River (Track 10).
📷 M. Hyde

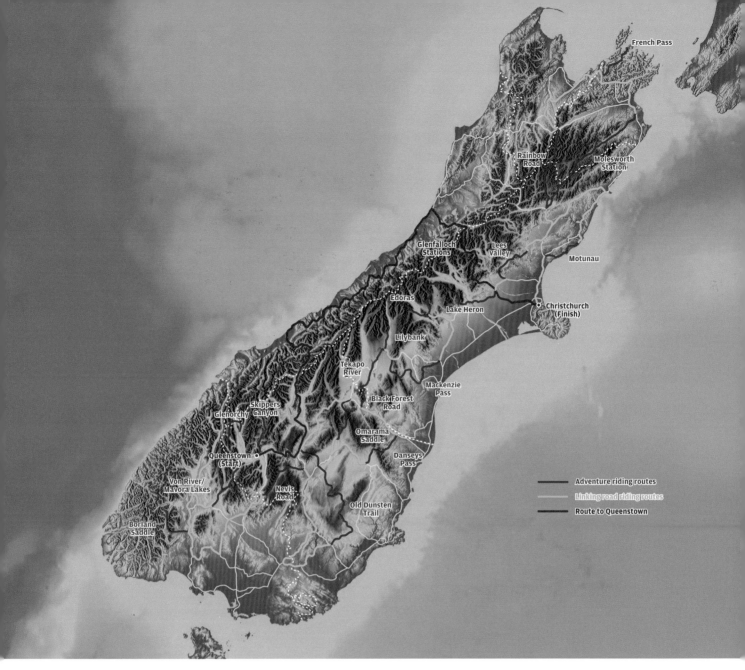

French Pass

Rainbow Road

Molesworth Station

Glenfalloch Stations

Lees Valley

Motunau

Edoras

Lake Heron

Christchurch (Finish)

Lilybank

Tekapo River

Mackenzie Pass

Skippers Canyon

Glenorchy

Black Forest Road

Omarama Saddle

Danseys Pass

Queenstown (Start)

Von River/ Mavora Lakes

Nevis Road

Old Dunsten Trail

Borland Saddle

——— Adventure riding routes
——— Linking road riding routes
——— Route to Queenstown

RECOMMENDED MAPS

For an advance-planning overview of the whole country:

New Zealand Road Atlas
Published by: Hema Maps
ISBN: 978-1877302329

For on-the-ride and detailed route planning, a digital map set sold on DVD:

Freshmap
Scale: 1: 250,000
Applications: PC, Mac, Garmin GPS

Chapter 5

Europe & the Middle East

There is some exceptional adventure riding to be had in Europe, and with the continent boasting arguably the best road network anywhere in the world it's easy to get to adventure destinations quickly. Europe also acts as the gateway for adventures in Africa to the south and Asia to the east.

The continent's mountain ranges are an ideal source of adventure riding. Located in south-central Europe, the Alps extend for almost 700 miles (1,125km) from the coastline of southern France (near Monaco) into Switzerland, northern Italy and Austria, then southeast through Slovenia, Croatia and Bosnia and Herzegovina, ending in Albania on the rugged coastline of the Adriatic Sea. Any ride here will be filled with stunning scenery, glaciers, lakes, mountains and valleys.

Further west lie the Pyrenees, which form the natural border between France and Spain and extend for about 270 miles (435km) from the Bay of Biscay to the Mediterranean. Here riders are rewarded with more than just mountainous terrain and twisting roads – this is a melting pot of Catalonian and French cultures, wonderful food and excellent wine.

The Apennines form the backbone of Italy and run the entire length of the country, while the Caucasus Mountains, located between the Black and Caspian Seas, dominate the landscape of Armenia, Azerbaijan and Georgia in southeastern Europe. The Ural Mountains, which stretch for 1,640 miles (2,640km), extend from the northern edge of the Russian Federation down through Kazakhstan, and form a natural border between Asia and Europe.

The Middle East sits at the crossroads where Africa, Asia and Europe meet. Recent political developments in the region are likely to have some impact on adventure travel, but it remains feasible to travel from Europe to Asia via the region assuming you're not taking the more northerly route through Kazakhstan. Be ready for sand dunes, oil pipelines, scattered oases and some of the hottest and driest places on the planet. ∎

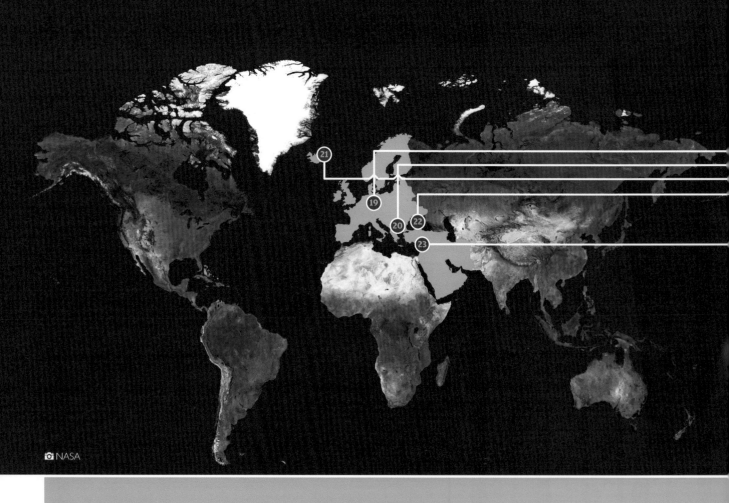

NASA

The Alps and Dolomites

An escape to Europe's highest mountain wonderland

Simon Race

For far too long I believed that 'adventure' journeys had to encompass dirt tracks, hardship, far-distant lands and loads of preparation. Recently, however, I've enjoyed interspersing my longer and further afield trips with some stunning routes closer to home. One recent gem was a spur-of-the-moment escape into Europe to explore and enjoy parts of the Alps and Dolomites. There are no particular routes that you should follow – the joy of these regions is that wherever you go the roads are sinuous and rewarding, the vistas and scenery sublime, and the hospitality, accommodation and camping sites warm, welcoming and good value. Whether you go for a long weekend or a longer break, and if you pick the timing of such trips well, the roads are often quiet and there for you to enjoy to the full whether you ride with a pillion, with a bunch of friends or on your own.

To give some insight into the area I'll explain where I went. I'm sure I missed a load of great places and roads, but therein lies this region's charm. There is so much to see and it is close enough to nip back again to continue exploring.

I started by hightailing it down through France to Lausanne. It's only 450 miles (720km) from Calais and within a day or two, using 'D roads' instead of the autoroute, I was in a wonderful Swiss restaurant on the shores of Lake Geneva examining my maps, working out how I could pack the maximum fun and mountain passes into the next few days. With nothing more on my agenda than a desire to encompass both the Alps and the Dolomites, I made a note of the location of a few of the famous passes in Switzerland and Italy and headed out with

no set route, no destinations in mind, no accommodation booked and a massive sense of freedom from 'routine'.

Keeping away from the motorways, I cut across from Lake Geneva towards Spiez and the Interlaken area. As a 'warm-up' for things to come I crossed the 4,900ft (1,500m) Juan Pass between Charmey and Boltigen. Through green and rolling scenery the road flowed wonderfully, passing through small communities and rural settings.

⬆ **Passo di Giau.**

⬅ **At the summit of Passo di Giau.**

⬇ **The San Bernardino refuge.**

Not wishing to linger in the busy and touristy town of Interlaken, I pushed on. Things stepped up a gear with the sensational 7,200ft (2,195m) Susten Pass between Innertkirchen and Wassen. This was a 'proper' pass, high in the majestic mountains, and complete with astonishing views and a welcoming restaurant at the top. This is a deceptively long pass and the west side is steep, with a great view of the Steingletscher Glacier that comes nearly down as far as the road itself.

→ **Across the top of the San Bernardino Pass.**

Shortly after descending I saw a sign to Andermatt. Why not? The bonus of heading this way was finding that Andermatt sits at the base of the 6,500ft (1,981m) Oberalp Pass – and this was the only way out of town to the east. Across the pass the road and the railway line entwine, switching sides frequently. How much better I felt on the bike, racing the train up the pass, fresh air in my lungs, sweeping through the bends rather than sitting in a sterile environment peering at the scenery through the windows of a railway carriage.

Following my nose from the base of the Oberalp in Sedrum I found myself in the charming village of Disentis, and the start of the 6,200ft (1,889m) Lukmanier Pass to Olivone. If I had done some research I might have found this wasn't going to be one of the highlights of the trip.

Wandering smaller roads brought me to the foot of the San Bernardino Pass in Mesocco. The architecture and the way the ladies were dressed told me I was close to the Italian border here. And the pass turned out to be a highlight of the day – but make sure you are not on the motorway, as that just dives through the mountain via a rather long and dull tunnel.

The southern side of the San Bernardino ended up being one of my favourites. The road runs mostly through the trees and it's not very wide, but it has a great surface, miles of fast and medium sweepers, and a

short but steep climb to the plateau at the top. Then there is a short stretch of twisties over the dramatic granite and water-filled landscape to the Refuge. The northern descent comprises a steep series of hairpins until you reach the base at the delightful village of Splügen where I found a wonderful hotel and restaurant to reflect on the day.

The following day started out with no gentle warm-up. Immediately on heading out of the village I was on the Splügen Pass to Italy, and it turned out to be one of the most demanding rides of the trip. Cresting at 6,900ft (2,100m), the Swiss side narrows through trees and then turns into a steep and narrow set of hairpins necessitating 'lock-to-lock' steering all the way to the top and the Italian border. On the descent there are a few villages and a few hairpins leading to a fast road beside a reservoir. There are a couple of dark galleries before the village of Pianazzo and it's here that things start to get interesting. A large number of these narrow galleries and unlit tunnels follow, some with bends in them or even hairpins on the descent to Chiavenna. The Maloja Pass from Chiavenna to Silvaplana – a gentle sweeping pass with nothing too technical to trouble one's ability or give one vertigo – was a welcome break.

The fantastic thing about this region is that no sooner have you completed one pass than you are immediately on to the next! There's no need to hunt out anything special – it simply falls into your lap, as did the Bernina Pass from

Pontresina to Poschiavo. The northern side is very fast, with great views of the mountains. But keep your eyes peeled for the one railway level crossing – you'll know you have reached it (if you aren't looking) when you get airborne if you are doing more than 30mph (48km/h). The descent back into Italy is sensational with fast, wide hairpins all the way down.

After an overnight stop in Fondo I noticed the landscape starting to change. And not only did the

⬆ **Looking back down the western side of the Susten Pass.**

⬅ **Descending the Susten Pass to the east.**

vistas change, but the riding did too. The roads were faster, with more sweeping bends, open and flowing with far longer views. As I approached the Dolomites via the Aprica Pass, the Passo del Tonale and the Passo di Mendola, the landscape could not have been more different. Compared to other mountains they seemed brighter, more colourful and more 'monumental'. Formed 200 million years ago, they reach more than 9,800ft (2,987m) up into the sky. Déodat de Dolomieu (1750–1801) discovered and defined the unique composition of the stone, giving the mountains their name. Now they are listed as a UNESCO World Heritage Site.

Once in the region I found wonderful passes like Passo del Pordoi, Santa Lucia and Passo di Giau, taking me to Cortina d'Ampezzo. I didn't linger long in the town of Cortina as I wanted to get back into the mountains.

ABOUT THE AUTHOR

Simon Race has been riding motorcycles since the age of 17. His wife, Susie, often flies out to join him for portions of trips or to meet him in certain cities. He currently owns a 2008 R1200GSA, a 2006 KTM 640 Adventure, a 2009 KTM 400 EXC and a 2002 Beta Rev 3 trials bike. This year he rode through Eastern Europe, Belarus, Russia, Kazakhstan and Mongolia. Next year he hopes to reach Magadan.

From an overnight stop in San Cassiano roads like the Passo di Falzarego, Passo di Valparola, Passo di Gardena, Passo di Sella, Passo Pordoi, Passo di Campolongo and the Jaufenpass (plus a fair haul on fast highways) sped me to one of my few 'must-see destinations' – Spondinia, and the start of the infamous Stelvio Pass!

The Stelvio Pass is one of the highest of Europe's Alpine passes, at a little over 9,000ft (2,743m). From Spondinia there are 48 hairpin turns on the northern side of the pass. The original road was built between 1820 and 1825 at the behest of the Austrian Emperor to connect the (former) Austrian province of Lombardia with the rest of the Austrian Empire, covering a climb of 6,100ft (1,859m). Since then, the route has changed very little. The hairpin bends, numbered with stones, are quite a technical challenge for riders.

Unlike many other mountain passes, where approaching from either direction offers a similar experience, with the Stelvio I'd read that it was best approached from the northwest side. It's only by coming from this direction that you get to drive up the famous wall of switchbacks, and also approaching from this side means you run through the heart of the Stelvio National Park on many miles of fast, sweeping roads before arriving at the foot of the pass.

It isn't one of the most beautiful passes, and nor is the northern side one of the most enjoyable. But it is a pass that has to be seen and the descent to Bormio is sensational, making the climb worthwhile! From Bormio I took the Passo di Foscagno to my night stop in Livigno.

The following day saw a few repeat passes I had done in the other direction at the start of my route. I again had a couple of key routes I wanted to ensure I bagged before I departed, and my run from Livigno took in the Forcola di Livigno, a re-run of the Bernina Pass, the Julier and another run over the San Bernardino to avoid the boring motorway and the dreadful tunnel.

My penultimate run was to be the St Gotthard Pass. But be sure of two things: first, that you exit the motorway to avoid the tunnel, and second, do try to find the old cobbled road instead of the modern highway over the pass. The new road up has some great wide hairpins and is a 'peg grinder's' dream to start with. Watch out, though, for the turn-off to the original and now disused 'Val Tremola' road – cobbles and bumps all the way and some astonishing history.

My final pass was the Furka. From Andermatt the pass starts with an approach along an arrow-straight road, running parallel to the railway line – great for finding that much under-utilised sixth gear again! The climb is narrow and steep with sensational views all around. The top is a real lunar landscape. On the descent a few great switchbacks led to the Hotel Belvedere. The hotel itself has a nice panorama restaurant and is a great place to stop to view the Rhone Glacier.

From here things got better and better. From steep switchbacks the route gradually becomes wider and smoother, cutting a long sweeping path along the valley for around four miles. Visibility forward is fantastic and the road surface is immaculate, so it's a road that you really ride with a big smile on your face. At Gletsch I did consider turning right to do the Grimsel Pass, but then decided to leave something for next time. By the time I got back to my start point in Lausanne I'd spent five wonderful days crossing 29 passes and riding 1,050 exhilarating and spectacular miles (1,690km).

RECOMMENDED MAPS

Motorcycle Atlas of the Alps
Publisher: Hallwag
ISBN: 9783828306493
Scale: 1:300,000

Tyrol – Dolomites Road and Panorama Map
Publisher: Freytag & Berndt
ISBN: 9783850842266
Scale: 1:450,000

South Tyrol – Dolomites – Trentino
Publisher: MairDumont Motorcycle Road Maps
ISBN: 9783829721547
Scale: 1:200,000

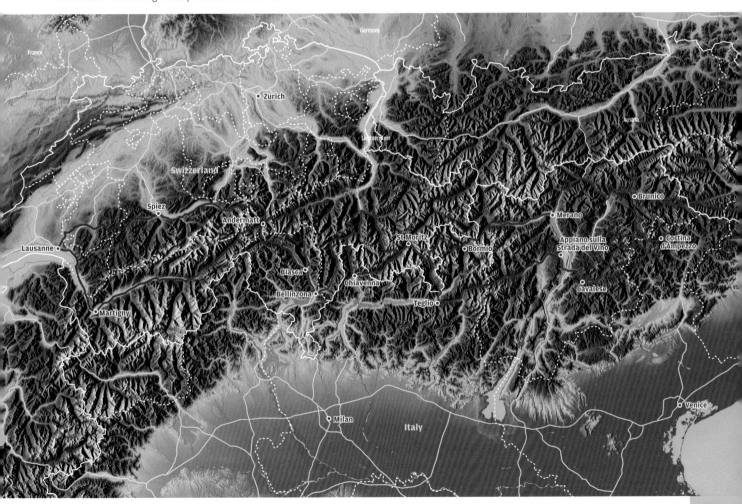

Greece

Adventure riding through the cradle of Western civilisation

Ilker Ecir

With its rich history, outstanding cuisine, hospitable people, countless gorgeous islands and wonderful coastline, Greece is the number one choice as a tourist destination for many people. Being a sailor I have been to many Greek islands and on every trip I rented a scooter to explore – something that I always enjoyed.

Now it was time to explore further and step on to the mainland. We planned a route consisting of Greece's major mainland cities and attractions, and added some extra flavour by including the famous island of Mykonos to our route. Our route was a circular one from Istanbul totalling 2,360 miles (3,800km), and it took 13 days.

Greece has mild, wet winters and hot, dry summers that are ideal for growing the olive trees that produce the world-famous Greek olive oil, but it is probably best for riders to travel either between April and June or September and November, so that there will be no need to change your clothes completely to see a nearby historical site or attraction.

Preparation for the trip starts with the paperwork. Depending on your country of citizenship and the country that your motorcycle is registered in, you will need a passport valid for at least six months, Schengen visa (if appropriate), international driving licence, temporary entrance card from customs and international traffic insurance (Green Card) along with a minimum €30,000 health insurance policy.

Greece consists mainly of mountains, which extend east into the Aegean Sea to form the peninsulas and hundreds of Greek islands. Even though you might have swum in the morning, a trip to your destination hotel can easily go through a mountain forest route with high elevations, so be sure to pack for cold conditions as well as warm weather.

Motorcycles, and especially scooters, are widely used

in all major cities and on the islands, and this means that motorcycle repair shops are common, especially in the bigger cities. All the same, make sure you take adequate tools, including a tyre repair kit, along with your standard toolkit. In the cities it's worth bearing in mind that parking spots are scarce and streets are often very narrow. Away from the cities, fuel stations often have limited opening hours and can be hard to find, so fill up in good time, especially if you're planning to ride through the night.

Although the bikes that we used on our trip were a Suzuki V-Strom DL650 ABS, BMW 1200GS and 1200RT, this route is entirely on good-quality asphalt, so any bike over 400cc can complete the journey without any difficulty.

Greek cooking, which is very similar to Turkish cuisine, is basically Mediterranean. Some suggestions to try

↑ **Mykonos has just 10,000 local inhabitants and a vibrant night life.**

← ← **Temple of Poseidon, built in 440BC.**

← **Chios is the fifth largest of the Greek islands.**

⬆ **The Epidaurus Amphitheatre was designed to seat some 15,000 people.**

➜ **Athens.**

include mezes, dolmadakia, Greek salad, fava, spanakopita, keftethes, boureki, tzatziki, gyros, moussaka, baklava, halva, and loukoumi. Locals like to drink ouzo, made from aniseed, which turns white when water is added, but beer and wine are readily available too.

The Greek islands

Our route through Greece started on Chios Island, which lies just 50 miles (80km) to the west of Izmir, Turkey's third most populous city.

Chios, the fifth largest Greek island, is famous for its Masticha liqueur and gum. There is a lot to see on this island, a highlight being the Monastery of Nea Moni.

If you plan to use a ferry between any of the islands, it's a good idea to purchase tickets in advance (from www.greekferries.gr) as some ferries are extremely small. The ferry we took from Cesme/Turkey to Chios was so small that only six motorcycles and a car would fit!

All the ferries that we went on had tie-downs, and staff were very helpful about securing our motorcycles in case of rough seas.

The next stop was the famous island of Mykonos, a three-hour ferry ride from Chios.

Mykonos is a very cosmopolitan island and is known for its extremely lively nightlife. Riders mostly do not wear helmets here. You can walk through the beautifully painted narrow streets which are full of shops, bars and tavernas or restaurants, as well as going to see the famous windmills of Mykonos and Little Venice. There are beautiful beaches and beach clubs like Sol Y Mar, Paradise or Nammos where you can enjoy the turquoise waters of the Aegean Sea. The island of Delos is just 30 minutes by boat from Mykonos and it is one of the most prominent mythological, historical and archaeological sites in Greece.

Mainland Greece

After enjoying the Aegean beaches for three days we took a five-hour ferry ride from Mykonos to the harbour of Rafina on the eastern seaboard of the Greek mainland. A spectacular road leads south from here to the 2,500-year-old Temple of Poseidon (God of the Seas) at the tip of the Attica Peninsula (GPS: N37 39.03 E24 01.36). According to legend, this is the place where Aegeus, King of Athens, leapt to his death off the cliff, giving his name to the Aegean Sea.

Greece is a country of gods and goddesses and full of mythology, so try to read a couple of books related to ancient Greece in order to get more out of the trip.

An hour's ride to the north brought us to Athens. As you approach the Greek capital you'll see the breathtaking Acropolis located at the highest point of the city. We found that it was a good reference point when riding around as it can be seen from everywhere, but be careful of the traffic and the drivers who change lanes every second. Founded in 1400 BC, Athens was named after the goddess of Athena. Both the Acropolis and the New Athens Museum are magnificent places to visit. The Plaka district is full of cafés and tavernas, and having dinner at one of these is a must.

From Athens we headed west towards the Peloponnese peninsula, which has technically been an island since the construction of the Corinth Canal in 1893. The Peloponnese is the heartland of Old Greece and it was here that the Greek War of Independence began. The canal (GPS: N37 55.30 E22 59.51) connects the Gulf of Corinth with the Saronic Gulf. Boat trips through the canal are a unique experience.

The Peloponnese

Once over the canal follow Route 70 south for about 30 miles to the Epidaurus Amphitheatre (GPS: N37 35.47 E23 04.44). This 15,000-capacity theatre is 2,400 years old. You can hear a pin drop on the stage from the back row.

Nafplio, the first capital of modern Greece, lies 25 miles (40km) west of Epidaurus. The Castle of Palamidi and Castle of Bourtzi are both spectacular sites to visit.

We continued our journey south 68 miles (110km) to Sparta, following fantastically entertaining and extremely windy mountain passes through forests. For those with an

⬆ The amazing Corinth Canal separates the Peloponnesian peninsula from the Greek mainland.

⬅ Beach on Elafonisos.

⬇ On the road leading to the village of Kosmas.

interest in military history, Sparta is a must-see destination. The Spartan social system and constitution focused completely on military training and excellence and was unique in ancient Greece. Its inhabitants, classified as Spartiates, underwent rigorous training and education. Spartan warriors had a formidable reputation in battle. Make sure you watch the movie *300* (about Sparta) before your trip.

With a population of just 500, the village of Kosmas (GPS: N37 05.30 E22 44.23) is a good place to stay after the never-ending winding mountain roads!

A minor detour to the small island of Elafonisos (courtesy of yet another short ferry ride) is worth it for

the beautiful sandy beaches and turquoise-coloured waters; Simos Beach is not to be missed.

Situated just to the north of Elafonisos lies the Peninsula of Monemvasia. The name Monemvasia means 'single entrance' in Greek because the only connection to the mainland is via a narrow 200m-long causeway. No vehicles except donkeys are allowed within the walls of the medieval fortress. For more good riding head west around the peninsula to the southernmost tip of Greece (GPS: N36 24.13 E22 29.12). The roads leading there consist of tight U-turns but they are of good-quality asphalt, and give spectacular views of the Aegean.

Due north lies Kalamata, the second-largest city of the Peloponnese in southern Greece. It lies 148 miles (238km) south-west of Athens, about 37 miles (60km) west of Sparta and 440 miles (715km) south of Thessaloniki. Famous for its succulent local dark olives and honey-eyed figs, Kalamata is a port city where you can find good accommodation and food, and also service your motorcycle if needed.

Among the highlights of a trip to the Peloponnese are the 16,400ft (5,000m) Diros Caves (GPS: N36 38.18 E22 22.51). You can take a gondola-like boat round them.

From Kalamata we headed due west to Proti then followed the coastal road north to Olympia, home of the first Olympic Games, held in classical times. Although the gigantic ivory and gold statue of Zeus is long gone, you can still see the site, which dates back to 700 BC, and the Olympia Stadium.

Before you leave the Peloponnese peninsula be sure to visit Patras, the third biggest city of Greece. It has a large student population, and features the Rio-Antirio bridge (the world's longest cable bridge) that crosses the Gulf of Corinth. You can also find a number of motorcycle repair shops in Patras should the need arise.

ABOUT THE AUTHOR

Ilker Ecir is the managing partner of a family-owned insurance company in Istanbul, Turkey. He studied business administration at San Diego State University in California, where he met the long-distance riding community, the infamous Iron Butt Association. Ilker rode some of the toughest long-distance Iron Butt rides, including Bunburner Gold – 1,500 miles (2,400km) in 24 hours; Border-to-Border Insanity – Canada to Mexico in under 24 hours; 100 CCC (Coast to Coast to Coast) in under 100 hours; and San Diego to Jacksonville Beach in Florida and back – 4,800 miles (7,725km) in 99.5 hours. Ilker's other rides include the Three Flags Classic, which takes in Mexico, the USA and Canada. He also has a keen interest in scuba diving, powerboat racing organisation and professional car racing.

Back to Mainland Greece

The road to Delphi from Patras has stunning views. Delphi is the site of the most famous oracle in the classical Greek world and also home to the Temple of Apollo, a must-see UNESCO World Heritage Site.

If you head to Meteora from Delphi you will ride through the Brallos Pass, considered to be the best motorcycle road in Greece – it has wide open turns with perfect surfaces and you may want to ride again. Meteora is the most important and largest complex of Eastern Orthodox monasteries in Greece. There are six monasteries built on top of natural sandstone rock pillars and all are open to visitors.

Our journey continued on to Ioannina, in Epirus in north-western Greece. Ioannina was the last Greek city that the Ottoman Turks left after the Balkan Wars. Important sights in the area include Nisaki Island on Lake Pamvotis, Ali Pasha's living quarters at the Monastery of Agios Panteleimon and the Aslan Pasha Mosque.

Before heading back to Turkey we visited Thessaloniki, the second largest city in Greece. Thessaloniki has a beautiful coastline full of cafés where you can stop and enjoy the view with your drink. It has numerous sights from Roman, Byzantine and Ottoman times, with the White Tower, Agios Demetrios Church and Ataturk House among those most worth visiting.

Greece offers some wonderful riding, great local hospitality and some of the most spectacular vistas anywhere in the world.

RECOMMENDED MAPS

Road Map of Greece and the Turkish West Coast (AA Road Map Europe 9)
Publisher:	AA Publishing
ISBN:	978-0749568436
Scale:	1:800,000

Greece – National Map
Publisher:	Michelin Editions des Voyages
ISBN:	978-2067143098
Scale:	1:700,000

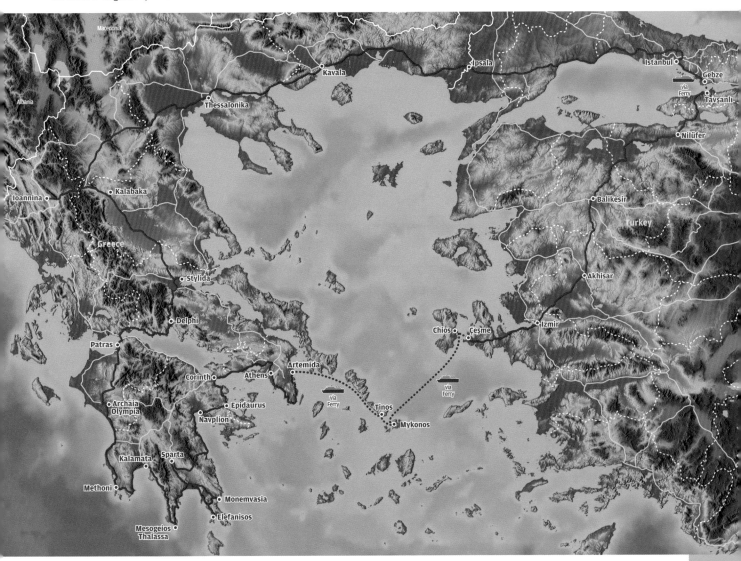

ROUTE: 21

Iceland
Land of fire and ice

Eythor Orlygsson and Robert Wicks

If you really fancy somewhere different to go adventure riding, then Iceland is the place. The landscape resembles the moon's surface. It is vast, dramatic and ruggedly beautiful with huge icecaps, glaciers, waterfalls, geysers and hot springs, raging rivers and lava-filled valleys as far as the eye can see. Iceland has roads and tracks that suit every rider and skill level and just two weeks spent there will allow you to cover a huge variety of terrain, with the added benefit of extended daylight hours in the summer (June–August).

For most people the natural starting point and entry into the country is the capital city, Reykjavik, which is best described as a vibrant city with a metropolitan feel to it but in some ways still resembling a small fishing village.

The best rides include:

- A lap of the island along the desolate 830-mile (1,335km) ring road.
- An expedition into the uninhabited and unforgettable Central Highlands.
- An exploration of the Western Fjords, the westernmost part of Europe.

Ring Road

Iceland's Highway One, otherwise known as the 'Ring Road' (local name: Hringvegur), encircles the island and is considered to be one of the most desolate and scenic routes in the world. The route goes through some extreme landscape and was only completed in 1974. This is one of the quietest and most scenic roads in Europe, and for almost all its length the road is two lanes wide with one lane in each direction. It is predominantly paved, except for a few sections on the eastern side, and along the way you can see majestic mountains, volcanoes and geysers, ocean views, wildlife and waterfalls. The country is renowned for its beautiful natural scenery and adventure activities that include snowmobiling on glaciers, horseback riding and ice climbing, and the ring road provides full access to all the country has to offer.

The southern part of the route is sometimes subject to flooding, caused by geothermal heat and volcanic eruptions melting ice under Iceland's inland icecaps. There are several other hazards to contend with, including blind curves and blind hills, single lane bridges and narrow passes. In winter, icy roads and sheer winds can make travel especially hazardous. Before setting off be sure to check the official road bureau websites and local weather stations.

Central Highlands

The uninhabited interior of Iceland is one of the very few relatively easily accessible such areas left in the world. It consists mainly of moraines, sanded areas, lava fields, lakes and glaciers. Road conditions in the interior change regularly and river crossings are more the norm than the exception. These should be forded with the greatest of care. Off-road driving is strictly prohibited, so be sure to stick to the marked tracks. The road system is constantly being improved and some of the mountain roads are passable by all vehicles during summer. In winter snowmobiles and

← It's best to stay on the road here; that's moss-covered lava on either side.

modified jeeps equipped with monster tyres make their way to every nook and cranny of the interior.

Sprengisandur

This part of the interior is the longest stretch of the Central Highlands between the north and south. It is generally very desolate and barren. Only where there is water will sparse vegetation be found. The greatest obstacles along the route are the unbridged rivers, which have to be forded. They swell when it is warm (as the glacial melting increases) and when it rains a great deal they can become very dangerous for those who have no experience.

Kaldidalur

The Cold Valley is the shortest of the three main routes across the Central Highlands from south to north. It lies between Ok Mountain and the Long Glacier and its highest elevation is 2,385ft (727m); the view from there is excellent on a fine day. It is usually passable for between three and five months of the year. A side road to the east from the main route leads to a hut at the edge of the Long Glacier, where the glacier tours start.

← Wide-open spaces make Iceland an adventurer's playground.

⬇ Directions on one of the interior roads.

Vatnajokull

Vatnajokull is the largest glacier in Europe with an area of about 3,127 square miles (8,100km²) and an average thickness of 1,312ft (400m). The icecap rises between 4,593ft (1,400m) and 5,905ft (1,800m) above sea level. A range of adventure activities and tours can be undertaken on and near the glacier.

Lonsoraefi

The uninhabited, mountainous area to the east of the Vatnajokull icecap is called Lonsoraefi. Its southern boundaries are the Skyndidalur Valley, the low Geldingafell Mountain in the north and the small Hofsjokull Glacier and the uppermost part of the valley of Vididalur in the east. A track which ends on the so-called Illikambur ridge connects the area with the main road.

Western Fjords

The Western Fjords are one of the island's hidden treasures, a peninsula on the northwestern corner of Iceland still largely unaffected by tourism.

Head out of Reykjavik on Route 1 in a northerly direction. This is a good A-class road with soft sweeping turns. Around 9 miles (15km) from the city limits take the right-hand turning on to Road 47 (GPS: N64 16.456 W21 50.305). From here there is a 4.5-mile (7km) road tunnel under the fjord, or you can ride along the fjord instead and enjoy the breathtaking scenery. One of the most interesting sights is an old whale slaughterhouse (GPS: N64 23.713 W21 26.110). Back on Route 1 continue

↑ Good off-road riding skills help as the terrain is varied and sometimes challenging.

↓ Breathtaking scenery and not a soul in sight.

Veidivotn Lakes

This region includes about 50 lakes of various sizes, many of which are crater lakes, fed and discharged underground because of the lava fields and porous rocks. To reach the area, you must ford the small river between the two Fossvotn lakes. The northernmost lakes are called Hraunvotn. This lake area is one of the most beautiful parts of the country.

north, riding through lush farmlands and shallow valleys, by salmon fishing rivers and through lava fields. Nearing the Western Fjords the road climbs over the first real mountain passes on the route before a gentle descent towards Road 68 (GPS: N65 08.802 W21 04.562).

Taking off on to Road 68 the way follows the coastline, around numbers of fjords, in seemingly endless turns. The route passes one of Iceland's richest seal breeding areas and the odd head can be seen popping out of the water; even whales can be spotted from time to time. Head for the quaint fishing village of Holmavik – with a hidden dark side of witchcraft and sorcery. Continue on Road 61 towards Isafjordur where the road climbs with ease over a mountain pass to the great fjords of the west.

The ride for the next 125 miles (200km) follows deep narrow fjords, with high mountains on one side and the shoreline on the other. The silence will surprise you.

Even though the Western Fjords are considered a 'cold' area, with no apparent geothermal activity, there are a few natural hot pools to choose from as well as several man-made pools with hot spring water. One of the area's most interesting places to stay is Heydalur, a farm hostel where an old barn has been renovated into a gourmet restaurant with cosy accommodation (GPS: N65 50.927 W22 38.769).

Across the bay the snowy coast is in full view and the Drangajokull Glacier shines like a gemstone on a crown. Stop briefly at the small farmhouse called Litlibær (GPS: N65 59.167 W22 49.000) on a fjord called Skotufjördur – it's a living museum. The road in this area is well maintained, with gravel sections adding to the adventure. There is never a dull moment on these roads – you are either busy negotiating turns or enjoying the view. Riding through the village of Sudavik one is reminded of nature's power – in January 1995 an avalanche swept several houses out to sea and killed 14 people; the scar runs through the entire old village.

Soon the town of Isafjordur comes to view. This is the largest town of the west, with several good restaurants and the only real hotel in the area.

If the roads leading here were not interesting enough for you, the real fun begins once the route heads to Road 60. Beyond the first tunnel it is apparent just how difficult it must have been to build the road in the first place – steep cliffs run straight up from the seafront, so the road has to climb over the mountains in tight steep turns, while a distinct lack of guardrails and single lane bridges make this a challenging route that commands your full attention.

The road climbs over mountains between fjords, seemingly almost carved into the hillside down by the shoreline around the fjords. Just when you think you have seen it all, the majestic Dynjandi waterfall comes into view. There is a campsite at the foot of the waterfall (GPS: N65 44.197 W23 12.538).

From here a desert-like landscape takes over as the route heads to Road 63 (GPS: N65 38.022 W23 14.775) and a good gravel road passing through small, charming fishing villages, before Road 62 takes over at the village of Patreksfjordur (GPS: N65 35.395 W23 58.309). You will

ADVENTURE MOTORCYCLING IN ICELAND

Most mountain roads and roads in the interior of Iceland have a surface of loose gravel. The same applies to some sections of the national highway, which also has long stretches of asphalt. The surface on the gravel roads is often loose, especially along the sides of the roads, so one should ride carefully and slow down whenever approaching oncoming vehicles. The mountain roads are also often very narrow, as are the bridges, which are only wide enough for one car width at a time. Mountain roads are often winding, and consequently journeys often take longer than might be expected.

- In Iceland the law prohibits all driving off road or on unmarked tracks in order to protect the fragile environment. Don't let that put you off, though – the tracks you can ride on are full of adventure anyway!
- A Green Card or other proof of third party insurance is mandatory for riders from some countries, so check before you depart.
- The general speed limit is 31mph (50km/h) in urban areas, 50mph (80km/h) on gravel roads in rural areas, and 56mph (90km/h) on asphalt roads.
- Fuel station opening times in the countryside vary from place to place; larger towns have automated pumps that accept credit cards, but it's advisable to fill up when you get the chance.
- The roads in Iceland can be divided in to five categories:
  - High standard wide paved roads, similar to British A roads.
  - Lower standard narrow paved roads, similar to British B roads.
  - Well maintained unpaved gravel roads.
  - Less maintained unpaved gravel roads.
  - Highland tracks only open during the summer, with extremely low maintenance, usually marked 'F' with unbridged river crossings.
- Most tracks into the interior remain closed until June because of wet and muddy conditions which make them totally impassable. Before embarking on any journey into the interior collect as much information as possible on the likely road conditions.
- The choice of accommodation is extensive and will suit most people's budgets. Make use of farm hostels in the coastal regions and mountain huts in the highlands.
- The only ferry to Iceland is by Smyril Line from Hanstholm in Denmark to Seydisfjordur in the northeastern part of Iceland, so ship your bike by cargo vessel to Reykjavik.
- Quality bikes for rent and full Iceland tours are offered by Biking Viking (www.bikingviking.is).
- Bike servicing is scarce, except in Reykjavik itself. Consider bringing essential parts with you to carry out emergency repairs. Spare spark plugs, oil filters and even engine oil are worth thinking about in case you have a mishap during a river crossing.
- Glacial rivers can be very difficult to cross. They are typically milky coloured with a strong current and are often unpredictable. Examine them thoroughly before crossing; the best time of day to cross is in the early hours of the morning.
- The weather changes rapidly and you need to be suitably prepared in terms of gear and adapting your riding style to cope with the conditions.

find yourself wondering why people might consider living in such a desolate area.

To get to the westernmost point of Europe, situated at Latrabjarg (GPS: N65 30.153 W24 31.907), turn on to Road 612 (GPS: N65 31.855 W23 46.962). The road gradually turns into a small track, with few easy river crossings. Latrabjarg rises straight up from the North Atlantic, a cliff inhabited by a variety of bird species like puffins that nest in every possible crevice of the cliff face. From Latrabjarg the Snæfells Glacier can be seen in full view, rising out of the ocean.

Backtracking on to Road 62 there are further mountains to pass before making it to the port of Brjanslækur. Here one can take a ferry across the bay to Stykkilsholmur on the Snæfellsnes Peninsula. It takes about three hours to cross and is a very relaxed trip as you take in spectacular views of puffins swimming around the ferry and even the odd whale breaking to the surface among the islands. Stop for a night at Flatey, an island halfway across the bay, where life appears not to have changed since the middle of the last century.

If the ferry is not for you, then ride the coastline, a five-hour trek to Stykkilsholmur. Shortly after the ferry port at Brjanslækur the route turns back into Road 60 (GPS: N65 34.569 W23 10.225) and an interesting mix of gravel roads in poor condition and recently rebuilt paved roads around fjords and over mountains for 125 miles (200km). This area is home to Arctic foxes, and even the odd eagle or falcon can be spotted.

Drop off Road 60 on to Road 54 (GPS: N65 02.658

⬆ **Few places in the world offer this sort of landscape.**

🔽 **Be wary of winter weather – not for the faint-hearted!**

ABOUT THE AUTHOR

Eythor Orlygsson was born in Reykjavik in 1966. He is a dedicated motorcyclist and experienced off-road rider who loves nothing more than travelling on two wheels. He is the manager of Biking Viking motorcycle tours, rentals and servicing. He also manages Iceland's Triumph dealership. He has explored most of Iceland's interior and highlands on both light enduro bikes and heavy adventure bikes and has over the years gathered an extensive knowledge of adventure motorcycling in Iceland. He likes to share his passion and gladly offers advice to travellers about routes and equipment.

W21 41.749) towards Stykkisholmur to ride around the Snæfellsnes Peninsula. This is a good gravel road at first, with jagged volcanic mountain ridges on one hand and the ocean on the other, while out in the bay the countless islands are clearly visible from the shore. Stykkisholmur is a charming small fishing village with a strong Danish heritage. Beyond the village is a farm called Bjarnarhof (GPS: N64 59.872 W22 57.737) at which you can purchase fermented shark – a local delicacy. Back on the road you will pass lava fields en route to the Snæfells Glacier at the tip of the peninsula. According to Jules Verne, the glacier is 'the entrance to the centre of the earth'.

You can ride around the glacier on Road 574 or, better still, cross the peninsula at the foot of the glacier on a mountain track named as F570 on your map. Shadowed by the glacier is the summer village of Hellnar (GPS: N64 45.069 W23 38.758), a small village with B&Bs, a campsite and a small café. The area is enclosed by beautiful lava formations on all sides. Head for the campsite at Arnarstapi or Hotel Budir on the waterfront. Take Road 54 again, heading towards Borgarnes, before making your way back to Reykjavik.

↑ **A typical Icelandic coastal village.**

RECOMMENDED MAPS

Iceland Road Atlas
Publisher: Ferdakort
ISBN: 9789979671893
Scale: 1:500,000

Iceland
Publisher: ITMB – International Travel Maps
ISBN: 9781553412458
Scale: 1:425,000

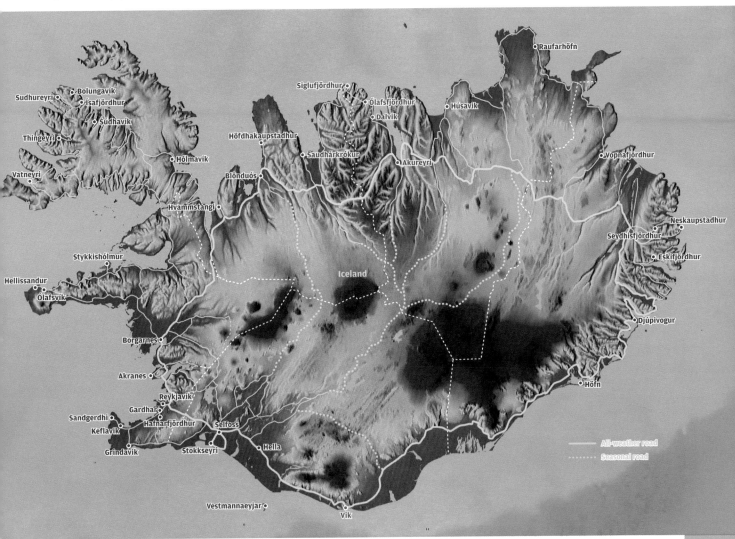

Touring Turkey

Adventures in the land of Atatürk

David French

First the good news: Turkey abounds with spectacular destinations, an unrivalled range of roads linking them up, a very genuine welcome and plentiful options to suit all pockets. Weather is predictable, food is incredible and the sheer diversity in everything from culture, altitude, sophistication and security gives endless choice. Given that my first encounter with Turkey was at the wrong end of a large and violent political demonstration, a predisposition to dislike the place and the people has been repeatedly and overwhelmingly overcome on every visit since.

On a rough scale, Turkey is more advanced than somewhere like Morocco; there's far more going on, far more common ground and far less culture shock for a western European. Remember too, that Mediterranean destinations like Italy, Spain and Greece gained their reputation and current allure when they looked more like Turkey does right now.

Taking it anti-clockwise, the west coast of this rectangular-shaped country is the most popular with tourists. This is where your mates are likely to be if they're holidaying in Turkey. Bodrum, Kusadasi and the surrounding resorts are up there with the best in Ibiza, but they're the least representative of the country. The southern part of the west coast has a stunningly scenic winding Mediterranean road connecting resorts varying from stellar to very grim Costa-styled concrete. The southeastern border is the jumping-off point for Syria, Jordan and Iraqi Kurdistan. This area is full of remote, scenic, but difficult to reach spots like Bahcesary. The roads from Sirnak to Hakkari and on up to the surprisingly modern city of Van are as spectacular as they are scenically remote. The northeast is more wide open and includes the Ishak Pasha Palace and the photogenic Sumela Monastery. The north coast, from Yakakent west to Amasra, is one of the most scenic stretches of coastal road on the planet and an absolute must-do if you have a bike in

TURKEY BY SASA LALIC

A visit to Cappadocia, best known for its unique moon-like landscape, underground cities, cave churches and houses carved in the rocks, is recommended on any trip to Turkey. The valley of Cappadocia was originally filled with volcanic ash that, over the course of time, eroded into peculiar natural formations and became a trademark of the area. Cappadocia is Turkey's most visually striking region, especially the 'moonscape' area around the towns of Ürgüp, Göreme, Uçhisar, Avanos and Mustafapaşa (Sinasos), where erosion has formed caves, clefts, 'fairy chimneys' and folds in the soft volcanic rock. The region is located around 34 miles (55km) southwest of the major city of Kayseri.

the area. In the centre of all this is Cappadocia with its cave buildings at Göreme.

As a world city Istanbul is simply a must-see, but by motorcycle is not the best way. Edirne, Ankara and the others are far more manageable. Some of the big cities are somewhat gritty (like Diyarbakir), others are more easily lovable (Malatya), some are off doing their own thing (Trabzon). Practically all have big quarters of apartment blocks which is partly why the eastern steppes are so empty of everything but occasional villages and shepherds.

Ruins, such as Ephesus, left by civilisations ranging from the Romans, Commagenes and an innumerable host of others litter a landscape which was already blessed with plenty of natural wonders, such as Pamukkale. Many of the cities and locations are mentioned in the Koran/Bible/Torah. More recently there is Gallipoli and its First World War history, which is worth a visit. Incidentally, if the west coast is your destination, take the car ferry at Canakkale and skip Istanbul.

← **Fascinating cave buildings at Göreme in the Cappadocia valley.**
📷 Sasa Lalic

↑ Ishak Pasha
Palace in the
east.

→ Roadside
castle on the
D975 south of
Van.

Thanks to the massive southeastern Anatolia Project (GAP), which involves the construction of 22 dams for irrigation and hydro-electric power, a large area including at least 35 towns will be flooded within the next few years. Hasankeyf is a picturesque example of one of these and well worth a visit. Go there and look at a place that soon will never be seen again.

On the theme of development, Turkey is racing along. Building sites, road works and general economic activity are changing the landscape at an increasing rate. Massive earthmovers are cutting new roads through awkward terrain that old roads had to go around or over. Older roads have more character but the new ones get you there faster.

Distances are large if you want to see the whole country, so unless you have a month it's better to concentrate on one region. The best time to visit depends on where you are visiting. Even in high summer the mountain passes in the east are chilly – best visited from May to September, and even then bring a range of gear to adjust to the temperatures. In winter the east is snowy with passes closed and remote areas often cut off.

Road quality is stunningly wide, featuring everything from tolled motorways to barely visible dirt tracks. Paper and GPS maps are fairly up to date and the very high level of infrastructure investment means good four-lane highways with frequent roadworks are often the case. Sand on roads is sometimes intentional, to deal with melting tar, and longitudinal road scraping happens occasionally. Coastal and mountain roads often lack barriers, so if your sense of self-preservation has been weakened by too long in the modern health and safety culture you may want to ease yourself in gently.

Driving standards are manageable outside urban areas. Lane discipline is weak, with drivers cutting corners; as usual, night riding is unadvisable and the usual trio of animals loose on national roads, slow unlit tractor-type things (aka Asian one-eyed buffaloes) and charging lorries are all there. Within large urban areas driving is rarely discourteous but still chaos, tailgating at speed, jostling and a general lack of competence compounded by simultaneous mobile phone use are ubiquitous. When riding, the word to remember is 'defensive'.

Turkey is a predominantly Muslim country. There is nothing obviously radical or anything to get concerned about. Women motorcyclists are fairly rare but not unknown, alcohol is not available everywhere but it is brewed (and well) in the country. The harder stuff (raki) makes for great sundowners. Hospitality includes regular glasses of well-brewed tea. After a few days you'll be looking for it.

Hotels (Turkish: 'otels') are easy to find and range from around £15 up to £50 a night. Parking varies, from inside some back room to on the street in front of the hotel. Provided you have a lock, and ideally also a lightweight bike cover, parking on the street is fine, especially if the reception is open all the time. WiFi is free practically everywhere with a roof, and mobile phone coverage is fine, although there are some limitations on phones if you are in the country for more than a few weeks. Short of a GS-911 Canbus diagnostic kit, the big bike dealers can provide almost anything you want.

To get there from the UK you have to nail it across Europe for at least two days and then cross over from Bulgaria, where a 90-day visa stamp costs just £12. Alternatively skip down to Italy and take a two-day cruise from Ancona to Izmir. As not every pillion is up for this it's worth considering arranging your motorcycle odyssey to rendezvous with family or friends who fly out on a sun-and-sand package deal.

The bad news

Sadly there is bad news. Notwithstanding the fact that there is now a law forbidding you to say otherwise, the nation's founder Mustafa Kemal Atatürk was a truly great leader. After seeing off the attempted capture of Istanbul

TOP ATTRACTIONS

- **Aspendos Theatre** – one of the best preserved ancient theatres of antiquity, built in AD 155 during the rule of the Roman Emperor Marcus Aurelius.
- **Patara Beach** – at 9 miles (14km), Patara is one of the longest stretches of sandy beach found anywhere in the Mediterranean. The beach is backed only by ancient Lycian and Roman ruins and swooping dunes.
- **Pamukkale** – meaning 'cotton castle' in Turkish, this is an unreal landscape in western Turkey, famous for its white terraces. They are made of travertine, a sedimentary rock deposited by water with a very high mineral content from the hot springs. People have bathed in its pools for thousands of years.
- **Bodrum** – with its sandy beaches, shop-lined streets and sophisticated restaurants, the city of Bodrum has long been the favourite seaside retreat in Turkey.
- **Mount Nemrut** – a 7,001ft (2,134m) high mountain in southeastern Turkey, near the city of Adiyaman, featuring the tomb sanctuary of King Antiochus I, Theos of Commagene.
- **Olüdeniz** – a small village located on the southwestern coast on the Aegean Sea. The beach is famous for its shades of turquoise and remains one of the most photographed beaches in the Mediterranean.
- **The Blue Mosque** – with its six minarets and sweeping architecture the Sultan Ahmed or Blue Mosque impresses from the outside. While still used as a mosque, the Blue Mosque has also become one of the most popular tourist attractions in Istanbul.
- **Library of Celsus** – the ruins of Ephesus are a popular tourist attraction on the west coast. The city of Ephesus was once famed for the Temple of Artemis, one of the ancient Seven Wonders of the World. The library was built around AD 125 to store 12,000 scrolls and to serve as a monumental tomb for Celsus, the governor of Asia.
- **Hagia Sophia** – dating from the sixth century, the Hagia Sophia was originally a basilica constructed for the Eastern Roman Emperor Justinian I. A masterwork of Roman engineering, the massive dome (102ft/31m in diameter) covers what was for over 1,000 years the largest enclosed space in the world.

← **Endless Greek and Roman ruins at Ephesus in the west.**

→ **Canyoning in the south-east between Sirnak and Hakkari.**

↓ **Sumela Monastery in the north-east Trabzon province.**

by the British and French in 1916 he went on to mould the modern democratic secular republic of Turkey from the crumbling remains of the Ottoman Empire. His life work remains unfinished, however.

Although improving (they haven't hung but did imprison Kurdish leader Abdullah Ocalan), Turkey does not have a good human rights record. From the people missing since the controversial partial occupation of Cyprus in 1974 to a recent case where an army sentry dog killed a 10-year-old girl, there is a lack of transparency and accountability about Turkish politics that doesn't fit well with being a modern democratic state, and particularly with joining the European Union. Several groups and courageous individuals like Vedat Sengol, a human rights lawyer in the city of Mus, work to improve the situation.

Dominating everything, however, is the Kurdish question. Almost one-fifth of Turkey's population is ethnically Kurdish and this doesn't fit well with Turkey's unified self-image. Kurdish customs, dress, language and identity are banned. Freedom of speech takes on a whole new dimension when your very language is disallowed. Thousands of Kurds went 'missing' in the 1990s. Military activity is very evident in the southeast. The Kurdish

WHAT BIKE?

Petrol stations are everywhere and unleaded is generally available so no big tank or catalytic convertor removal requirements are necessary. Petrol station attendants have to log your registration before dispensing fuel and credit cards are widely accepted.

Good tall suspension is a big help in dealing with gravel diversions and the ubiquitous speed bumps. To balance this, if you are going to get there on the same bike then good medium to high speed touring ability is useful. As Turkey doesn't have a daytime lights law, figure out how to disconnect the headlight bulb from any hardwired-on bikes, or endure endless reminders from other drivers flashing you.

Unless you are really intent on exploring then road tyres are fine; anything else will wear out before you get there anyway. Bike dealer distribution beyond Istanbul and Ankara is minimal but the levels of mechanical skill and resourcefulness are naturally high, as would be expected from a strong self-sufficient agricultural nation.

Ponder the options for a while and then take a BMW R1200GS like everyone else. I jest. Several Dutch riders I met were doing fine on extremely overloaded 2009 model 660cc Teneres. For getting to Bodrum you could take a GSXR-1000 and get along fine.

population is concentrated there, with the result that if you tell almost anyone in the western half of the country that you are going east, they'll warn you of lawlessness. As usual with that sort of warning, it's patent nonsense.

For travellers there is little to worry about. Even during the recent conflicts, in May 2010, which resulted in the deaths of Kurdish fighters operating on the Iraqi border and Turkish army personnel, travel in the border area was quite safe. If there's a real problem, the frequent checkpoints put in place will turn you back. Compared

with the risks of motorcycle travel, however, your chances of sustaining anything worse than mild inconvenience and delay are insignificant.

In this crazy world the problems of motorcyclists don't amount to a hill of beans but for us they are, of course, severe. Motorcycle touring as we know it is effectively illegal in Turkey. Yes, you read that right. Motorcycle touring as we know it is effectively illegal in Turkey. This doesn't mean you can't go motorcycle touring in Turkey, as you would anywhere else; it just means that, depending on

↖ **Climbing Mt Nemrut in the south-east.**

↓ **Kurdish town of Hasankeyf, due to be flooded by the controversial Ilisu Dam.**

David French is an accomplished adventure motorcyclist who between 1990 and 2007 visited every European country by motorcycle except Malta. Some of his adventures include a circuit of Japan, a three-month tour in Southeast Asia, a solo Baltic journey, two African trips and a solo tour of eastern Europe. His most notable recent trip was in May 2010, a 6,200-mile (10,000km) three-week round trip from Wroclaw, Poland around Turkey to the Iraqi-Kurdistan side of the Iranian border. He has held various roles in the motorcycling world, including as a committee member of the Federation of European Motorcyclists Associations (FEMA) from 1992 to 2002. He is a director of the Motorcycle Outreach Charity and was the joint organiser of the largest motorcyclist demonstration in Dublin in 1995. He is a regular contributor to motorcycling magazines.

your mileage and exposure, you are likely to be stopped by the police and fined. The reason? Speed limits.

Outside urban areas, where the limit is a standard 31mph (50km/h), motorcycles in Turkey are subject to lower limits than cars. On open national roads the limit for motorcycles is a ridiculous 43mph (70km/h) whereas cars are allowed to travel at 56mph (90km/h). On motorways motorcycles are limited to 50mph (80km/h) while cars can do 75mph (120km/h). As motorways are relatively rare this means you are legally required to travel at no more than 43mph (70km/h) between cities. Try this tomorrow morning and see how long you sustain it. Removing the gear lever may help.

In practice the motorways are rarely monitored for speed so you can carry on as usual. National roads are a different story, however, and if you spend more than a week in the country you'd be doing very well not to go through a radar trap where an advance police vehicle equipped with video and radios lies in wait, with another to flag you down and prosecute. Occasionally police will apply the car limits to bikes, but don't count on it. The guidelines are that 10% over the limit is acceptable so you'll

Endless winding coastal roads on the northern Black Sea coast

get away with 48mph (77km/h), but you'd be prosecuted at 50mph (80km/h).

All of the half-dozen European motorcyclists I met in Turkey had fallen foul of this and been prosecuted, some several times. Penalty points don't accrue to foreign licences but the fines do add up. As a guide, it's about 130 Turkish lira (£55) for 10km/h and 270 TL (£125) for 20km/h over the limit. Being pulled in for doing 50mph (80km/h) on a four-lane road while a Turkish driver overtakes you with kids hanging out the windows of an overloaded banger is hardly an infringement of your human rights, but it does sour the tourist experience. Fines are payable at the border.

For some more information on motorcycle touring in Turkey see the piece on *Horizons Unlimited* by Turkish rider Paulo Volpara: http://www.horizonsunlimited.com/country/turkey/

To summarise, if you have the time and enjoy motorcycle travel, Turkey is one of the most rewarding countries you can get to. The speed limit is insane but try to see it as a tourist tax. Protest to the representatives back home, but go there anyway.

← **Taking a break by the Black Sea.**

RECOMMENDED MAPS

Turkey 758
Publisher: Michelin
ISBN: 9782067156999
Scale: 1:1,000,000

Turkey
Publisher: ITMB – International Travel Maps
ISBN: 9781553414407
Scale: 1:1,100,000

Turkey Road Atlas
Publisher: Mepmedya Yayinlari
ISBN: 9789759137311
Scale: 1:400,000

📷 All photographs courtesy of David French

Syria and Lebanon

Journeys through antiquity

Ilker Ecir with Murathan Yildiz

oth Syria and Lebanon had always attracted my attention, with their open desert and mountain roads, ancient history, untouched archaeological sites, bazaars, and Levantine cuisine. After an extensive East Anatolia trip in August 2007 my good friend, Murathan Yildiz, and I decided to explore Turkey's neighbouring country Syria and continue further to the 'Paris of the Middle East', Beirut in Lebanon.

The round trip from Istanbul was a total distance of 3,540 miles (5,700km) and took 17 days. Contrary to what we sometimes hear, both Syria and Lebanon were peaceful, with hospitable locals, beautiful nature and excellent cuisine, although at the time of writing uprisings have changed things considerably in the region and access is limited, at least for the time being.

The extreme heat (43°C/110°F) in this region can be a real challenge from June to August. In order to be able to wear protective riding gear and not be subjected to the 'oven-effect', it is best to travel either in spring (from March to May) or autumn (from September to November). Also bear in mind that the differences between day and night temperatures can be quite significant, especially in the drier inland areas, where the nights can be surprisingly cool.

For this trip you must have a passport valid for at least six months. Whereas the Syrian visa must be applied for prior to the trip at the respective Syrian consulate, the Lebanese visa can usually be obtained at the border – although this doesn't apply to citizens of certain countries. Since you will have to re-enter Syria after Lebanon, you must get a multiple-entry Syrian visa.

Most importantly, the bearers of passports with Israeli visas or entry/exit stamps will not be allowed to enter either Syria or Lebanon.

Furthermore, you must have an international driving licence and a Carnet de Passages en Douane that identifies your motorcycle. You also need to purchase liability insurance at the Lebanese border. Passing through Syrian or Lebanese customs can take up to two hours.

In general terms, Syria is a flat desert plateau with a narrow coastal plain fronting the Mediterranean Sea. Turkey borders it to the north, Lebanon and Israel to the west, Iraq to the east, and Jordan to the south. It consists of mountain ranges in the west and farther inland an area of steppe. In the east is the Syrian Desert, bisected by the Euphrates valley. Between the humid Mediterranean coast and the arid desert regions lies a semi-arid steppe zone extending across three-quarters of the country, which is on the receiving end of hot, dry winds blowing across the desert.

Lebanon is a coastal country intersected by mountains, which offer magnificent routes for motorcyclists. The country stretches along the east side

COUNTRY FACTS

Population:	18,500,000 (Syria)
	4,250,000 (Lebanon)
Capital city:	Damascus (Syria)
	Beirut (Lebanon)
Currency:	Syrian pound (SYP)
	Lebanese pound (LBP)
Languages:	Arabic is the official language and Armenian is a common language for both Syria and Lebanon. There are significantly more English and French speakers in Lebanon than in Syria.
Religion:	Muslim 89%, Christian 10% (Syria)
	Muslim 60%, Christian 39% (Lebanon)

⬅ **Play us a song, you're the banjo man.**

⬇ **Coalition forces normally turn right at this junction.**

ADVENTURE MOTORCYCLING IN SYRIA BY SASA LALIC

Entering Syria, a new world begins. Just a few kilometres over the border a man in a pick-up truck starts shouting and waving. It didn't seem to matter that we couldn't understand him but he soon revealed his intentions – as he passed us he dropped a handful of cherries into my palms and said the word which would follow us throughout this journey – 'Welcome, welcome!'

▓ **Entry into Syria by motorcycle costs €100 – this includes insurance and the relevant paperwork.**
▓ **The Syrian notion of a 'highway' is somewhat different from traditional western experiences. Motorcyclists are everywhere, mostly on smaller bikes, and they randomly execute their turns with little or no consideration for other road users. Sometimes we found it easier to conform to the kamikaze driving style.**
▓ **If you ask for directions to Palmyra, no one will even be able to guess what you are talking about. It is essential to call the city Tadmur in order to get any useful information. The road then takes you to Damascus. It's worth mentioning that the scenery on this desert route is absolutely mesmerising. Spend at least a day in Palmyra, the oasis in the heart of the Syrian desert.**
▓ **From Damascus to Palmyra is about 150 miles (240km) and there isn't a single gas station in sight, so don't forget to refuel.**
▓ **Fuel is considerably cheaper than in Europe but often the fuel is lacking in quality. Poor Syrian fuel makes taking octane booster a must.**
▓ **I cannot speak highly enough of Syria, but only if you correct our mistake and stay on the road for at least a month, if not more!**

Sasa Lalic hails from Serbia and works for the national railways. He has been riding bikes since the age of 14. His first bike was his grandfather's Tomos 50cc and today he rides a Honda Dominator.

of the Mediterranean, its length almost three times its width. Lebanon's mountainous terrain, proximity to the sea, and strategic location at a crossroads of the world have all been decisive factors in shaping its history.

Thanks to the Syrian Department of Transportation, the tarmac throughout the country is of high quality and for off-road enthusiasts there are stunning open desert roads to enjoy across the country. In this part of the world 125cc motorcycles are very popular and repair shops are never in short supply, but they tend to specialise in the small-capacity machines. Plan, therefore, to carry a good range of spares, including tyre repair kit, fuel pump, air filter and levers. The one exception on the route is Beirut, where pretty much everything is available.

From Turkey a good entry point into Syria is at the Yayladağı border crossing. Yayladağı is a town and district with a long history dating back to the Hittites. It also plays host to Topraktutan, Turkey's southernmost point. Head to Latakia, the principal port city of Syria and a good destination for the first night's stay, but no more than that. Latakia is located 216 miles (348km) north-west of Damascus and 116 miles (186km) south-west of Aleppo.

An easy 45-minute ride east from Latakia gets you to the citadel of Salah Ed-Din which dates back to the tenth century. Of particular note is the fortress's 92ft (28m) deep ditch that was cut into rock by the Byzantines. The castle itself is situated in high mountainous terrain, on a ridge between two deep ravines.

Another 40-minute ride, this time along Route M1 to the south of Latakia, will take you to the 1,000-year-old Marqab Castle, located at the top of a hill. The ride to the top is very good, with magnificent views of the Mediterranean coast.

Some 30 miles (48km) inland lies the ancient town of Masyaf, a fictional depiction of which featured in the

⬇ **Qal'at Ja'bar**
(Jabaar Castle).

← Local Syrian transportation and not a Touratech sticker in sight.

↑ Crac des Chevaliers – real life Age of Empires!

video game *Assassin's Creed*. After this, head north-east out of Masyaf past the national hospital and after three miles turn left and head north on Route 50 to Apamea, located on the right bank of the Orontes River. Apamea overlooks the Ghab valley and was built in 300 BC. Most of the uncovered ruins in it date back to the Roman and Byzantine ages. It is most famous for its high walls and the main thoroughfare that is more than a mile long and lined with extensive columns. There is a selection of reasonable accommodation on Route 56, which runs south-east towards Hama.

Hama is famous for its gigantic 66ft (20m) *norias* ('wheels of pots') on the Orontes River; they were used to lift water up to the aqueducts to irrigate gardens and farms.

At this point on the route, you are close to one of Syria's most interesting sights, the so-called 'Dead Cities', a group of 650 abandoned settlements dating back to before the fifth century AD and containing many remains of Christian Byzantine architecture. Important dead cities include Qal'at Sim'an, Serjilla and al Bara, all of which have overwhelmingly intact structures. Most sites are now easily accessible and in recent years many roads have been asphalted.

There is a beautiful and relaxing short-cut asphalt road from the Dead Cities to the Qasr ibn Wardan that goes through an open plateau of farms. The sixth century Byzantine castle, church and military complex has a unique architectural style. Also of interest are the beehive houses made from mud, poles and stones on the way to Homs, which lies some 30 miles (48km) due south of Hama. Homs is the third largest city in Syria and you can find good accommodation and services. The Ottoman-built Khalid ibn al-Walid mosque, local souks (bazaars) and the two clock towers are interesting sights here.

Head west for 25 miles (40km) from the city centre of Homs on Route M1. The road runs north of the large Quattinah Lake. Follow directions to Al-Nasrah and the famous Crac des Chevaliers, which is arguably the best preserved medieval military castle in the world. Atop a 2,130ft (650m) hill with spectacular roads, it is a UNESCO World Heritage site that you definitely would not want to miss.

In this area the border with Lebanon is less than a

Dura-Europos

GPS: N34 44.45 E40 43.38

Located on an escarpment above the Euphrates river, ruins of the city offer stunning views of the Euphrates River and the desert plateau. The importance of the Euphrates River is very clear at this location. At this point you are just 27 miles (43km) from the border with Iraq.

Qal'at Ja'bar

GPS: N35 53.55 E38 28.51

The 12th century Jaabar Castle has spectacular views of Lake Assad and the Euphrates. Boat tours on Lake Assad are available for sightseeing and swimming. The nearby archaeological city Ar Rasafah is also worth a visit.

Suleiman Shah's Tomb

GPS: N36 38.20 E38 12.28

Suleiman Shah is the grandfather of Osman I, the founder of the Ottoman Empire. Suleiman Shah was drowned while crossing the Euphrates River searching for a homeland for his people in 1086. In accordance with the 1921 Ankara Treaty, the tomb and nine acres of land has been accepted as a Turkish territory.

A final stop should include Aleppo - the most populous city not only in Syria but also in the region. Aleppo's Citadel is the major attraction, and the city has countless souks, khans, hammams, madrasas and mosques that need at least two full days to explore. The famous Aleppo soap is a fitting end to any Syrian adventure ride.

mile from Route M1. Lebanon has taken impressive strides towards becoming a fully independent, sovereign nation and shaking off its image as a Syrian puppet state, and many hope that Syria has finally abandoned its vision of Lebanon as part of 'Greater Syria'. Lack of clarity on the border and Syria's control of much of this region indicates that Syria has not wholly embraced Lebanon's autonomy. Ill-defined borders and checkpoints present issues from time to time and it is best to carefully research where best to cross into Lebanon given the fluidity of the situation.

Political issues aside, Lebanon has some wonderful sights. At an altitude of 3,838ft (1,170m) and situated in the east of the country is the Baalbek Temple in the Bekaa Valley. It is the largest and most noble Roman Temple ever built.

On the west coast lies Beirut, which deserves the title 'Paris of the Middle East' with its multi-cultural and multi-religious structure. It is the centre of new trends, fashion and shops, luxury cars, entertainment and nightlife – including the Buddha Bar! In complete contrast to Syria, helmet law is strictly enforced throughout Lebanon. Many riders will choose to avoid the city and enjoy the countryside instead.

Head south-east from Beirut on a 31-mile (50km) ride along a beautiful winding mountain road which will lead you to the magnificent Beit Ed-Dine Palace, built by the Ottoman Emir Bashir Shibab II and widely regarded as Lebanon's leading tourist attraction.

At this point you can head east and back across the border into Syria and on to the oldest continuously occupied city in the world – Damascus. It is like stepping into a time machine, taking visitors back to ancient times with its untouched and unparalleled texture, culture, bazaars,

➔ **Palymra – an oasis in the desert from the age of antiquity.**

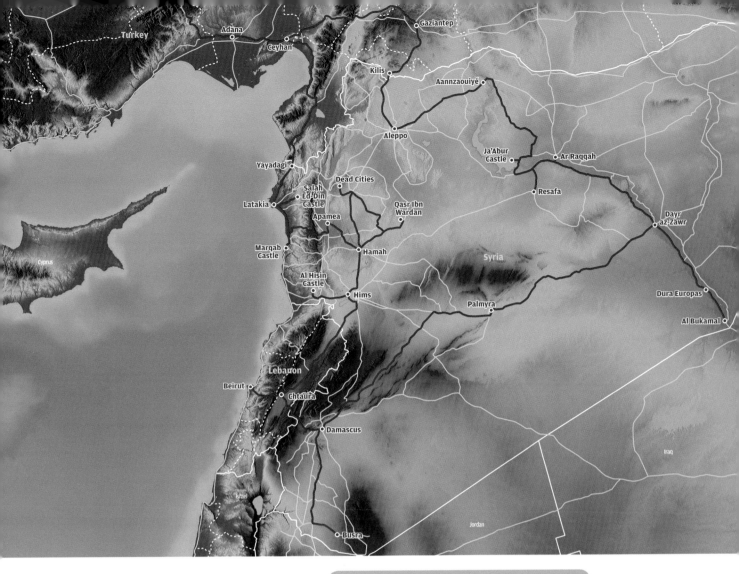

restaurants and shops. Azem Palace, Al-Hamidiyah Souk, Khan As'ad Pasha, Architect Mimar Sinan's Suleymaniye Mosque, al-Hejaz railway station and Nour A-Din Hammam are just a few of the sights, with Umayyad Mosque being the most important of all in Damascus.

An 87-mile (140km) ride to the south of Damascus towards the Jordanian border is the 3,400-year-old Bosra. A magnificent, well-preserved Roman Theatre and one of the oldest mosques in Islam, 'Al-Omari Mosque' is well worth seeing. Another worthwhile excursion from Damascus is Maalula, some 31 miles (50km) out and almost 5,000ft (1,600m) above sea level.

Situated to the north of Maalula lies the Monastery of Saint Moses the Abyssinian (Mar Musa). The route here runs through the desert and it can get extremely hot, so be sure to carry extra water. The main church in the compound hosts precious 900-year-old frescoes and the monastery accepts guests for overnight stays.

From Mar Musa, head back to the main road, Route 7, and turn left to head in a north-easterly direction and enjoy the 95-mile (152km) ride to Palmyra that runs through the Syrian desert. Situated right in the very centre of Syria, this was once the last stop of the caravans on the spice road before reaching the Mediterranean.

RECOMMENDED MAPS

Syria Road Map
Publisher:	Freytag & Berndt Maps
Scale:	1:700,000
ISBN:	9783707909838

Syria and Lebanon Travel Map
Publisher:	Cartographia
Scale:	1:1,000,000
ISBN:	9789633529621

The gigantic archaeological site with its temples and ruins is simply overwhelming and considered the country's finest tourist attraction.

Local delights

The main dishes include meze, mutabbel, za'atar, kabab, manakish, kibbeh, hummus, tabbouleh, mujaddara, shanklish and baklava. The local drinks are Ayran, Jallab and Arabic coffee (known as Turkish coffee), plus Arak and Almaza beer – which are alcoholic. *Narghile* (waterpipe) is commonly smoked with different tobacco flavours. Locals usually salute you by saying 'Ahlan Wasahlan' meaning 'Hello and Welcome'.

Chapter 6

North America

The northern half of the American continent offers much to interest intrepid adventure riders. The entire region is one of dramatic contrasts – from the frozen north of Alaska to the arid states of Nevada, Arizona and New Mexico in the southwest. The result is a continent full of routes to excite and challenge all tastes. The wealth of national parks, forests and outdoor activities will certainly enhance any itinerary. No carnet is needed and the low cost of fuel is a real bonus.

The west coast plays host to a large section of the Pan American Highway as it winds south from Prudhoe Bay, Alaska to its final destination at the tip of Argentina. If a five-month epic adventure like the Pan American is too much, consider a run from either the east or the west across the USA or Canada – almost all of which can be completed off road. You might take in the UNESCO World

Heritage national parks of Jasper and Banff, before heading through the Rocky Mountains, the wonders of Colorado and Montana, past Mount Rushmore and the spectacle that is Niagara Falls.

If you prefer your adventures a little more dusty, head south to the Mohave Desert and Death Valley, which holds the record for the highest reported temperature in the western hemisphere at 56.7°C (134°F). Or perhaps you might enjoy a pilgrimage to the mecca of speed at Bonneville and its famous salt flats before heading off to the Grand Canyon and perhaps Tucson in Arizona – the jumping-off point for adventures in Mexico and South America.

Adventure riding possibilities in North America are endless and the fact that there is a single currency and no language barrier to contend with make the continent a very popular choice. ■

NASA

Alaska and the Yukon

North America's adventure paradise

Simon Race

Should this northwest corner of North America be the start, the mid-point or the end of an adventure? That debate could continue for ages. All that really matters is that it should feature on the adventure motorcyclist's 'bucket list', for this is territory that should not be seen from the windows of a cocktail bar on a cruise ship! It is a region that discloses its majesty, sensational scenery and wonderful character to those who dare to explore the interior.

My journey, like many from overseas, started outside Anchorage airport's cargo terminal as I assembled all my 'worldly possessions' that had just been freed from their crate in a damp car park. Although many border crossings and customs formalities can be lengthy and troublesome, entering Alaska with my bike could not have been simpler. From arriving at the cargo depot to riding into the city took only 90 minutes. So never let that aspect of travelling here deter you. Alternatively, several companies will rent you a bike – including one company that actively encourages riders to get off the beaten track – whereas others don't allow bikes to leave the asphalt highways.

Although many riders will be keen to head off into the wilds as quickly as possible, there are some sensational day rides and shorter journeys around Anchorage, all of which heighten the anticipation and expectation for the days to come. The Kenai Peninsula, for example, offers spectacular day-trip options to Homer and Seward – riding alongside the spectacular Turnagain Arm – while heading through Palmer up to Independence Mine State Park is another sinuous and beautiful route where, if the weather is good and the route is open, the more adventurous can return via Hatcher Pass.

Ask most bike riders about Alaska, and whether they mention 'Deadhorse', Prudhoe Bay, 'the Dalton' or 'the Haul Road', the vast majority will be talking about a route running north from Fairbanks taking in the Elliott Highway to Livengood and then the James W. Dalton Highway onwards to the oil fields of Prudhoe Bay. This is, indeed, a magnificent objective for adventure motorcyclists. But rushing headlong towards this 'Holy Grail' of Alaskan adventure riding means many miss some of Alaska's gems.

Along the Parks Highway from Anchorage to Fairbanks one can stop to explore the small town of Talkeetna, Denali National Park, and even Skinny Dick's 'Halfway Inn' – a tavern run by one of America's most irreverent bar owners. And a great side trip along the lesser known

↑ Nagley's Store in Talkeetna, a good place for a break...

← Bear Glacier on the way to Stewart & Hyder.

← The view towards the old mine in Independence Mine State Park.

→ 'Downtown Wiseman' signpost.

→ Looking south on the Dalton, just below the Brooks Mountains.

↓ The old gold dredge at Chatanika on the Steese Highway.

Steese Highway before heading to the Arctic Circle and the Beaufort Sea heightens the rider's anticipation for what's to come later.

The Steese runs from Fox through Chatanika to Central and Circle, and starts with some magnificent sweeping asphalt bends before switching to hard-packed gravel to break the rider into Alaska's dirt gently – myriad wonderful trails head off this quiet highway that are all worthy of exploration and many are easy to do on even the biggest of dual sports bikes. As a bonus to those interested in Alaska's mining heritage there are some evocative relics to be found too, such as the mighty Gold Dredge and Museum at Chatanika and the small local museum at Central.

Having retraced one's route to Fox it is time for 'the main event'. The build-up starts with some sensational sweeping bends and spectacular scenery on 'the Elliott' en route to Livengood. Thereafter 'the Dalton' proper starts, offering the rider an astonishing mixture of vistas and riding conditions. This mostly gravel highway stretches 414 miles (662km) through rolling, forested hills, across the Yukon River and the Arctic Circle, through the rugged Brooks range and over the North Slope to the Arctic Ocean. Built during construction of the trans-Alaska oil pipeline in 1974, the Dalton is one of the most isolated roads in the United States. There are only three towns along the route: Coldfoot at Mile 175, Wiseman at Mile 188 and Deadhorse at Mile 414. Fuel is available at the Yukon River bridge (Mile 56), as well as at Coldfoot and Deadhorse.

Even within the recognised 'seasons' Alaska has an amazing ability to deal you a surprise or two ... a day, or night, of heavy rain can change this magnificent road from benign scenic experience to one that is feisty, troublesome and an extreme test of man and machine. It's the calcium chloride they use to finish off the grading work that does it. This remarkable substance makes the surface as slippery as ice when wet. But when it dries, astonishingly, it becomes as hard as concrete and as smooth as a billiard table. And I, like many others, experienced both aspects!

I'd elected to take my time. Not because I couldn't handle the conditions – from Livengood to Coldfoot the road and weather conditions could not have been better – but because there was so much to see. It is a road that yields wonderful wildlife to the patient, observant and cautious. I saw grizzlies, caribou, Dall sheep, Arctic foxes, musk-ox, ptarmigan, owls, ground squirrels, porcupines and plenty of rabbits. I broke my journey at Yukon River Camp and had a fascinating evening chatting with a 'local' family who had paddled the Yukon for dinner. Stories of times past, trapping and prospecting added to the richness of my impressions of life on the Dalton.

A lot of people elect to stay at Wiseman, just short of the Brooks mountain range, but I found it fascinating to spend an evening talking with the truckers at Coldfoot Camp. The following morning the road changed dramatically. First it climbed through the dramatic amphitheatre of the Atigun Pass as it crossed the mighty Brooks range. Then the final stretch took me through the vast Arctic tundra to Deadhorse.

It was on this stage where I had my proper 'Dalton Experience' – mud, rain, slipping, sliding, more rain and even more mud … it started as 'light drizzle', which quickly turned to a torrential downpour. And all the while as this epic battle between blue skies and thunderclouds played out the road deteriorated. In truth I know I got 'bad' rather than 'really bad' conditions, but it was challenging enough. The solution seemed to be to get up on the pegs, stick it in third or fourth gear, gas it and hang on. At 40–50mph (65–80km/h) it was 'wriggly', but I kept the faith and let the bike set the course and all went

well, although the mud continued for approximately 60 miles (95km). Finally the sun came out and the beauty of the tundra was revealed. Small stretches of tarmac were interspersed with gravel – and more mud – but it was incredibly beautiful and astonishing to think where I was: at the top of the world.

My return, a couple of days later, having explored Deadhorse, was a revelation. The calcium chloride had 'done its thing'. The stretch that had been so slippery was like a proper highway. It was dry, smooth and excellent progress was made. However, two miles from the end of the road the Dalton served up the usual last-minute surprise – a final two miles of slimy, slippery mud.

On reflection, I wrote in my trip journal that 'it is an astonishing road. It makes you really appreciate the hardiness of the workers who built it and, indeed, the value of the oil for such an operation to be commissioned and completed in such a fashion.' To build a 414-mile (662km) road through such wild and remote land in five months was an amazing feat. Engineers overcame permafrost, mountain ranges and the relentless flow of the Yukon River in just 154 days. And, without knowing it, those engineers have created a fabulous road for motorcycle adventurers to ride...

It probably is no harder than other roads out there, but the sheer diversity of wilderness and mountain range that

DID YOU KNOW?

- Alaska was purchased from Russia in 1867 for $7.2 million by the then Secretary of State, William H. Seward.
- Alaska has the highest mountain in North America – Mount McKinley at 20,320 feet (6,193m).
- 5% of the state is covered in glaciers.
- Alaska is the largest state in the USA at 586,412 square miles (1,518,800km2) – over twice the size of Texas.
- It's about one-fifth the size of the contiguous 48 states. Alaska is about 1,390 miles (2,236km) long and 2,210 miles (3,556km) wide.
- Barrow, 800 miles (1,300km) south of the North Pole, has the longest and shortest day. When the sun rises on 10 May it doesn't set for nearly three months. When it sets on 18 November, Barrow residents do not see the sun again for nearly two months.
- The highest air temperature recorded in Alaska was 38ºC (100ºF) at Fort Yukon in 1915. The lowest temperature, –62ºC (–80ºF), was recorded at Prospect Creek Camp in 1971.
- Alaska is almost as close to Tokyo, Japan (3,520 miles) as New York City (3,280 miles), and it's just 55 miles east of Russia.
- Prudhoe Bay, on the northern Alaskan coast, is North America's largest oil field.
- Nearly one-third of Alaska lies within the Arctic Circle.

one encounters alongs its route is simply breathtaking. It is a road that can change from benign scenic experience to a more significant challenge from one day to the next. It is a road that yields wonderful wildlife to those wishing to moderate their riding to see it. I feel it is more than just a 'badge' to be worn – one shouldn't feel it is just about 'getting to Prudhoe'.

So how to follow that? Well, not by taking the Alcan Highway all the way out of the state, that's for sure. While I'm certain it was once an adventurous road, the Alaska-Canada Highway no longer offers the variety of conditions and challenges that I was seeking. Its 1,390 miles (2,224km) are impressive and it traverses some spectacular areas, but I wanted to explore roads 'less travelled' which would take me through smaller towns and remoter areas.

The advice I had been given was that it was inevitable that I'd have to ride sections of the Alcan from time to time, but that the Alaska and Yukon experience would be enhanced if I took roads with hugely evocative names such as the Denali Highway, the Top of the World Highway, the

Klondike Highway and the Stewart-Cassiar Highway. The first of these required a little backtracking down the Parks Highway from Fairbanks to Cantwell. But it was worth it. Linking Cantwell on the Parks Highway to Paxson on the Richardson Highway, the Denali Highway is a lightly travelled 133-mile (212km) easy gravel road. It is scenic and remote – but pretty well maintained.

Along the way, in good weather, there are stunning views of the peaks and glaciers of the central Alaska range, including Mount Hayes (13,700ft/4,175m), Mount Hess (11,940ft/3,639m) and Mount Deborah (12,688ft/3,867m). After crossing the Susitna River, the road runs along the toe of the Denali Clearwater Mountains and then winds through the geologically mysterious Crazy Notch to the MacLaren River, where there are fine views north to MacLaren Glacier. Thereafter, the last 45 miles (72km) snake through the Amphitheatre Mountains, cresting at MacLaren Summit, at 4,086ft (1,245m) – the second highest road in Alaska. If you are lucky, 15 miles (24km) from the finish (I am told) there is a

⬇ **Looking west from the Parks Highway near Cantwell.**

'pull-out' where (in clear weather) one can gain a final view of the Wrangell Mountains, the Chugach Mountains and the Alaska range. I'll have to return to see that one.

At Paxson one is faced with a choice. Head north on the Richardson Highway to Delta Junction to connect with the Alcan to Tok, or south from Paxson to intersect with the Glenallen to Tok Cut-off. Both are roughly 180 miles (288km). I can't compare them as I've only ridden one of them, but I'm led to believe the southern route and the Tok Cut-off is the more interesting and scenic of the two. However, if you want a fix of the straight and flat Alcan this is your chance. From Delta Junction there's 108 miles (172km) of the straight stuff to get your teeth into.

At Tok I was obliged to head out of town on the Alcan. But only for 12 miles (19km), mind you. Looking at the map there's a route that leaps out at you. Snaking through some wonderful terrain were the Taylor Highway and the unpaved Top of the World Highway linking places called Chicken, Poker Creek, the Fortymile Mining District and Dawson City in Yukon Territory. With evocative names like that I didn't think twice.

The first 60 miles (96km) of the Taylor Highway comprise a delightful paved section meandering through some wonderful scenery with extensive, sweeping vistas. The remainder of its 96 miles (154km) is gravel. The first highlight after finding you are virtually alone as you head out into the wilderness and away from the Alcan is a tiny community called Chicken. The settlement is called Chicken as the original settlers couldn't agree on the spelling of their chosen name – Ptarmigan! In winter the population is about 15 and in the summer the numbers soar to between 30 and 50 – you can grab a great breakfast, as I did, at the downtown Chicken Café.

The border crossing into Canada at Poker Creek couldn't have been simpler. 'No, I don't have any guns or drugs. Correct, I am not planning on staying in Canada longer than I should. Yes, I agree – it is cold and looking like it is going to pour. Cheerio...' And I was in. New favourite road: the Top of the World Highway.

I must admit I was sceptical when I heard tales of this road. With its name I wondered whether I was in danger of mismanaging my expectations. Not a bit of it – it ran the entire ridgeline, with sweeping sinuous curves and some astonishing, far-reaching views. It was so good I even contemplated going back to do it again on my day off in Dawson. But I was in no fit state to do that having fallen into some exceptionally good 'bad company' in the Downtown Bar the evening I arrived.

Arriving in Dawson City is a bit like stepping back in time to the heyday of the Yukon Gold Rush. History surrounds you everywhere – streets with boardwalks, saloons with 'swing doors' and a raft of historic sights. Dawson is definitely worth exploring rather than rushing through. In wandering the town I learned that the Klondike Gold Rush started in August 1896 when three Yukon 'Sourdoughs', George Carmack, Dawson Charlie and Skookum Jim, found gold in Rabbit Creek, now called Bonanza Creek, and changed the history of the Yukon for ever.

Thirty thousand (some say fifty thousand) pick-and-shovel miners, prospectors, storekeepers, saloon keepers, bankers, gamblers, prostitutes and con men from every corner of the continent poured through snow-choked mountain passes and down the Yukon River to stake their claim to fortune on creeks with names like Eldorado, Bonanza, Last Chance and Too Much Gold. Most seekers found no gold at all. But the prospect of sudden riches was not all that mattered. For many of those who made the incredible journey the Klondike represented escape from the humdrum (like me), and the adventure of a new frontier. At its height, in 1898, the Gold Rush turned Dawson into a thriving city of 40,000. By 1899 it was all over and the town's population plummeted, with just 8,000 people left. When Dawson was incorporated as a city in 1902, the population was under 5,000.

It was only in the early 1950s that Dawson was linked by the Top of the World Highway to Alaska, and in 1955 with Whitehorse, along my next stretch of road that now forms

↑ **Downtown Chicken. The cafe does an excellent breakfast.**

BIKE CHOICE

For the majority of rides in Alaska any form of bike will do. Most roads are tarmac and those dirt highways that are to be found are graded and in good condition. However, I'd advise that roads like the Dalton, the Dempster and the Top of the World Highways would be so much more enjoyable if one was astride a 'dual sport' or dirt-oriented bike. And, although not strictly essential, decent dirt tyres will, again, make life so much easier for the rider. If one wishes to stray further from the dirt highways into the hills on old mine tracks the more 'dirt-oriented' the bike is the more enjoyable the experience will be. I found the BMW R1200GS Adventure an excellent choice – at home on the dirt, supremely comfortable on the long tarmac stretches and able to make it from gas station to gas station without having to carry spare fuel.

Dalton Highway

The 424-mile (682km) Dalton Highway begins at Mile 73 on the Elliott Highway, 84 miles (135km) north of Fairbanks. The Dalton Highway is unique in its scenic beauty, wildlife and recreational opportunities, but it is also one of Alaska's most remote and challenging roads. It's definitely not for the timid or the unprepared. The Dalton Highway is one of the last great adventure roads in the United States. If you have the right bike and plan ahead, it can also be one of the most satisfying rides of a lifetime – mostly gravel, two lanes, hilly in places, bumpy in many, lonely and with few facilities along the way. Riders need to watch for ruts, rocks, dust in dry weather, potholes in wet weather, and trucks and road maintenance equipment at all times.

Top of the World Highway

This is a 79-mile (127km) long highway, beginning at a junction with the Taylor Highway near Jack Wade, Alaska, and travelling east to the ferry terminal in West Dawson, on the western banks of the Yukon River. The highway is only open during the summer months. Its name comes from the view one gets as it skirts the crest of the hills, giving views down on the valleys. It is also one of the most northerly highways in the world.

Dempster Highway

This road is also referred to as Yukon Highway 5 and Northwest Territories Highway 8. It connects the Klondike Highway in Yukon, Canada to Inuvik, Northwest Territories on the Mackenzie River delta. During the winter months, the highway extends another 121 miles (194km) to Tuktoyaktuk, on the northern coast of Canada, using frozen portions of the Mackenzie River delta as an ice road (the Tuktoyaktuk Winter Road). The highway crosses the Peel River and the Mackenzie River using a combination of seasonal ferry services and ice bridges. The highway begins about 25 miles (40km) east of Dawson City, Yukon on the Klondike Highway and extends 457 miles (736km) to Inuvik. Much of the highway follows an old dog-sled trail. The highway is named after Royal Canadian Mounted Police Inspector William Dempster who, as a young constable, frequently ran the dog-sled trail from Dawson City to Fort McPherson.

Alcan Highway

The bombing of Pearl Harbor in December 1941 led to construction commencing on this highway as a military necessity, as Alaska was considered vulnerable to a Japanese invasion. The Alcan Highway stretches in a northwesterly direction from Mile mark 0 at Dawson Creek, British Columbia through Yukon Territory to Mile 1,520 at Fairbanks. The highway is open and maintained year round; it is asphalt surfaced, but the condition ranges from poor to excellent with many gravel breaks, poor shoulders and bumps.

part of the Klondike Highway. Again, as with the Dalton, these pioneers had created not only an important lifeline to remote communities but superb biking roads as well.

The ride out of town started magnificently, but in truth there was little chance of the entire day competing with the ride in – and this was reflected in a subtle, but significant, change in the 'feel' of the journey. This might sound daft, but in preceding days I had felt as if I were an 'adventurer'. Gradually I could feel myself becoming more of a 'traveller' and, dare I say it, a 'tourist'. But there were still a couple of stunning elements to come before the adventurous riding was left behind.

Just outside Dawson City is a fantastic viewing point called the 'Dome'. If you are in this neck of the woods do make the detour. It is well worth it, particularly in the early morning as the mist hangs below you in the Yukon River Valley. Thereafter one encounters the hugely tempting turn-off for the Dempster Highway. On this occasion, although part of me was crying out to return to the 'adventurous stuff', I stopped for a photograph and headed on my way, thinking the Dempster could wait for another occasion.

I did the same in Carmacks. Although hindsight says I should have turned off to follow the Robert Campbell Highway to Faro, Ross River and, via remote gravel roads, Watson Lake. Instead I did the 'hard yards' on the Alcan through Whitehorse to Watson Lake. It's probably the only regret I have about the trip.

Things improved from Watson Lake onwards when I took the Stewart-Cassiar Highway, which stretches from the Cassiar Mountains in northwestern British Columbia to the Skeena River and offers some impressive scenery. Wild rivers, deep canyons, magnificent glaciers, clear lakes and pristine areas distinguish the region. Unfortunately – or fortunately, depending on how you look at things – this route has been upgraded in recent years and is now

⇲ The sign at the entrance of a wood carver's site on Turnagain Arm near Anchorage.

⇓ Entering Hyder, Alaska.

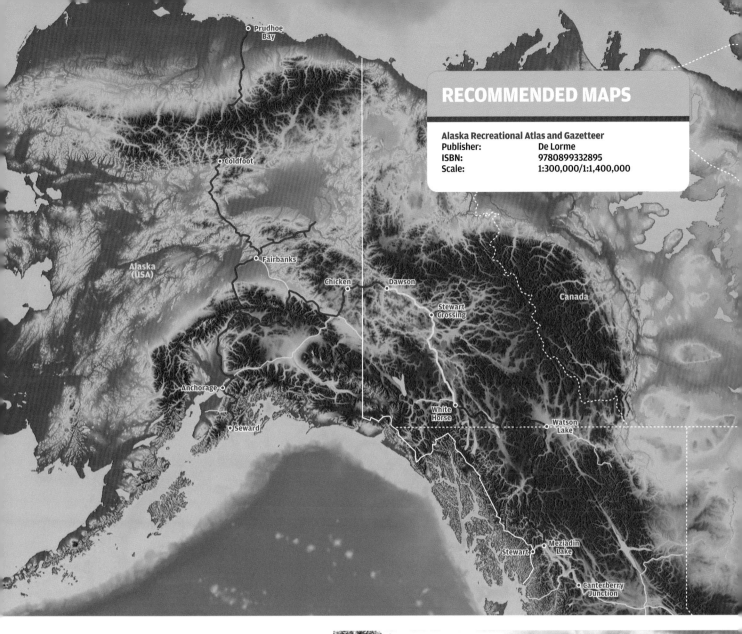

RECOMMENDED MAPS

Alaska Recreational Atlas and Gazetteer
Publisher:	De Lorme
ISBN:	9780899332895
Scale:	1:300,000/1:1,400,000

completely hard-surfaced except for a two-mile stretch of gravel on either side of the Stikine River bridge and another five miles just south of the Yukon border that is scheduled to be completed very soon.

The Stewart-Cassiar Highway runs west of the Skeena Mountains and east of the Coast range, connecting the spruce and Jack pine forests of the Yukon with the great northwestern rainforest. At Dease Lake the highway crosses the continent's other great divide, where the waters stop flowing north through Jack pine forests ending up in the deltas of the treeless Arctic and, instead, flow west into the misty rainforests of the Pacific Ocean.

Just before Meziadin Lake is the last jewel in this area — from Meziadin Junction I turned off the main highway on to the road to Stewart and Hyder. It snaked through gorges and canyons — following the Bear River, past the Bear Glacier and the town of Stewart back into Alaska, where — in the quiet community of Hyder — I was able to reflect on the magnificence of Alaska and the Yukon and prepare myself for the continuing evolution of my ride into more familiar and well-travelled areas of Canada and the United States.

Canada to Mexico

Off-road adventure through America's untamed West

Ramona Schwarz

In late 2006 the founder of Touratech, Herbert Schwarz, embarked on yet another adventure to test his company's products under extreme conditions. This time he was looking to test a range of equipment designed for lighter enduro bikes, with specific emphasis on their suitability for long-distance travel. He chose a route from Cananda to Mexico as the test and then set about finding a riding companion. 'We were looking for a woman who had the experience, the time, and the guts to ride off road from Canada to Mexico in four weeks,' he recalls. Herbert rang up Ramona Eichhorn [later Schwarz], who was no stranger to Touratech's products, having previously ridden with a set of their aluminum panniers around the world for six years. She takes up the story from here.

I asked Herbert what made him think of me and he replied: 'I know a handful of women who are all very good motorcycle riders. But our motto will be: no asphalt, no fast food and no hotels. We won't get started before November, so there will be snow in the mountains around Washington by then and we'll have to camp in the icy cold. I've read your own adventure travel articles so I see you enjoy this kind of stuff and that you won't give up at the first obstacle. Plus, I assume that you know how to make a fire...'

When I asked what bike I would be riding, Herbert replied it would be the BMW G 650 X challenge. I'd never heard of it before but then realised the bike hadn't even come out yet. In fact, it wouldn't be available in Germany before March the following year. As Herbert filled me in

with the technical details of the single cylinder machine I realised this was the opportunity of a lifetime and an offer I could not refuse.

Two photographers would accompany us. Arnold Debus would ride the same bike as me, serving as a moving 'spare-parts inventory' – if anything went wrong with my bike, he would simply donate the relevant parts. The second photographer was Helge Pedersen, well-known adventurer and author of *Ten Years on Two Wheels*. He would ride a BMW HP2, the same bike that Herbert would be on.

The idea for the route came from a conversation

↑ **Wandering through a narrow canyon in Nevada is lots of fun.**

← **A well-deserved stop after a long day of standing on the footpegs and a sign reading 'Caution 4x4 High Clearance Recommended'. Just wondering what technical challenges will await us on the track ahead.**

However, the team decided to make two important modifications: not only did we intend to ride Jerry's trail from the opposite direction, including side trips, but we also chose a different starting point: Victoria on Vancouver Island in Canada (Jerry's original trail starts/ends in Idaho, near the Montana border).

Our start along the Pacific coastline was a cold one as we took the ferry towards Seattle, and a few hours later the city's silhouette, with its trademark Space Needle, emerged from the dark water. What better place to say farewell to civilisation and comfort than a rustic biker's bar in Seattle? That's where we met Phil – quite a character, with a remarkable appearance: white engineer's coat, shoes held together with duct tape, and a seemingly never-ending cigarette in his hand. His long grey hair matched his beard. Following his passion for old English motorcycles, he was running a small bike shop in Seattle. After a few beers and bike talk, he insisted on giving us a little tour through his workshop, where we immediately felt at home. The dusted shelves were full of antiquated machine tools, every one telling a story, and now-yellowed posters, with glamorous ladies wearing the same white-toothpaste smile since the 1970s, were plastered all over the walls.

In order to get to Riggins, in southern Idaho, to pick up Jerry's trail, we had to feed our GPS with an alternative route from Seattle across the Cascade Mountains which extend from southern British Columbia through Washington and Oregon to Northern California. The fact that we were in the right place at the wrong time of the year – the beginning of winter in the northern hemisphere – made it a real challenge, just as much for the riders as for the motorcycles. On Stevens Pass, an icy wind was blowing thick snowflakes on to our visors. We had brought screws for our tyres in case we needed makeshift spikes for the ice, but we were able to manage without them.

From the town of Ellensburg, Washington, we followed

⬆ Sometimes, it was so cold that icicles formed under Ramona's front fender.

between Herbert and Tom Myers, Touratech's US importer. Tom knew of off-road enthusiast Jerry Counts who had been on an extraordinary mission for ten years. After a great deal of on- and off-road research, Jerry and his friend Dave Hutchings linked a network of dirt roads and wagon trails used by the early explorers of America's untamed West. Their idea was to map out a continuous off-road connection from the town of Tecaté in Mexico up to the Canadian border, with ever-changing extremes of terrain and climate, and a great diversity of landscapes. Part of the trail followed historical routes, such as those travelled by the Pony Express riders, or the Lewis and Clark Trail.

➡ With Nevada we enter another, much drier, world.

a gravel road to a narrow canyon. At the bottom of the gorge we found a remote camping spot next to a stream, and turned in for the night. The next morning, tent and motorbikes alike were covered with a layer of fresh snow. We wiped down our gear and equipment and took the rocky trail out of the valley into the mountains. The sky was milky grey and only the noise of our engines cut the silence. In tricky terrain like this – washouts, snow and deep ruts – light enduro bikes really are the best choice. Even though the seat height of 36.6in (93cm) took some getting used to for a 5ft 6in (167cm) rider, I was impressed by how easily I could steer the bike around huge rocks. Mostly, though, I rode standing up.

On the way to Hell's Canyon, in Idaho, we rode through misty forests of pine and fir trees, skirting mud pits and water holes. Fountains of water and dirt sprayed from underneath the bikes, giving them a new coat of brown paint. Suddenly, the weather changed from rain to sunshine, and we came around a corner to behold a spectacular view of the barren landscape, with the rays of the setting sun catching the mountains. A narrow ribbon of gravel wound

its way downhill to the Snake River, which has cut a 125-mile (200km) gorge into the Wallowa Mountains. Much of the range is designated as the Eagle Cap Wilderness Area, part of the Wallowa-Whitman National Forest.

Shortly before nightfall we reached a small village with a solitary gas pump and a 'mom-and-pop' store nearby – fortuitous because we were ravenous. However, the notion that we would be able to get some dinner turned out to be an illusion: their supplies – consisting mainly of fishing tackle, ammunition and rainwear – did not exactly constitute the elements of a palatable dish. A sign for strangers read: 'If we ain't got it, you don't need it.'

After a bridge crossing from Nevada into Oregon, our route continued to the Strawberry Mountains. We surmised that there must have been a major forest fire in this spooky landscape, as charred tree trunks reached up into the clouds amid patches of mist and a light drizzle. We felt like ghost riders. When the rain eventually stopped, we were soaking wet. Looking for a spot to pitch our tent, we saw the glow of a fire through the tall pine trees. Was it just a mirage? Actually, it turned out that a few locals had set up camp so

⬆ **Following professional racer Jonah Street through a river near Ellensburg, Washington.**

village. Even though there were still residents, most of the wooden houses were abandoned, with smashed windows, leaking roofs and paint peeling off the facades. A few 'Closed' signs and an orphan swing in one of the trees were symbols of the melancholy that permeated this place. We were relieved to get away from this strange town and ride on lonesome gravel roads through the wide open landscape up to Steens Mountain in Oregon, named in 1860 after United States Army Major Enoch Steen, who fought and drove members of the Paiute tribe off the mountain.

The hills were newly covered in snow and the scent of sagebrush was in the moist air. It was so cold that icicles formed under my front fender. Too late, we noticed that the snow on the road had lost all traction, and the gravel was frozen with a thin layer of ice. Taking a left turn, Herbert and I crashed in synchronisation – luckily no one was hurt. At 9,500 feet (2,895m), higher than the highest pass in the Alps, we sat atop a large boulder looking down into a crater-like basin and had a chuckle about the crash.

In Nevada, the next state on our map, we felt as though we were on another planet. A sandy track snaked up and down to Black Rock Point, a striking formation rising from the flat land. The hot springs next to it turned out to be an ideal place to camp – a natural bathtub for rinsing off the dust of the last few days.

It was after midnight that a fierce dust storm blew two of our tents (fortunately without occupants) out into the desert. After a sleepless night we started a search operation and discovered one tent floating in a smelly swamp and the other stuck in a thorn bush out in the desert. Later that day, Herbert and I flew across the cracked surface of the saltpan at 95mph (152km/h), kicking up clouds of dust and feeling like we were chasing our own shadows.

⬆ **Immersed in the challenge of taking on winding, sandy trails.**

⬇ **Where the HP2 feels most at home; in rocky and sandy terrain.**

they could go hunting early the next morning. They took pity on these BMW riders caked in mud, and invited us over to their fire to warm up over a cup of bourbon.

In an attempt to do three things at the same time – make coffee, take photos and dry all our wet gear – I suffered a minor disaster. I had put our damp clothes to dry on wooden sticks near the fire, but had unfortunately underestimated the enormous heat a fire can produce, especially if you put your things too close. Three minutes of distraction were enough to burn big holes in Herbert's socks and melt the plastic material of my brand-new riding boots.

Continuing on our route, we passed a long-forgotten

⬆ **Kicking up clouds of dust in the Black Rock Desert, Nevada.**

We had heard that extraordinary phenomena take place in Death Valley, and we decided to find out for ourselves. Rocks weighing up to 660lb (300kg), moved as if by an invisible hand across a flat and dry lake bed, had left strange tracks in the cracked surface without any plausible explanation. In the kingdom of rattlesnakes and scorpions, nature tantalised us with high sand dunes and bizarre colourful rock formations. Framed by barren hills and in the midst of a dried-out salt lake is Badwater, the lowest point in the USA, at 280ft (85m) below sea level. In the Mojave Desert, temperatures can reach extremes of hot and cold – as high as 57°C (135°F) in the shade one day in 1913. When we stopped for gas, the attendant introduced us to his pets – a scorpion, a snake and a tarantula.

In California, we experienced an unforgettable night among Joshua trees. The setting sun had painted the desert sky a bright orange, and in the foreground stood the unmistakable silhouettes of black Joshua trees. These cacti-like plants can grow up to 60ft (18m) and to an age of 900 years – a unique phenomenon. Sitting in the sand around a fire, we watched one shooting star after another race across the clear sky. Orion was watching us from above; it was simply magical.

Unfortunately all good things have to come to an end.

⬅ **Trying to solve the mystery of the so-called 'racetrack' in Death Valley: rocks weighing up to 660lb are moved as if by an invisible hand across a flat and dry lake bed, leaving strange tracks in the cracked surface.**

ABOUT THE AUTHOR

Ramona Schwarz was born in East Germany in 1976. 'Growing up under that Communist dictatorship, with brainwashing, indoctrination, oppression, manipulative propaganda and teachers trying to break me, are still vivid memories,' she says. A nonconformist couple from the neighbouring village were Ramona's solace and inspired her to think for herself. At 13 the fall of the Berlin Wall 'set her free', but she soon realised that living the typical rat race and a 'conventional life' simply wasn't for her, so when her boyfriend presented her with the opportunity to ride a 640 KTM Adventure around the world with him she didn't have to think twice. 'To begin with, I had to learn to ride. The notion that all my worldly possessions would fit into two panniers was a fascinating idea,' she recalls.

The world soon became her home and she learned to get by with very little, making money as a travel writer and photographer. 'I slept under the stars, bathed in cold rivers, warmed myself by the fire and learned to trust my gut feeling,' says Ramona. After five years on the road Ramona and her boyfriend parted company. A year later she met her husband, Herbert Schwarz, the founder of Touratech, who was working on the Canada to Mexico project. Ramona and Herbert have two children and their latest adventure has seen the whole family cycling across Cuba.

⬇ Crossing to California and dry at last.

⬈ Teakettle Junction in Death Valley, California.

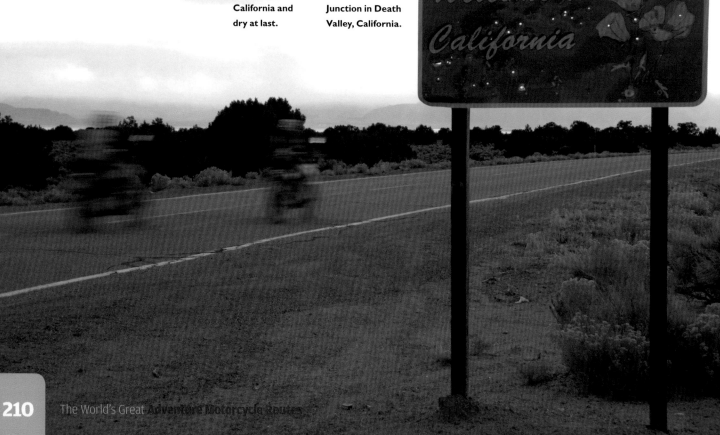

When we crossed the Mexican border, our odometers were witness to the 3,265 memorable miles (5,254km) we had ridden through snow, mud, water, sand, salt and gravel. In four weeks, we had ridden across five states – Washington, Idaho, Oregon, Nevada and California. The ride had been a great success, with many products tested that would soon feature in the Touratech catalogue. Sitting on the kerb in the town of Tecaté we clinked two bottles of local beer and saluted a great adventure.

General

Jerry Counts and Dave Hutchings joined dirt roads and old paths along which the pioneers travelled west, to create a fully traversable route from Mexico to Canada. Asphalt roads appear only occasionally, a path to gas and food supplies. Depending on the time of year, their tours lead from the Mexican town of Tecaté to Nevada (in spring) or from Nevada to Canada (in late summer). We rode the trail on our own, from the opposite direction (north to south), including side trips.

Board and lodging

For outdoor enthusiasts who like to sleep under the stars, carrying camping gear is essential. Those who join the tour do not need to rough it, since accommodation can be provided in motels along the way. For more information about the tours check out www.mex2can.com.

Roads and biking

The terrain is a mixture of everything one can think of in terms of off-road riding: hard-packed gravel roads, winding single trails with deep sand, washouts, deep ruts, big rocks, river crossings, and a very small portion of asphalt. Most ideal is a light, comfortable and reliable dual sports bike, able to hold enough fuel to cover a minimum of 130 miles (210km). You should know the basics of motorcycle maintenance and be able to fix a flat tyre.

How to get there

Those who ride the tour are responsible for getting themselves to the start (Tecaté or Fallon, close to Reno). Assistance is offered with transportation and truck rental around Los Angeles, as is transport from Canada back to LA.

RECOMMENDED MAPS

For obvious reasons the tour organisers are protective of the trail co-ordinates. Navigation is based on following a standard dual sport road with turns that are based on mileage.

For any riders wanting to try this route independently, good maps can be sourced from publishers including: Reise Know-How (Regional Touring Map series), Benchmark Maps, Rand McNally and DeLorme. Check www.stanfords.co.uk for more information.

Trans Canada
Riding the Labrador Highway

Craig Carey-Clinch

I'm sure that there's been many an occasion when folks have thought about riding the iconic coast to coast journey across the United States. But riding across Canada? This was a journey which had only recently come on to the radar, as realisation dawned that the country was not all prairies and the long straight Highway One once the Rocky Mountains were left behind.

We all have some idea of what Canada might be about. The dramatic mountains in British Columbia and Alberta, perhaps? Freezing cold winters? Lakes and forests filled with bugs? Or perhaps merely a good skiing destination... But what else does the country have to offer that would attract overland riders? In August 2009 I was asked to research and conduct a Trans Canada journey for motorcycle overland travel company GlobeBusters. The only things we knew for sure were that Canada offered one of the widest transcontinental rides on the planet, that there was a large flat bit in the middle, that we wanted to explore the little known Labrador Territory in the east, that there were lots of trees, and that only one of us had decent enough French to deal with Quebec. Distances were clearly huge – entering Canadian airspace less than halfway through our flight to Vancouver just reinforced this view.

Collecting our R1200GS from Vancouver customs was a straightforward procedure and we were soon free to explore that gem of the far west, where modern skyscrapers huddle on the small island which makes up 'downtown'. This is the most cosmopolitan and modern of cities, surrounded by water and with mountains

TRANS-LABRADOR HIGHWAY

The Trans-Labrador Highway is located in the provinces of Newfoundland and Labrador. It is the primary public road in Labrador and one of the few in that part of the province. For almost its entire length the route runs through dense wilderness, with no roadside services between communities. Anyone attempting to ride the route in winter should plan accordingly, as weather and road conditions can be extremely unpredictable.

tumbling into broad rivers as they stretch into the distance. It's also a city which retains an air of the frontier, enhanced by the regular float plane services that fly in and out of the city centre.

We might have embarked on the journey to research a ride east, but we started by heading west, via ferry, to enjoy a day on sleepy Salt Spring Island, where wine and spices grow in reminder of the variable Canadian climate, where winter does not universally mean a frozen wasteland. Indeed, southern British Columbia sometimes enjoys much milder winters than the apparently temperate UK.

A further short ferry ride and we drifted lazily up Vancouver Island on excellent roads, enjoying the feel of Canadian highways – a little like US roads, with the same cars, trucks, fast food stores and road signs, but distances were marked in kilometres, not miles, and the

← **The Athabasca Glacier, Alberta.**

← **Mount Robson, British Columbia.**

↑ **The Icefields Parkway, Alberta.**

↓ **Trestle Bridge in The Labrador.**

buildings were flying provincial flags, the Canadian flag and (surprisingly often) the Union Jack, rather than Uncle Sam's stars and stripes.

We took the time to plunge into the mountains in search of fast twisting highways, the township of Gold River and some forest trails which we hoped would take us northwards to Port Hardy. Forest fires put paid to the plan, though. Summer 2009 was marked by extensive fires which resulted in road closures and evacuations. A morning spent riding mud and stone fire trails in the mountains north of Gold River resulted in miles of choking smoke and a ticking-off from a wild-eyed ranger, who proclaimed that we should 'get the hell out, 'cos BC's on fire!'

The 'Inside Passage' ferry, as it's known, offers one of the most dramatic of sea voyages. Linking Port Hardy with Prince Rupert in the north, it navigates the network of islands and fjords which run up the Pacific coastline in the northwest, staying away from the open sea as much as possible. This means an exciting 19 hours of precise navigation as the full-sized, ocean-going ferry tackles narrow passages where steep mountains tumble into the sea. Each narrow passage, sometimes little wider than the ship, is taken at maximum speed; the ferry sails past small native fishing villages, hunting outposts and around the twists and turns of the route, heeling over with a harsh list as knots are maintained. It's easy to imagine the helmsman gripping the wheel, with sweat on his brow, as he maintains a thousand-yard stare and refuses to move the engine room 'telegraph' away from the 'full ahead' position.

Prince Rupert is a good place from which to start the Trans Canada properly. In the far north of BC, it's only about 20 or 30 miles (32–48km) from the southernmost Alaska border and heading east, through mountains reminiscent of the Scottish Highlands, we passed the junction for Hyder and Bear Glacier in Alaska. Much of the journey east at this point runs through rich rolling countryside and vast agricultural tracts, interspersed with more hilly areas of deep forest and picturesque lakes. Reaching Prince George, we joined the GlobeBusters Trans Americas 2009 group. Led by Kevin and Julia

Sanders, the team was bound for Tierra del Fuego, five months' riding away. Our plan was to ride with them for a few days until we headed east for Calgary.

The Rockies were a clear landmark of the journey and anticipation built as we headed southeast from Prince George, following the excellent highway as it slowly gained height and vast mountains rose to eye-watering heights in the distance. Entering the Rockies proper, we paused at Mount Robson and viewed its snow-covered peak while dodging tourists trying to park their badly driven RVs.

Jasper, Alberta may have its eye on the tourist dollar, but it's a tidy place, with plenty to see and an excellent stopover to allow a diversionary ride to Lake Maligne, along a route which leads into the heart of the Rocky Mountains. Tree-lined back roads offered a relaxing ride, although we had to watch out for local wildlife such as elk, bears and clusters of tourists blocking the roads as they frantically photographed anything that vaguely looked mammalian.

The 170-mile (274km) route between Jasper and Banff takes in the best that the Rockies have to offer. The Icefields Parkway sometimes rises to 10,000ft (3,048m) and the road winds past waterfalls, glaciers and broad, deep lakes of bright ultra-marine blue. Distant glaciers could be spotted as we traversed several ranges of mountains, thrusting their craggy peaks far into the sky. We stopped to view the Columbia Icefield and noted the number of tourist 'ice crawler' buses which seemed to have left numerous dirty tracks in the ice.

Banff also trades on tourists. A quaint town where unemployment means departure for the person involved and everything is rather 'pretty' in a pseudo-alpine mountain town sense, it's a good, if expensive, place to spend the night, with a wide choice of restaurant food and plenty of accommodation.

From Banff the road steadily descended away from the Rockies, taking us out into the open prairie of eastern Alberta and Saskatchewan. These are broad, open farmlands and endless roads track their way across the vast prairie, a scene which is only broken by the occasional farm, grain tower or town. But far from being dull, the vast skies above grabbed attention as weather systems formed and dissipated within our sight. The 'Land of the Living Skies' leaves the rider feeling both humbled and awed at the small space we occupy on a large planet. We elected to cross this section of prairie in one hit and nearly 600 miles (965km) after Banff we finally reached Saskatoon, just as a massive electrical storm hit and the city was put on 'hurricane watch'.

We headed north, the idea being to take the most northerly roads from this point, in order to move our ride away from the beaten track and into wilderness areas of the country; to explore ancient forests and boreal landscapes. Leaving open farmland behind, we entered a picturesque area of pine forests and lakes. Long distances between settlements were travelled via both tarmac and dirt roads and broken by the occasional stop for fuel and food.

We left Saskatchewan and entered Manitoba at the silver mining town of Flin Flon. This was as far north as it's

possible to get in this part of the country, with nothing but lakes and trees between us and the Arctic ice. After two days of Manitoban forests, where we took several diversions to see particularly dramatic lakes and to visit some native Inuit settlements, we emerged further south near Winnipeg. We were trying to avoid the main Trans-Canada Highway, but the 'Trans-Can' provides the only real road route into Ontario. However, we discovered a poorly maintained secondary route, the original pioneer trail, which led us through beautiful, peaceful, hilly and wooded country and limited our exposure to the modern highway to just a few miles of fresh blacktop as we crossed the border into Ontario.

The next few days saw the land gradually change to much more scenic territory, as altitude was slowly gained and rocky outcrops and hills started to appear. The route weaved its way around countless lakes, through vast forests and took us to a variety of daily destinations, which all offered something new to see – from hunting lakes to waterfalls, views into the northern United States and even a vast sculptured goose at Wawa. Lake Superior was a new landmark on the route east, a road shadowed by mountains for the first time since Alberta and offering excellent riding along well-paved twisting routes, unencumbered by the vast amounts of traffic that Europe often sees.

Entering Quebec, we found ourselves in France with a Canadian flavour. Buildings were 'francophone' and the dialect unfamiliar. The reappearance of pavement cafés, unseen since Vancouver, was welcome, as was the natural friendliness of the Quebecois. Our route again took us northwards, through territory that led through endless forests of Jack pine, along terrain that was moulded by glaciers.

We changed tyres to off-road specification in Quebec City. This was in preparation for a long-awaited landmark

⬇ **Sweeping roads in British Columbia.**

of the adventure – the Labrador Highway. The Labrador is among the world's youngest lands, in geological terms, having only recently emerged from the glaciers. It's little known outside Canada and only a few European riders have traversed the 750-mile (1,207km) gravel route between Baie Commeau and Red Bay. It carries its own mystique for motorcyclists in the Americas.

After a day off in Forestville, we turned on to the Trans-Labrador Highway. The first two hours were spent steadily winding our way upwards through the hills to a welcome breakfast at the hydro-electric dam at 'Manic 5'. Then the

tarmac was left behind as we headed down the piste in the direction of Labrador City. The route was hard-packed mud and the going was good.

Altitude was slowly gained as we rode through a land that's clothed entirely in endless forests and has been carved by massive forces over millennia. The piste took us through mountainous areas where very few visit who are not concerned with the harsh daily lives of mining or frontier living. That said, huge articulated lorries were frequent enough to present a notable hazard, the huge 'semis' being driven at high speed along the gravel and drifting through the bends.

We rode across the Quebec border and into the provinces of Newfoundland and Labrador to our night stop at Labrador City, a town that didn't exist 50 years ago and is entirely focused on the endless work to tame the 'bush'.

After another day of excellent gravel road riding, with the occasional patch of deep stones to remind us to avoid complacency, we reached the hydro-electric town of Churchill Falls. This is a company town, which serves the huge underground hydro-electric plant. Electricity from here feeds much of lower Canada and New York State.

And then it was on to Goose Bay, a pioneer town that was established prior to the Second World War around a large Royal Air Force base that was built as a staging post on the old Atlantic air route. Nowadays it's the major settlement in Labrador and offers good local services, as well as excursions to native areas and 'interpretive centres', as they often call museums in North America.

With the section of highway between Goose Bay and Cartwright Junction still under construction, we embarked on a wheezing and ancient overnight ferry, which deposited us in cold early morning light in Cartwright town, where a decent cooked breakfast fortified us for the final long section of gravel highway.

So far the ride had been great, sometimes a bit tricky, but nothing that the average rider couldn't tackle with care. But as the month changed from August to September so did the weather, and later that morning we found ourselves riding into the tail end of Hurricane Danny, which had lashed the American east coast a few days earlier. What we'd hoped would be a triumphant ride out of Labrador turned into a long and difficult day's struggle along a soaked piste which had very deep gravel stretches, leaving us unable to appreciate the stunning views, as the piste led us across high open moorland territory, dotted with lakes and rugged outcrops of rock. We were glad to leave the gravel behind later in the afternoon as we arrived in Red Bay, soaked and tired but exhilarated at completing the Trans-Labrador Highway.

After a 36-hour delay to allow the sea to calm down, we took another ancient ferry to Newfoundland and the road southwards through the Gros Morne Mountains. A night stop at Rocky Harbour meant a meal of locally caught fish and a chance to familiarise ourselves with the Newfoundland dialect – not quite Irish, not quite English West Country – a wonderful burr which was a

delight to listen to. Our long ride to St John's, the capital of Newfoundland, the following day also reminded us of home, with a landscape reminiscent of Scotland, the west coast of Ireland and Cornwall as we covered big miles to reach shelter before a further forecasted hurricane hit the area.

Finally arriving at St John's we stopped at Cape Spear, a mile or two from the city, the most easterly place on the American continent and only 1,800 miles (2,900km) from our home. Then it was time to celebrate in suitable style, with fresh lobster and British Columbian wine as the rain started falling and the wind howled outside.

Leaving the oh-so-English St John's was a wrench, but there were more miles to ride before finishing our journey in Halifax, Nova Scotia – this time westward. We departed via the overnight ferry to North Sydney, Nova Scotia. 'New Scotland' lives up to its name. The mountainous Cabot Trail was an unexpected high point of the journey and the route westward passed through softer mountains and alongside deep blue lakes before we joined our first motorway since Vancouver, passing near towns such as New Glasgow and Truro before arriving in historic Halifax, 6,700 miles (10,789km) and 22 riding days from Vancouver.

RECOMMENDED MAPS

Canada Back Road Atlas
Publisher:	MapArt
ISBN:	9781553686149
Scales:	Various

Canada West
Publisher:	Hildebrand
ISBN:	9783889892782
Scale:	1:1,500,000

Canada East
Publisher:	Hildebrand
ISBN:	9783889892775
Scale:	1:1,500,000

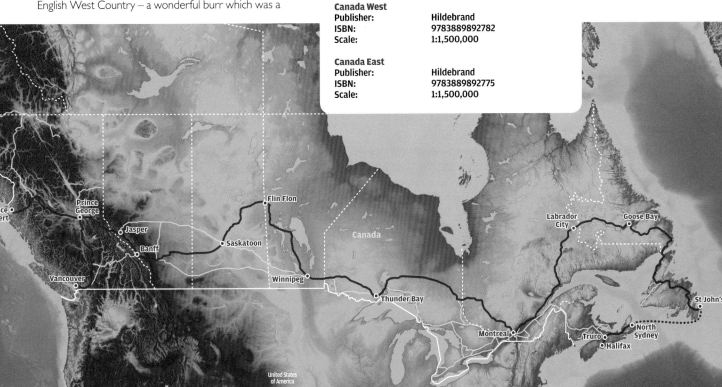

Colorado

Adventure trails in the San Juan Mountains

Oliver Ruck

When you think of Colorado, images of majestic mountains and treacherous shelf roads come to mind. Nowhere is this truer than in the San Juan mountain range near Silverton, Colorado. These mountains include the third highest unimproved mountain pass in the state and some of the most famous adventure riding routes in the world. Colorado is the only US state that lies entirely above an elevation of 3,281ft (1,000m), which in itself gives an indication of some interesting terrain for the adventure rider. To the west of the Great Plains of Colorado rise the eastern slopes of the Rocky Mountains with some 54 peaks that are 14,000ft (4,267m) or higher in elevation.

The state boasts four national parks, six national monuments, two national recreation areas, two national historic sites, three national historic trails, a national scenic trail, 11 national forests, two national grasslands, 41 national wilderness areas, two national conservation areas, eight national wildlife refuges, 44 state parks, a state forest, more than 320 state wildlife areas, and numerous other scenic, historic and recreational attractions.

Colorado is also home to three of the most challenging adventure biking trails: Black Bear Pass, Engineer Pass and Imogene Pass. Whether you have just begun to explore the freedom of the path less taken or you are an experienced veteran, you will discover an experience you will always remember in Colorado.

Black Bear Pass

Total distance: 8.68 miles (13.9km)
Elevation: 8,996ft (2,742m) to 12,472ft (3,801m)
Season: June to September

Black Bear Pass is one of the more difficult trails in the state of Colorado and is recommended only for the most

daring adventure riders. Legend has it that more than one hundred years ago a prospector found gold up on the side of the mountain and he built this road in order to get his wagons and supplies up from Telluride. The trail includes a 'one-way-only' section – downhill (east to west, except for a couple of days per year when the path is reversed). In order to complete this trail it is strongly recommended you conquer Engineer Pass and Imogene Pass first (see below) to gain experience with the local terrain and altitude. Black Bear Pass tests the strength, skill and courage of any rider.

The notorious trail starts from Highway 550 (also known as the 'Million Dollar Highway') north of Silverton. The start of the trail is marked with a famous sign that reads: 'Telluride – City of Gold. 12 Miles – 2 Hours. You don't have to be crazy to drive this road – but it helps.' The track winds its way up into the mountains and eventually reaches Telluride, cresting at an elevation of 12,840ft (3,910 m).

The ride up to the pass from Highway 550 is typical of any trail in the region and very enjoyable as you pass over the mountain from Silverton. Larger adventure bikes can power through the terrain to get to the pass sign. It's a two-way road all the way to Ingram Falls. This is your last chance to question your sanity and turn around.

After the pass, the ride gets serious. Advanced terrain will challenge even experienced dirt bike riders, while large adventure bikes will be pushed to their limits during the descent to Telluride, which is a well-known ski and summer resort some 360 miles (576km) southwest of Denver.

Shortly after the initial descent from the pass, the trail officially becomes a 'one-way-only' path down. Returning to the summit is dangerous and nearly impossible. A

⇐ **The top of the steps at Black Bear Pass.**

⇐ **The start of Black Bear Pass from Highway 550.**

challenging obstacle awaits riders as soon as they gain sight of Telluride, far in the distance. The steps of Black Bear Pass rapidly drop to a right-hand turn at the edge of a cliff with little room for error. In 2004 a jeep slipped off the slope near the beginning of the switchbacks and fell several thousand feet, killing two of the passengers and severely injuring two others. From experience, it's best to walk the

steps before attempting to traverse the rocky ledges, which are likely to test your riding skill to the limit; the steps are very steep, all shale, and include a 90° turn. It's difficult to slow for this turn, but you must – there are no guardrails and all that's in front of you is sky. Slow down well in advance and ease your way around the right hand bend. The snowmelt and rains throughout the season coat the slippery steps and add yet another dimension to the challenge.

This area must not be taken lightly because an error may be fatal, but a great reward waits at the end. The bottom of the steps is a popular photo and social gathering spot for two- and four-wheeled enthusiasts. The lookout at the bottom of the steps offers a great view of the switchbacks descending to Telluride, nestled in the valley 4,000ft (1,220m) below you. Looking back up the steps you won't believe that you dared bounce down those rock ledges! You will soon have to cross the stream which you avoided going down the cliff. As one rider put it: 'If you make it down the steps, the rest will seem like a piece of cake and you can go into the first bar you come to in Telluride, clean out your shorts, and knock back a cold one – you're gonna need it to settle your nerves after that experience!'

One of the reasons this pass is 'one way only' is because of the tight corners that have to be navigated on the switchbacks; 4WD vehicles have a difficult time turning sharply enough to maintain the path and avoid falling off the edge along the switchbacks. Bikes with large turning radii must approach the switchbacks with caution: any error is not forgiven.

A large waterfall and historic hydro-electric power station can be seen on the way down. Bridal Veil Falls sits in the middle of the switchbacks and is the tallest waterfall in Colorado at 365ft (111m). These switchbacks on Black Bear Pass are some of the most exciting riding you can experience in the San Juan Mountains. The extremely narrow and steep road proves an amazing addition to any rider's list of conquered trails.

Engineer Pass

Total distance: 31 miles (49.8km)
Elevation: 7,813ft (2,381m) to 12,805ft (3,902m)
Season: June to October

Engineer Pass is part of the 'Alpine Loop' – the longest route in the San Juan region – with views that are truly amazing and features for both new and experienced adventure riders. The trail takes you from Highway 550 just south of Ouray (GPS: N37 59 16.60 W107 38 56.25) to the town of Lake City, Colorado (GPS: N38 01 37.25 W107 19 10.63). Engineer Pass has had a rich history of transportation for the mining industry since its completion in 1877. Along the route you can get close to many old mining structures, making for some great pictures and a good excuse to catch your breath, while amazing sights such as a ghost town and an abandoned dam line the road up to the pass.

Engineer Pass can be divided into three different types

← One of many amazing mining structures along Engineer Pass.

of ride, each with significantly different difficulty levels. The main trail runs the full length from east to west and can be ridden in either direction. There is a bypass route through Animas Forks which starts at GPS: N37 56 01.52 W107 34 06.81 and meets up with the main trail at GPS: N37 57 37.90 W107 34 32.65. This bypass route can be ridden east with less difficulty. Finally the eastern section of the trail, starting at Lake City, can be ridden west to the pass both early and late in the season for a spectacular view of

← One of the steep drops on the Engineer Pass.

↑ The top of Engineer Pass.

the mountains; this is one of the few passes kept open by snow ploughs.

The start of the main route south of Ouray on Highway 550 is barely noticeable off the east side of the highway, especially considering the beauty and danger of the Million Dollar Highway. The beginning of this main section will test the limits of any rider on a large adventure motorcycle. During the summer months rain is expected almost every day and the trail will be wet. The track withstands heavy rain very well, however, and mud is not as much of a concern as the aggressive rocks.

The section of Engineer Pass directly east off Highway 550 is recommended for smaller dirt bikes and experienced or very determined larger adventure bikes. High tyre pressures are recommended because, even during rain, traction is not an issue, but the need to keep

↓ Oh Point on Engineer Pass.

up momentum will inevitably cause heavy hits to both tyres and suspension. One piece of advice on the first section: it's best not to slow down or look back because stopping is only likely to make progress more difficult. 'I have no pictures or video of the difficult section because I was too busy hanging on for dear life,' says Oliver.

The western section of the trail soon joins with the bypass route that comes from Animas Forks. This bypass route is more suited for larger adventure bikes with experienced riders. The high altitude will drastically decrease the performance of any motorcycle and rider here, and you need to be prepared, both mentally and physically. The trail from here to the pass is highly recommended for its amazing scenery and intense riding experience. The route quickly takes you above the tree line, past Poughkeepsie Gulch and into classic Colorado mountain terrain.

Once at the top of the mountains you will see a trail leading over a ridge to an overlook; this is the 'Oh Point' (GPS: N37 58 11.78 W107 35 35.82). The view from this overlook is unparalleled and superior to the view from the pass. Even if you approach the pass from the east you must make your way to this overlook – it is within view of the pass and is positioned at 13,000ft (3,962m), at least 200ft (61m) higher than the Engineer Pass itself, which is situated at GPS: N37 58 24.97 W107 35 07.58. During the off-season this pass is sometimes ploughed to allow access, even when there is 10ft (3m) of snow!

The eastern side of the pass parallels Henson Falls Creek all the way to Lake City. This ride crosses the original Capitol City, which aspired to become Colorado's capital.

Engineer Pass should be at the top of the list for any adventure rider, but note that only experienced riders should tackle the west side of the pass while new riders can enjoy the scenery on the east side.

Imogene Pass

Total Distance:	11.78 miles (18.9km)
Elevation:	8,740ft (2,664m) to 13.114ft (3,997m)
Season:	July to September

Imogene Pass, also in the San Juan mountain range in Colorado, is one of the best kept secret wonders of the region. The pass runs directly from Telluride across a 13,114ft (3,997m) mountain towards Ouray. It is the third highest unimproved pass in Colorado that is passable by vehicles. The route has only one option for travel and starts at GPS: N37 56 24.29 W107 48 42.31 out of Telluride and ends on a dirt road leading to Ouray at GPS: N37 58 30.00 W107 43 24.03. (This path can be run either way, but highly recommended is the start from Telluride.)

This route should be attempted by small dirt bikes or expert adventure riders, but anyone riding it should travel with a friend in case the mountain gets the upper hand. Later in the season snow drifts may form near the summit making progress difficult or impossible. With heavy jeep traffic on this pass a clean line has developed on the extreme outer edge of the path, tempting motorcyclists.

← **Once past the rock ledges the worst part of the trail is over.**

The inside line will often be rocky but stable compared to the smooth and treacherous outer line.

Imogene Pass goes through a forest on quick shelf roads that snake up the sides of the mountain to the tree line, gradually becoming more difficult. High tyre pressures are recommended to prevent pinch flats on larger bikes, and a healthy respect for the edge of the road is demanded of even the most experienced rider. Proper road etiquette is required when passing other vehicles – you may encounter 4WD vehicles and the rider or driver on the ascending path will always have the right of way.

↓ **The steel sign at the top of Imogene Pass.**

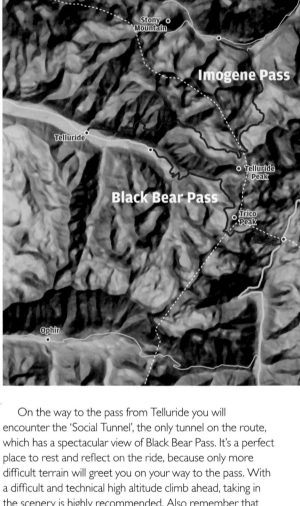

↑ The old mailbox at the top of Imogene Pass.

→ A stream along the north side of Imogene Pass.

ABOUT THE AUTHOR

Oliver Ruck is a mechanical engineer from the Dallas Fort Worth area in Texas. He has always enjoyed mountain biking, hiking and car racing. Throughout his life he has had a passion for travel and the desire to experience people and nature up close and personal. Unsurprisingly, then, this combination led him to adventure riding. He loves to share stories and advice and promotes adventure and dual sport riding whenever possible. 'Planning gear and routes is a large part of my trip experience to ensure maximum potential from any ride, especially if they don't go as predicted,' he says.

On the way to the pass from Telluride you will encounter the 'Social Tunnel', the only tunnel on the route, which has a spectacular view of Black Bear Pass. It's a perfect place to rest and reflect on the ride, because only more difficult terrain will greet you on your way to the pass. With a difficult and technical high altitude climb ahead, taking in the scenery is highly recommended. Also remember that this is a high alpine environment, so be sure to bring plenty of water, food and appropriate clothing.

From here the trail becomes rocky and loose with short sections of technical ledges to climb. High altitude will severely decrease engine power as you climb to the summit, over 13,000ft (3,962m) above sea level. Carburated bikes must have proper jetting to sustain reasonable power at these heights.

North of the 'Social Tunnel' you will encounter the ruins of a massive mining site, the Tomboy Mine. Today the town is a pile of wood and metal, but the iron will of the

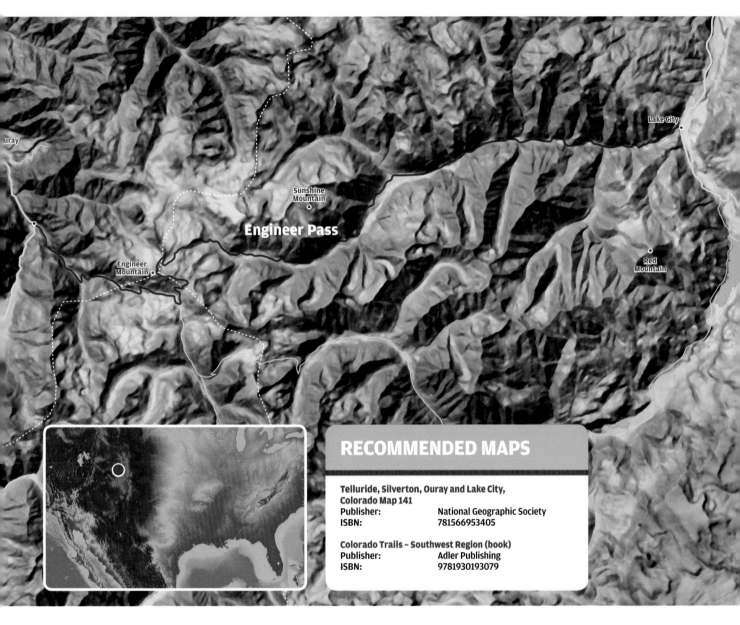

Engineer Pass

Sunshine Mountain

Engineer Mountain

Lake City

Red Mountain

Uray

RECOMMENDED MAPS

Telluride, Silverton, Ouray and Lake City, Colorado Map 141
Publisher: National Geographic Society
ISBN: 781566953405

Colorado Trails – Southwest Region (book)
Publisher: Adler Publishing
ISBN: 9781930193079

miners who hauled equipment up and ore down must be appreciated. North of Tomboy the trail intensifies to a rocky technical section. A large bike with minimal suspension will cause its rider problems in this area. Luckily there are often other people on the trail who can assist during tough sections. It is not recommended to tackle this section alone.

The climb to the summit is spectacular. The colours and terrain conjure images of alien planets and amazing landscapes. The view from the peak of Imogene Pass is, by some margin, the most dramatic of any Colorado trail. Up there an old lookout has decayed into ruins and a large coil of cable is the last remnant of long-distance alternating current power lines constructed over Imogene Pass to carry power from the Telluride area to the Camp Bird Mine. The ancient mailbox at the top of the pass displays the emblems and scars of many adventure clubs.

On the north side of the pass a lookout over the Red

Mountains is a great place to pause and enjoy the view. There may be patches of snow here year round.

Travelling down the north side of Imogene Pass will require proficient brake modulation and choosing a line that will allow the suspension on your bike to work for you. There are several lines you can choose from on this wide path, but note that 4WD vehicles have carved difficult tracks alongside the easier tracks, so keep a sharp eye on the trail.

The route to Ouray rapidly descends into a valley with numerous deep puddles and rock formations. With the daily seasonal rains the trail is guaranteed to be saturated but not slippery, though wet boots are to be expected.

Imogene Pass can take most of the day, especially if you wait for rain to subside during the morning before you start from Telluride. This pass should not be missed by any traveller and can offer the most spectacular views in Colorado.

All photographs courtesy of Oliver Ruck

Trans-Am Trail
Off-road riding across America

Sam Correro

Imagine riding 5,000 miles (8,000km) on remote dirt tracks, with sparse fuel availability, and you could be forgiven for thinking this was somewhere in Africa or Asia. In reality, though, this challenging adventure is available in the continental United States and it's called the Trans-Am Trail. The good news is that you don't need a passport and you certainly don't need to cross any international borders with this adventure.

The Trans-Am Trail (TAT) is made up of a series of interconnecting routes using dirt roads, forest tracks, farm roads, dried-up creek beds and abandoned railroad grades in the outback of the rural USA, all of which have been scouted and mapped to form the route. It has taken the best part of 12 years and thousands of miles of riding to assemble the 'puzzle'.

The route currently starts in northeastern Tennessee and snakes its way westward, dipping into Mississippi before shifting north through Arkansas and into Oklahoma, west to Colorado, Utah, Nevada, a short stretch in California and ends at the Pacific Ocean in southwestern Oregon. You ride from east to west across very remote areas of the country, meeting people along the way and stopping at places such as Oark, Arkansas which has just one store and a post office. The food is local and fantastic, the people are genuine and friendly. The route is approximately 5,000 miles (8,000km) with an average of 225 miles (360km) per day. All of the TAT is on public land and roads and this requires a road-legal motorcycle.

The first half of the trail is not exceptionally technical but challenges come with the rain – it gets muddy and the water crossings are deep. Beyond Oklahoma the TAT gets more challenging as it nears the Continental Divide.

Writing for motorcycleusa.com, Scott Brady says: 'What makes the TAT so exceptional is how Sam planned this remote route, while still providing fuel stops within

the range of the typical dual sport motorcycle. In addition to the fuel stops, each leg of the trip includes a technical portion of riding, if even for 15–20 miles (24–32km), which allows for a highlight each day.'

Into Nevada the route gets rugged and remote, with hundreds of miles of the trail only ridden by those braving the TAT. The three most important things to monitor when you ride are the weather, your fuel reserves and your navigation, which at times can be intense – routes may be blocked by trees, closed for logging or gated off by a private landowner. The navigation system itself is based on roll chart, trip odometer and supporting maps. The trip odometer is reset back to zero at each and every turn and has a map of the intersection. Also printed on the roll chart are the GPS co-ordinates to confirm the intersection.

The best time of year to travel depends on when you cross the Continental Divide in Colorado (if you choose to ride across Colorado, that is). There is a snow window in the Colorado Rockies from late June to early September and this is the best time to get through. The states of Utah,

← The remains of a three-storey mine shack on the road to California Pass.

← One of two rock slides blocking the route towards the end of the trail in Oregon, 2007. Sam is continuously reviewing parts of the route to ensure the trail remains accessible.

Some frequently asked questions

What is the 'best' motorcycle to ride on the Trans-Am Trail?

I would not recommend any motorcycle smaller than 400cc – anything smaller and you are always going to be looking for the next fuel stop. A KTM 640, BMW F650 Dakar, Honda XR650L or XR650R, or indeed any capable single-cylinder dual purpose machine of a similar size would be ideal. A KTM 950/990 or BMW GS Adventure will cope admirably – they have the framework to support a decent load and the fuel range to travel unsupported, but riding the TAT on a large adventure bike is always going to be physically demanding. Some of the sections will be challenging on a bigger GS or KTM, although bypasses are offered so larger bikes can avoid the very technical sections. In essence you need a dual purpose bike that you can handle through deep sand, mud, loose gravel, rocks and snow. It's important to be sure your motorcycle is in good shape prior to your departure. A tune-up and safety check are a good idea (fresh oil, clean air filter, good tyres and the right pressures).

Does my motorcycle have to be street legal?

Yes. Your motorcycle must be street legal.

When is the best time of the year to ride the Trans-Am Trail?

If you want to cross Colorado, Utah and Oregon, then your snow window will be late June to early September. Keep in mind the desert heat in Utah and Nevada. Also, snow on the high passes of Colorado usually doesn't melt enough to allow passage until later in June.

Can I ride from west to east?

No. The TAT maps and TAT roll charts are specifically designed for navigation from east to west, regardless of which state or what part of the trail you decided to start in.

⬆ **The trail starts relatively gently in Tennessee and into Mississippi.**

⬇ **The amazing Crater Lake in Oregon. Take a short detour off the trail to this must-see volcanic lake; it's five miles across and at its deepest nearly 600m deep.**

Nevada and Oregon also have that 'snow window', but keep in mind that no two years are the same for snowfall. The state of Oklahoma has a lot of rural dirt roads and for the most part it stays dry and rideable, but if you are caught in a rainstorm the mud becomes impassable and you must get out on a paved road.

Andrew Sarakatsannis from Fort Thomas, Kentucky has ridden the trail and is full of praise: 'Riding Sam Correro's TAT was a no-hassle, easy-to-navigate, good time that should be experienced by all riders. It has something for everyone from the beautiful scenery and winding trails, to all the great people you will meet along the way. Anyone who rides the trail will surely ride away with some new friends and some wonderful memories that will both last a lifetime.'

⬆ **Heavy rain can leave parts of the trail impassable.**

⬈ **The cattle grid that marks the state line between Nevada and California also marks a great sense of achievement.**

How many miles should I plan to ride each day?

The average day's ride is about 225 miles (360km) – and that's a full day from 7.00am to 6.00pm.

What about fuel stops?

Gas is plentiful in the eastern sections of the Trans-Am Trail, with nothing over 100 miles (160km) between available fuel stations, and an average of 60 miles (97km) between stations. One day in Nevada there is a 180-mile (290km) run between fuel stations. It's important that you review your TAT maps each night, locate the fuel stops and plan your fuel stops for the following day. Be aware, if you get a late start and are riding at night, some fuel stations may not be open. When in doubt, be sure to fill up your tank when it reaches halfway. Many areas of the trail are remote – do not wait until your tank is almost empty before thinking to refuel.

What about accommodation?

If you ride the recommended daily distance, there will be a motel either on the Trans-Am Trail or easy to find just off the trail, each and every night. It is important to locate and

⬆ **The trail follows the spectacular Cinnemon Pass over the Rockies in Colorado.**

⬅ **Ensure you manage your fuel stops; finding gas in remote parts can be difficult. Members of the 'Strong City' religious community gave me fuel in New Mexico after I missed my gas stop and ran out 90 miles short.**

↑ **Reaching Port Oreford in Oregon is the end of the trip of a lifetime.**

plan your overnight stay – do not risk getting caught in the outback after dark. Review your route each night to locate the preferred overnight stay. Motels shown on the TAT maps are typically modest, yet adequate accommodation.

What about camping?

Many riders prefer to camp when riding the Trans-Am Trail, so for an added sense of adventure, pack your tent. Campgrounds, state parks and national parks are not listed on the TAT roll charts.

What about bike maintenance?

Moab in Utah is about the halfway point of the entire Trans-Am Trail, and an appropriate place to change oil,

ABOUT THE AUTHOR

Sam Correro is a retired pharmacist based in northeast Mississippi on Lake Pickwick. He has been riding motorcycles for 40 years. 'The Trans-America Trail reflects my passion for adventure and my love of motorcycles,' he says. Sam wanted to share the route with other riders and he started with a simple and proven idea of cross-country navigation using a roll chart and odometer. He slowly improved on the format and added GPS information. 'What started with just exploring the "outback" and linking bits of road together has now turned into one of the great adventure rides,' he says.

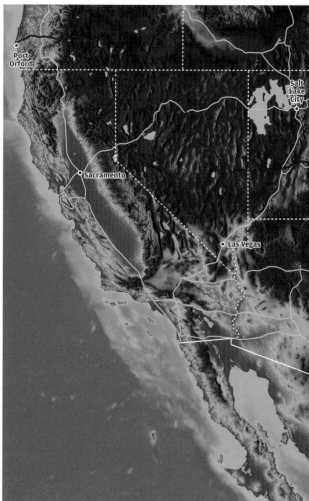

buy new tyres or get any other repairs done that your motorcycle might need.

Do I need knobbly tyres?

Yes – knobblies are best, but a good dual sport tyre would be OK in the eastern sections of the trail. The Continental TKC80 or Dunlop D606 are advised.

Do I need a GPS?

No. A GPS unit is not required to navigate the Trans-Am Trail, but it is recommended to have one. The main mode of navigation is the TAT roll chart and odometer, which is simple, basic and very accurate. A GPS would be added reassurance and a very good back-up. TAT roll charts are key, though, as they tell you ahead of time what to look out for.

Do I need a roll chart holder?

Yes. Get one with a wide and long window so you can view a big section of the TAT roll chart before you have to advance it.

How do TAT roll charts work?

The TAT roll charts are 2.25in (5.6cm) wide. Load one day's ride at a time, usually from motel to motel. The charts are sent to you on 8.5 × 11in (21.25 × 27.5cm) sheets of paper, not rolls, with three columns of navigation information per page, which you will need to cut into rolls. This is done for a very important reason – it's equally important to review both the TAT maps and the TAT roll charts as an integral part of your planning process. If the TAT roll charts arrived already rolled, you couldn't look at them without unrolling them to reveal various areas of the trail.

Do I need to pack food and water on the motorcycle?

Yes. Pack extra water and bring some food or energy bars. Also, matches and a flashlight would be a very good idea – and an adequate first aid kit goes without saying. Hydration systems are recommended – especially important in the arid climates of Colorado, Utah and Nevada.

What gear is recommended?

You must be able to keep dry and warm, even in the summer months. In the high elevations of Colorado, summer temperatures can be cold, even in July and August. If caught in the high elevations after dark, temperatures can drop significantly.

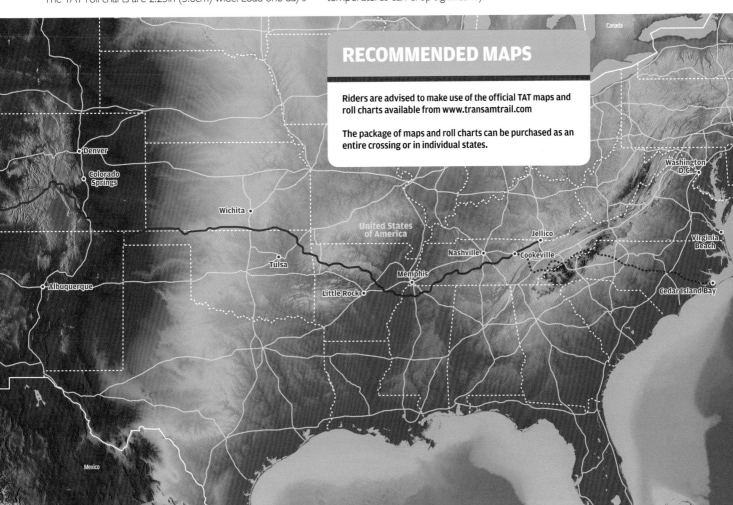

RECOMMENDED MAPS

Riders are advised to make use of the official TAT maps and roll charts available from www.transamtrail.com

The package of maps and roll charts can be purchased as an entire crossing or in individual states.

Chapter 7

South & Central America

South America is the planet's fourth largest continent and a real favourite with adventure riders. Main routes in countries such as Brazil, Chile and Argentina are well surfaced, while roads in the more mountainous regions of Peru, Ecuador and Bolivia tend to be less forgiving. The continent is generally pretty safe and no carnet is required for travel, which makes life a fair bit easier and cheaper.

Arguably the biggest challenges lie in the Amazon Basin, which covers about a third of the continent. Running through its heart is the Amazon River and its more than 1,000 tributaries, so get used to river crossings if you're headed this way.

The traditional north-south-north traverse along the continent tracks the Andes Mountains, which at some 4,500 miles (7,240km) extend all the way from Panama to the southern tip of South America. About midway down the continent lies the Atacama Desert. Sparsely populated and totally barren, it is positioned high in the Andes of Chile. This small desert is a cold place and one of the few deserts on earth that doesn't receive any rain. It's approximately 100 miles (160km) wide and 625 miles (1,000km) long.

Located between the Andes and the Atlantic Ocean, and about 1,000 miles (1,600km) in length, Patagonia stretches south from the Rio Negro River to Tierra del Fuego and the Strait of Magellan. It's mostly rugged, barren land, famed for its beauty and striking mountain scenery – riding here is a breathtaking experience. Finally, Tierra del Fuego represents something of a pilgrimage for adventure bikers, lying as it does at the very tip of South America and regarded as 'the end of the road' for riders heading south.

Central America is the tapering isthmus of southern North America, extending from southern Mexico to Panama, where it connects to Colombia. The Pacific Ocean lies to the southwest, the Caribbean to the northeast and the Gulf of Mexico to the north. Most of Central America rests atop the Caribbean Plate. The terrain here is rugged and dominated by a string of volcanic mountain ranges – eruptions and earthquakes occur from time to time.

Most countries in the region are still well off the beaten track, but certainly worth visiting. The area is inexpensive and devoid of major tourism, but there's a host of great attractions, including fine beaches, colonial cities, diving, trekking, rafting and indigenous highland villages to discover.

At the southernmost point in Central America lies the notorious Darien Gap – a large area of undeveloped swampland, ravines and impenetrable jungle that effectively separates Panama from Colombia. It measures some 100 miles (160km) long and about 30 miles (50km) wide and should not be attempted without a thorough understanding of the physical challenges involved. ■

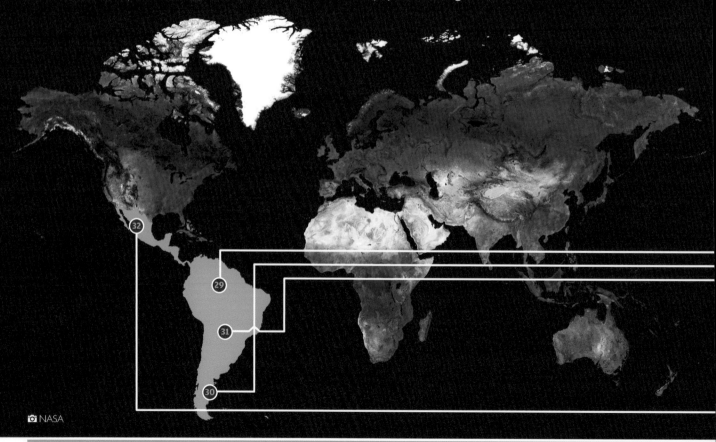

NASA

Trans Amazon

Through the 'green hell' on two wheels

Joe Pichler

The Amazon Rainforest Basin encompasses some 2,700,000 square miles (7,000,000km²), more than half of which is covered by rainforest. The region includes territory belonging to nine different countries, although the majority of the forest is contained within Brazil (60%). The Amazon represents over half of the planet's remaining rainforests, and it comprises the largest and most species-rich tract of tropical rainforest in the world.

Entry is possible from several different countries, the easiest of which are Ecuador and Brazil. To enter from Ecuador, the journey is likely to begin in Quito, a unique city rich in history which should certainly be explored if you have the time. From a Brazilian perspective, it's likely you will depart from Sao Paulo or Rio de Janeiro and head for the likes of Manaus, Belem, Macapa, Boa Vista, Porto Velho or Rio Branco as a base. Manaus and Belem have the most infrastructure for tourists.

Depending on your route, it's almost inevitable that you will spend time on a boat of some sort – the Amazon rainforest is full of rivers, including the biggest one on the planet, responsible for 25% of the fresh water that goes into the oceans. The Amazon is, in fact, so wide that in some places you can't see the other side of the river. Boats vary in size and you can pay for a small, reasonably priced cabin or travel the way the locals do and sleep instead in a hammock on the deck!

Fortaleza, on Brazil's northeastern coast, was the starting point for my journey and it took five days to sort out the customs formalities before I could finally get the sand under my tyres. I headed about 930 miles (1,500km) west to Belem and the mouth of the Amazon. Tons of fish from the Amazon are traded here at the harbour market

THE TRANS-AMAZONIAN HIGHWAY

The Trans-Amazonian Highway (official designation BR-230) is 3,290 miles (5,300km) long, making it the third longest highway in Brazil. It was originally planned to be a fully paved highway but financial pressures and high construction costs have left only part of the road paved. Travel on the non-paved stretches of the highway is extremely difficult during the region's rainy season (October to March) and in the dry season there are often serious potholes. Construction of the highway was very challenging because of the remoteness of the site, and the project has been criticised for indirectly causing a great deal of deforestation. Today the highway offers an overland route into remote areas of the Amazon.

and 'herbalists' sell everything imaginable (and quite a lot that is unimaginable) from the natural apothecary of the rainforest. I steered clear of the local Viagra and opted instead for a pot of organic anti-mosquito cream; I felt I was more likely to be needing that over the next few weeks.

There wasn't a lot of traffic on my route – a few lorry drivers raced across the potholed track like maniacs, and I encountered a number of other motorbikes. They are best described as 'moto taxis'. On a ramshackle bridge I met Carlos, the proud owner of a Yamaha 125, which he used to transport goods and passengers. Riding pillion on these poor tracks is certainly not the most comfortable way to travel, but it's a lot cheaper than a normal taxi, and business was going well. It was good to know that there was an alternative should my occupation as a speaker ever

← **The new road ends in Codo el Pozuzo. We continue along the Rio Pozuzo by boat. The KTM is loaded onto a wobbly canoe with outboard drive.**

← **Rain has turned the Trans Amazon into a mud track.**

↑↑↑ **The Kayapo still live a traditional life.**

↑↑ **Relaxing in a hammock on one of the large river boats.**

↖ **Brightly coloured macaws near the banks of the Rio Pacu.**

↑ **Colca canyon close to the source of the Amazon.**

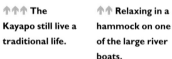

TIPS FOR TRAVELLING IN THE AMAZON

■ Buy local bug repellent but check the make-up of the product to ensure it does not harm your health if used constantly over many days. Take a good quality mosquito net.

■ Always carry plenty of water, given the heat and long distances between stops.

■ Learn a few words of Portuguese. You won't find many people speaking English in the Amazon rainforest, so it's good to learn some basic words – and locals will always appreciate the effort.

■ The Amazon rainforest region is a very poor place. Carry a moderate amount of local currency as you won't find much use for your credit cards or travellers' cheques. Beware of crime in the bigger cities.

■ Be aware of the logging trucks – they are tempting to overtake, but be sure of what lies ahead before making a move.

■ Don't take any seeds or plants from the forest.

■ Be sure to get a yellow fever shot at least ten days before you depart and take malaria tablets.

come to an end – if people stop coming to my shows, I'll be able to start an exclusive business in Brazil with my KTM Adventure.

Heavy night-time downpours are commonplace here and turn dusty tracks into mud very quickly, making progress of any kind extremely challenging. Lorries seemed to get stuck regularly and the only solution for them was to wait several hours for the mud to dry out. They simply couldn't understand what I was doing there. In their eyes, I had to be completely mad to travel this hellish route voluntarily – and even more so on a motorbike. And there were times when even I thought they had a valid point. I felt pretty exhausted as I reached Itaituba, on the bank of the Tapajós River in the heart of the Amazon. Translated, the name means 'the gravel place', which is quite appropriate. The humidity here is insane – above 80% almost all year round. The rainy season runs from December to April, while the driest months are from July to October.

The first thing on the list was a shower, and I slowly started to feel normal again. I recall it being a Saturday night and the road was teeming with Brazilians who were ready to party; the end of the week is always marked with good food and vast quantities of beer. I was sitting talking to a group of people that included the owner of a local mine, a totally inebriated bush pilot, the local radio reporter and a priest. When he heard of my plans to travel through the Amazon to Peru he stopped talking and immediately blessed me. That was about the most

religious of his undertakings as we headed off together to an open-air party.

Riding in the rainforest can be a lonely experience. On one stretch of road there wasn't a single township for 250 miles (400km), just a couple of guesthouses, thinly disguised as shacks. But I did encounter four cars, as well as two long black and yellow snakes. And, to top it all, the road at one point was blocked by a toll barrier and I had to pay the equivalent of $5 to continue my journey along the Trans-Amazonian Highway.

The route took me from Rio Madeira to Xapuri along a good asphalt road; the hardest part of the route was now behind me. This is where Chico Mendes lived and died (murdered in 1988) – he was the boss of the local rubber tappers and fought valiantly against the destruction of the rainforest.

My route took me to Rio Branco, which lies just north of the border with Bolivia, before heading towards Puerto Maldonado in Peru. In 1990 when I rode this route for the first time it had potholes in which my bike sank up to the handlebars. Today it's part of the Interoceanic Highway (or Trans-Oceanic highway) – a transcontinental highway in Peru and Brazil that is under construction and entails the renovation and construction of roughly 1,615 miles (2,600km) of roads and 22 bridges. When completed, it will create a connected highway from the Peruvian ports of San Juan de Marcona, Matarani and Ilo to the Brazilian ports of Rio de Janeiro and Santos.

I reached the Peruvian Amazon lowlands at Puerto Maldonado where I had a visitor from home: my wife Renate had flown in to join me for the rest of the journey.

The next few days were a real challenge as we rode from the tropical rainforest to the icy heights of the Andes. We spent a few days in Chivay at 11,482ft (3,500m) to acclimatise and prevent altitude sickness. Then we set off for the Nevado Mismi, an 18,363ft (5,597m) mountain peak of volcanic origin. A glacial stream on the Mismi was identified and confirmed as the most distant source of the Amazon River so it had a special meaning to travel there, more than 4,700 miles (7,600km) from the start point.

The next leg of the journey would run from Pucallpa to Iquitos along the eastern edge of Peru, but this four-day trip had to be done by boat – nothing too comfortable,

⬆ **Often the petrol is of a dubious quality, and is sold from barrels.**

⬇ **Some of the bridges are still under construction and are just loose boards.**

→ **The Carretera Marginal de la Selva is in a sorry condition and we have to ride through countless water holes.**

⬇ **The freighter *Lucho* is in an appalling condition and completely overloaded, but it's the only way to get from Iquitos to the Brazilian border.**

because rusty old tubs and creaking wooden boats are the norm. Iquitos is the largest city in the Peruvian rainforest. The city can be reached only by plane or boat, with the exception of a road to Nauta, a small town some 63 miles (100km) south.

Before we departed countless lorries unloaded their precious cargo throughout the night until, finally, 700 tons of freight had been loaded on board. There was just enough room for my KTM between the plantain and coconut palms. The passenger deck was a mass of hammocks; this was not the place to be if you suffered from claustrophobia. The boat, called *Henry 3*, pulled in at every tiny village along the shore. For the people who live in these places, the boat is their only link with the outside world – and a good way to do business. Every time we stopped, a crowd of sellers stormed the boat offering tropical fruit, grilled fish and freshly baked cakes. Their goods also included live parrots, stingrays and turtles!

In Iquitos we transferred to a freighter that was in an appalling condition, but it was the only way we could get to the Brazilian border. It was completely overloaded – so much so that in some places the hammocks were hung on two levels. The ubiquitous chickens, turtles and parrots were joined by two live pigs, and the place started to smell like a farmyard. It was an obstacle course to get to the

toilets. Bent in half to pass under the hammocks, stepping over children asleep on the floor, and past squawking chickens – enough said!

The boat trip ended in Santarem and it wasn't long before we found ourselves back where the journey had begun 100 days earlier. We had travelled more than 2,200 miles (3,500km) on boats down the Amazon and ridden some 8,700 miles (14,000km) through one of the world's most amazing landscapes.

RECOMMENDED MAPS

Amazon Basin
Publisher:	ITMB – International Travel Maps
ISBN:	9781553410478
Scale:	1:3,300,000

Brazil – The Amazon
Publisher:	Nelles Verlag
ISBN:	9783865742063
Scale:	1:2,500,000

Brazil Adventure Map
Publisher:	National Geographic
ISBN:	9781566955454
Scale:	1:4,200,000

Buenos Aires to Ushuaia

Plains and plateaus on Ruta 3 in Argentina

Brian Clarke

The coastal Ruta 3 from Buenos Aires to Ushuaia is an iconic motorcycle journey. This is a road of challenges, changing surfaces, inclement weather, endurance and views that cannot be imagined until seen. Once in the plains and plateaus of Argentina you will see a strip of asphalt in front of you that disappears into space, the heat-hazed horizon moulding into the sky without a visible join.

Ruta 3 is one of two main routes you can take to get to Ushuaia from Buenos Aires, the other being Ruta 40. An inland route, Ruta 40 is less direct and takes longer to ride, but is arguably even more spectacular. Ruta 40, however, terminates before Tierra del Fuego and so Ruta 3 becomes the only route for the last leg to Ushuaia.

The route begins in Buenos Aires, the famous capital city of Argentina. It crosses the provinces of Buenos Aires, Río Negro, Chubut, Santa Cruz and Tierra del Fuego and measures a distance of 1,892 miles (3,045km). It's best to allow six to ten days to cover the route at a reasonable pace, leaving time to take in the sights.

If you haven't ridden in Argentina before, the YPF chain of fuel stations will become your friend – it's a modern, popular chain that regularly offers WiFi, small delis and mediocre coffee. Don't try to fill up with fuel yourself – it's an offence and you have to let the attendant do it. We left the port late and only managed 47 miles (75km) to Canuelas before calling it a night. Our hotel room was clean, smart and had secure parking. The only drawback was the nearby nightclub – they party hard and into the early hours in these parts, so make sure you take plenty of earplugs for both on and off the road.

The first major section to undertake was Canuelas to Viedma, a distance of 570 miles (917km). The roads were in great condition and the weather was on our side. April to September are the colder months and the best time to ride here is from November to March. The skies were crystal clear and a sharp blue, with plenty of green fields, trees and vegetation to look at. Ruta 3 isn't one big black straight strip of tarmac the whole way; it does work its way through some towns and villages, so don't be afraid to ask the locals for directions. South Americans are the friendliest, most helpful people you could ever hope to meet. On plenty of occasions folks walked up to us for a chat or to lend a helping hand. Make sure you learn a few basic Spanish phrases like 'Donde esta…?' ('Where is…?') to get you on your way.

I wouldn't recommend Viedma as a stop-off point. I didn't examine the whole place, but the Hotel Cristal was definitely not a good indication – peeling paint, dirty beds, lots of damp and a venue where mosquitoes like to meet up for a drink (on you).

The next leg ran from Viedma to Gaimen – around 312 miles (502km), a great seven hours on the bike. It is on this stretch that the vastness of Argentina really hits you. The road seems to be eternal. You come to a slight incline and get excited at the prospect of a different view over the hill, but it is always the same – flat as far as your eyes can see. Some say this is 'boring'; I say it is 'different'. How often do you get to ride on such roads, in such landscapes? Not often, I bet, so take it all in and appreciate it because if you are heading north after Ushuaia it all changes dramatically.

Believe it or not, but Gaimen is a Welsh-speaking village in the province of Chubut, slightly west of Trelew. It's a gorgeous town and full of friendly people who seem to be very proud of their Welsh heritage. This is a popular spot

← **Riding high in Argentina – 4,800m up in the Andes on the way to San Pedro de Atacama.**

← **Rush hour in old-town Buenos Aires.**

- Download the workshop manual for your bike and keep it on a memory stick.
- A thermos for a hot coffee in the morning if you are camping can also be used as a hot water bottle.
- Instead of a separate video camera just take a good compact camera with video capability.
- Best piece of equipment – EXO2 StormShield heated gloves.

to stay for whale and orca spotting on the east coast. It's also a fossil hot spot. A couple of days here would be a pleasant experience and I would definitely like to visit again. We stayed in a B&B called Gwesty Tyni. It was slightly out of town in a quiet spot down a long gravel drive. The rooms were fantastic and Diego, the owner, was warm and friendly and spoke good English. The place had a very relaxed feel and I wouldn't hesitate to stay again.

The route further on is more smooth tarmac and vanishing skylines. Some sections are very lunar and change from rocky roadside walls to beige hills that break up the flat landscape. Comodoro Rivadavia is a popular stop-off point as one heads south. It is right on the Atlantic coast and is known as the 'capital of the wind'. It is also home to South America's largest wind farm. Around this point the wind certainly becomes more noticeable and it can get pretty violent at times. The city is quite large and provides a good opportunity to get any mechanical work done or hunt for spares.

Leaving here at dawn is a good option as you can ride along the coast with an amazing sunrise to your left, bathing you in warmth and blazing up the horizon with colour. You go up and down beautiful winding roads in the mountains,

following the coast, taking in fuel at Fitzroy and again at Tres Cerros. Wildlife here is more common with llamas, foxes, wild horses and birds of prey. Seeing them is fantastic, but make sure you always have one eye on the road when there are llamas around – there is always one with suicidal tendencies that wants their last sight to be a Pirelli.

You can refuel again at Puerto San Julian, 250 miles (400km) south of Comodoro. Always take advantage of the gas stations, even if you have plenty in the tank, as you can easily get caught out on some of the longer stretches. It's nice to stretch the legs and have a coffee every 100 miles or so, too.

I got lucky on a part of this route when I overtook a police car that was hidden in a line of cars in front of me. Not that bad, you may think, but it was up a hill, on a blind bend and over double lines! He steamed up behind me, overtook and then disappeared. South American cops do have a bit of a reputation so I was imagining a serious fine or worse, but this cop was either lazy or late for his dinner.

At times the strong wind felt like it was trying to rip my helmet off and chronic neck ache from fighting it all day is a common occurrence. It's not so bad when it is a constant wind, but when the blasts are intermittent it is pretty taxing. It was 470 miles (756km) south to Rio Gallegos, the capital of Patagonia and another popular place to stop. The city sits on the estuary of the Gallegos River, 1,638 miles (2,636km) south from Buenos Aires. It's a bustling place with a good selection of restaurants and 'supermercados' to stock up on food for camping.

The next stint was the last, in order to make it to Ushuaia. I would recommend putting on an extra layer or some heated gear at this point as the temperature does drop quite consistently from here on. It was about an hour to the first border from Rio Gallegos. If this is your first border crossing it can be a little daunting, but as they go this one was not too bad. It was all done in one building, which

→ Colourful accommodation in Buenos Aires.

View from 'the end of the world'.

certainly makes it easier (some crossings in South America are extremely confusing as parts of the process may be in different buildings and some miles apart). Be sure to have all your paperwork ready, join the queues, collect the forms and fill them in as best you can. It's a good idea to have plenty of photocopies of all your documents as some borders request them and charge for copying them. Have a few spare pens handy, too, then just smile and go with the flow. If you know it's going to be a tedious affair before you get in there, the reality will be less stressful.

It took me an hour and a half to get through this one, but I had a large group in front of me so it could have been quicker. Some borders can take much longer, so try to get to them as early as possible – you don't want to be entering a new country and searching for hotels or a campsite in the dark. Your passport gets a bit of a pounding during this part of the journey: out of Argentina and into Chile, out of Chile and back into Argentina, and the same on the way back north.

Then it was another windy ride to the infamous Strait of Magellan – a navigable sea route immediately south of

No Tiger tokens at this gas stop.

Ushuaia Harbour.

The end of Ruta 3 in Tierra del Fuego.

ABOUT THE AUTHOR

Brian Clarke has spent 20 years as a mechanic and is very passionate about various forms of martial art. He is also a snowboarding addict, having visited the Alps, Pyrenees and the Rockies. His goal in life is to see as much of the world as he can, and is continuing his travels through Canada and the USA and may go on to settle in Australia.

mainland South America and north of Tierra del Fuego. The waterway is the most important natural passage between the Pacific and the Atlantic Oceans, but it is considered a difficult route to navigate because of the unpredictable winds and currents and the narrowness of the passage. There's a roll-on roll-off ferry to get you across. I didn't pay on the way south but did going back – not sure why, but it's not expensive. Because of the wind it can get pretty choppy but it was a sturdy old brute so it was quite safe. It took about 25 minutes to cross the 3-mile (4.8km) stretch of water and there was a café on the other side for a rest and a hot drink.

Once back on the road you may want to look out for Cerro Sombrero. It's a right turning just before the road turns to gravel and a good stop for fuel as it's a fair way until the next one. The road was now hard-packed gravel for 120 miles (193km). I was riding a Tenere, which lapped it up, and I found it to be good fun chipping along at 50mph (80km/h). The landscape was like Mars and could easily be mistaken for a *Star Wars* movie backdrop. It became a bit difficult to appreciate the views while trying, at the same time, to concentrate on the gravel. There were lots more jagged mountains to the right and the glistening Atlantic to the left.

You think to yourself that you couldn't be any more amazed, but then Mother Nature does it again. The road got twistier still here and there were petrified forests on both sides of the track. We caught the sun going down between the mountains with a lake below – simply stunning! The road rose up and down the mountains, again taking my breath away. The black winding tarmac snaked south with a colossal drop to the right and a huge reservoir shimmering away below. It was here that the cold really started to bite, but soon we were in Ushuaia, the southernmost city in the world. Be sure to visit the 'end of the road' sign for a photo!

📷 All photographs courtesy of Brian Clarke

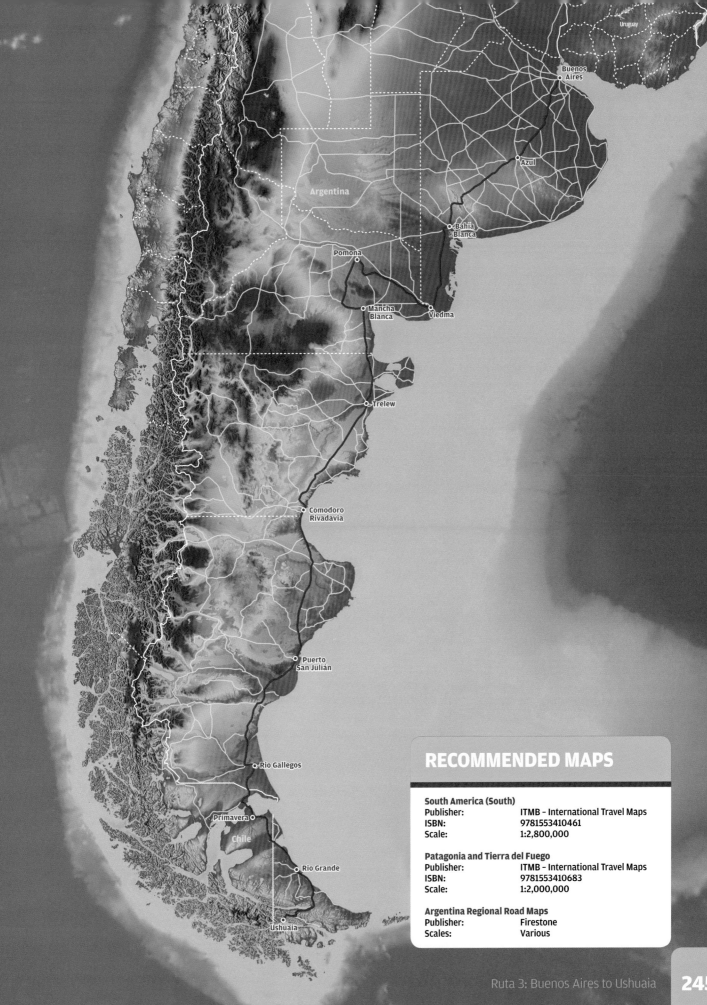

Argentina

Buenos Aires

Azul

Bahía Blanca

Pomona

Mancha Blanca

Viedma

Trelew

Comodoro Rivadavia

Puerto San Julián

Río Gallegos

Primavera

Chile

Río Grande

Ushuaia

Uruguay

RECOMMENDED MAPS

South America (South)
Publisher: ITMB – International Travel Maps
ISBN: 9781553410461
Scale: 1:2,800,000

Patagonia and Tierra del Fuego
Publisher: ITMB – International Travel Maps
ISBN: 9781553410683
Scale: 1:2,000,000

Argentina Regional Road Maps
Publisher: Firestone
Scales: Various

Uyuni to San Pedro de Atacama

High-altitude adventure in Bolivia and Chile

Chris Smith and Liz Peel

The ride from Uyuni in Bolivia to San Pedro de Atacama in Chile is a challenge – a feast for the senses and the stuff of adventure, not to mention great pub stories. At elevations from 11,500ft–16,400ft (3,500m–5,000m) the route takes in seas of salt, smoking volcanic cones and lagoons of vivid greens and reds. The high desert landscape of the Atacama is unforgiving, a dripping painter's palette of colour, and one of the most memorable rides on the planet. The high altitude dry desert reaches 21°C (70°F) during the day, dropping to –9°C (16°F) during the night.

Travelling northwest from Uyuni towards the salt flats (or salar, in local language) before turning south, the route crosses approximately 350 miles (563km) of desert and will take four to eight days depending on your pace and riding ability. This is more of a short expedition than a ride from A to B and that mindset will serve the rider well. The prepared will look back on this journey in years to come with pride and fond memories; the unprepared, and those who just blindly ride off into the desert, will need an element of luck to see them through. It's highly recommended that the route isn't undertaken alone and a minimum of three riders is ideal. Despite the lagoons there is no drinkable water en route, and at least one fuel drop will be needed. The local jeep tour operators will drop fuel off at the ranger station at Laguna Colorado for a small fee if you provide the jerry cans (also available in the town). There is a petrol station at the western edge of town on the road to Potosi.

At 11,689ft (3,653m), the town of Uyuni is at first sight a dusty little staging post that serves adventurous backpackers looking for guided tours of the salar and beyond into what is now known as the 'Southwest Loop'. It would be a struggle to describe Uyuni as being picturesque, but it does have a number of redeeming features that offer the traveller a few comforts. More importantly, it also offers enough in the way of amenities to prepare both bike and rider for the route ahead.

Along the quiet central main street are hostels, hotels and tour operators all vying for your business. Some hotels and hostels are better than others, but all will accommodate the motorcyclist and his or her bike. On the south side of the street, towards the famous train graveyard, is a relatively secure vehicle yard where bikes can be left while staying in town. There are a number of eateries to be found in the town, serving a range of food from budget boiled rice and chicken – a Bolivian staple – to American pizza. The Cementerio de Trenes (train graveyard) some 1.8 miles (3km) outside town is well worth a visit. Great iron hulks left over from the age of steam now spend their days stripped down and slowly rusting in the salt-laden air. It's a melancholy place but fascinating at the same time. Despite the train tracks and the mineral industry, which they served, the old steam engines look stranded and out of place, which is all part of their attraction.

The high altitude and mineral-rich air, not to mention the salt of the salar, demand that a bit of bike preparation is a good idea before leaving the town. Give your bike a good check over for any loose bits and don't be afraid to use some thread lock to ensure that you get to San Pedro de Atacama with all your bolts in place. Sections of the route are rough in places. Give your bike a good hose down with cold water (warm water will more readily dilute any salt already on your bike and just wash it further into the nooks and crannies). Mask off brake discs and calipers and then treat the bike to a liberal dose of WD40, readily available in Uyuni. Don't forget to do the underside. Finally, remove any excess lube from the drive chain to prevent the dust of the desert forming a grinding paste. For those with a shaft drive bike it's one less thing to worry about.

← **Crossing the Ferrocarril de Antofagasta a Bolivia.**

← **A sheltered camp nestled between the rocks adjacent to the Arbol de Piedra or Stone Tree.**

**Camping
on the Salar
de Uyuni.**

**Frozen waves of salt
lap the edges of volcanic
islands on the salar.**

SALAR DE UYUNI

Salar de Uyuni is the world's largest salt flat at 4,086 square miles (10,582km²) and sits at an elevation of almost 12,000ft (3,700m). The salar was formed as a result of transformations between several prehistoric lakes. Over time Uyuni developed a thick salt crust of brine on top composed of lithium, magnesium and table salt. Half of the world's lithium is to be found in the brine under Uyuni's salt flats; this is extracted for use in batteries and medicines. The salt is scraped up from the sheer level surface of the flats into piles where it dries better and is easier to cart away. Today the salt flats serve as the major transport route across the Bolivian Altiplano, and they are a major breeding ground for several species of pink flamingos.

As you will need to carry all your own drinking and cooking water give consideration to what food is suitable to take on the route. Foods such as pasta and rice, while light and high in energy, require a good deal of water to cook. Local cheeses, bread, crackers, biscuits and tinned tuna are all easily purchased in the town. Don't forget to take all your rubbish away as nothing breaks down in the harsh desert environment.

Uyuni to Colchani
North-northwest, 14 miles (23km)
The route begins via the well-used dirt road north-northwest to Colchani on Route 602. Once at Colchani turn west and on to the Salar de Uyuni where, depending on the time of year, you will either be greeted by a flat expanse of crisp white salt or an unbroken lake of water

**In the heat of
the day where sky
meets the earth.**

**James flamingos feed
on the algae-rich waters
of the lagoons.**

just a few centimetres deep and perfectly rideable.

The salar is an amazing landscape of brilliant white salt broken only by majestic ships of volcanic rock, trapped and immovable. You may find cones of salt piled up by local workers, drying in the sun. As soon as you turn on to the salar your senses are attacked. The horizon stretches for ever and the sky is twice as blue and twice as big. What would appear to be as slippery as ice under your wheels is solid and full of grip. If you have never ridden on perfectly flat salt before you will soon find yourself giggling as your confidence and speed grow. Should you be there in the wet season, and when the air is still, you will find yourself riding across the world's biggest mirror, as the sky is reflected in the water beneath your wheels.

Colchani to Hotel de Sol; to Isla de los Pescadores
West 7.5 miles (12km); West, 50 miles (80km)
Set out west across the salar towards the Hotel de Sol. The hotel is built from solid blocks of salt; even the tables are made of salt. Rooms can be pre-booked in Uyuni or you can take your chances and just turn up if you want to stay. If you do stay at the Hotel de Sol it will be a short day's ride and you may wish to push on, due west to the Isla de los Pescadores (Fish Island) instead. This is a favourite stopping-off point for jeep tours and you won't find yourself alone there until later in the day. On the plus side, you will see plenty of admiring faces, shocked to see that you have reached the island under your own steam.

If the salar is dry you can take your pick of camping spots for several hundred square miles. If not, you can camp on the Isla de los Pescadores itself or on one of the nearby smaller islands. All the islands comprise ancient, and not so ancient, lumpy lava which doesn't lend itself too well to camping. However, there are flat and softer spots to be had if you look. There is also some small, basic accommodation on the Isla de los Pescadores itself but it is often full or closed. Camping is a better option and finding a spot on the salt will not be difficult in the dry season. Camping on the salar is an experience not to be missed. The wind can pick up and it is nearly impossible to drive a tent peg into the salt so free-standing tents tethered to the bike are a bonus here. Make sure you have your camera ready for the amazing sunsets, too.

Isla de los Pescadores to Villa Martin Colcha
Due south, 49 miles (79km)
Leaving the Isla de los Pescadores ride due south across the salar over octagonal patterns formed by low-pressure ridges in the salt. You may also find bubbling springs of mineral-laden water pushing its way up though fissures in the salt. Some of these springs hollow out the salt below as they rise up to the surface, so it's advisable to leave a metre or two between yourself and them as you ride by, for fear of your front wheel disappearing down a hole.

As you reach the southern limits of the salar you will meet a constructed road of salt which will carry you over the higher pressure ridges where salt meets desert rock and the landscape changes from white to dull ochre and

→ **The Train Graveyard on the outskirts of Uyuni reflects the rich history of the region.**

→ **Shattered rocks and sharp sand cover the valley floors.**

→ **Elusive vicuna populate the high altiplano amongst the smoking volcanoes.**

dusty orange. As the road turns from salt to dust it will take you to the village of Villa Martin Colcha, nestling in among the hills. You'll see the occasional young Bolivian soldier watching you ride on with envious eyes as he stands on guard duty at the military checkpoint. As the road progresses away from the salar the route is obvious, but the going can be tough on the gritty sand for heavily laden bikes, or if riding two-up.

Villa Martin Colcha to San Juan
South-southwest 24 miles (39km)
There are a number of tracks through the desert between Villa Martin Colcha and San Juan. Pick a well-used one and keep heading southwest, crossing the railway track as you get closer to San Juan. At times you will find yourself covering vast expanses of flat ground between distant volcano cones shimmering in the heat haze. The sense of freedom and isolation is almost overwhelming.

The desert village of San Juan is 3.4 miles (5.5km) further south from a fork in the road that goes off to the southwest before reaching the railway tracks. This is the route that you will want to take the next day, having stayed overnight in San Juan, if you choose to do so. There is a small hostel (or *alojamiento*) in the village where rooms can be rented for the night. Electricity is intermittent and generally only on for a few hours in the evening. Petrol is often available in both San Juan and Villa Martin Colcha if you ask around; expect to pay over the odds, though.

San Juan to Laguna Canapa via Chiguana
Southwest, 52 miles (84km)
Having stayed overnight at San Juan, head back north over the railway line to pick up the track to Chiguana across the salar. The track goes southwest, roughly following the line of the tracks to the south for 19 miles (31km), or 15 miles

(25km) if missing out the overnight stay at San Juan.

At Chiguana cross over on to the south side of the tracks again and pass through the military checkpoint. The soldiers take their work seriously but they are generally friendly and relaxed.

Leaving Chiguana, follow the line of the railway southwest for approximately 1.8 miles (3km), after which the track will take you further south and away from the railway towards a chain of lagoons approximately 31 miles (50km) distant. The road between Chiguana and the lagoons is of mixed terrain but the route is generally easy to make out, with some sections being constructed dirt road. During the wet season, and for a month or so after it, some parts of the route can be muddy, especially around the edges of some salars. Other sections are firm and fast, gravel riverbed, sand or rocky. If that isn't enough, there are even a couple of sections of fine bulldust, which billows up like talcum powder as your wheels cut through it. This is a route with riding variety and scenery all the way.

Approximately 33 miles (53km) from Chiguana you will reach Laguna Canapa, the first of five lagunas in a chain. There are two smaller lagoons before Canapa, making seven in total. Any of the lagunas offer wonderful camping opportunities beside the blue, red and green waters and flocks of Andean, Chilean and James flamingos. All of the lagunas – Canapa, Hedionda, Charcota, Honda and Inco Corral – are distinctive from each other, with Canapa and Charcota being the most popular with tour guides. You will not be overrun by visiting tour groups and it is easy to put a little distance between yourself and them to find somewhere quiet for the tent. Laguna Honda is the obvious choice for Honda riders, but other lagoons are arguably more scenic. The laguna waters are heavy in mineral content and algae and not fit for drinking, even when filtered.

⬆ **Teamwork is often the only way to keep going through the deep sands.**

Laguna Canapa to Arbol de Piedra (Stone Tree)

Southwest, leading south to southeast, 37 miles (60km)
From Laguna Canapa continue southwest on Ruta de las Joyas Alto Andinas before the road turns south to southeast. The main route remains easy to follow, but tracks divide regularly and then come together again as vehicles taking the route previously have searched for the line of least resistance across the desert. Smoking volcanoes and fumaroles are all around in a landscape seeping colours that bleed into one another like melted chocolate sundaes. In the distance Volcan Ollague stands at 19,242ft (5,865m) on the Chilean border. Llamas, vicuna and guanaco, all members of the camelid family, can be picked out from the landscape as they forage for the meagre pickings that the desert scrub offers.

As you follow the route from the lagunas to the Stone Tree, it is well worth pulling over on high ground for a few moments, turning off the bike engine and walking some distance away. It is all too easy to keep following your front wheel and not to appreciate where you are. Stop and absorb the silence, beauty and isolation for a while. It is a unique experience and

if you're with friends, go off in different directions. It's something to do alone.

The track will lead you over more rock and desert, beside stone escarpments and sand dunes that wouldn't be out of place in the Sahara, before finally reaching the Arbol de Piedra in the Desierto Siloli. The Stone Tree stands apart from other rock formations, which rise up from the sand. Fashioned by wind-blown sand, the soft stone has been carved into a petrified sapling of some height. The rock formations beside the Stone Tree make an ideal and sheltered place to camp. The Stone Tree is another popular stop for the tour groups but they soon move on and you will have the place to yourself by late afternoon. A number of high dunes are also within spitting distance and it can be an entertaining challenge for experienced riders to reach to the top on a bike and look around at the view.

If you wish to continue, Laguna Colorada is only 11 miles (18km) further on and Huayllajara Hostel Altiplano is 6 miles (10km) further south beyond the park entrance, where there is accommodation and basic snacks to be had.

↑ Celebrations
at the Chilean
border.

⬇ Sometimes it's nice
to just appreciate
where you are.

Arbol de Piedra (Stone Tree) to Laguna Verde
South, 66 miles (106km)
From the Arbol de Piedra the road soon reaches the
fringe of Laguna Colorada beside a park ranger's station.
The laguna is a brilliant liquid red carpet over pure
white sodium shores. If you have arranged for fuel to
be brought out to the laguna by a tour operator, this
is where you will find it. If not, it will be at Huayllajara
Hostel Altiplano, to the south of the lagoon. The ranger
station is the better option for fuel drops, though, as it's
easier to track down.

Leaving Laguna Colorada and still on the easy to
follow dirt road on the western shore, the route takes
you on to the Sol de Manana geyser basin, approximately
21 miles (34km) beyond the ranger station. The geyser
basin is a primeval cauldron of spitting and boiling mud
pools and fumaroles. The air is thick with the sulphuric
smell of rotten eggs and the earth's crust is thin and
perilous in places. For fear of being boiled alive as the
ground gives way around the mud pools, it's best to keep
back and view the scenery with respect. Under your
feet the world is literally creating itself and it's another
opportunity to appreciate the wonder of where you are.

Southeast and then due south from the Sol de
Manana geyser basin it's a short 12-mile (19km) hop to
the hot springs of Termas de Polques and the Salar de
Chalviri. The hot springs are a comfortable temperature
for soaking tired muscles while taking in the view of
snow-capped volcanoes and pink flamingos.

Leaving the Termas de Polques and Salar de Chalviri,
Laguna Verde is 22 miles (35km) further on to the
southwest. The road once again divides and rejoins itself
time and time again, as different tracks have been taken
between the volcanoes across the lava and ash fields.
Other sections are more discernible as a maintained
dirt track, bounded by lines of piled grit sand where
earth movers have pioneered a more identifiable route,
although it is not always more spacious.

The shores of Laguna Verde are another reasonable
camping option, having covered in the region of 60 miles
(100km) since the Stone Tree, although there is little
shelter to be had from the cold winds when they pick
up. The laguna this time is a vivid blue-green set against
a backdrop of carmine reds and dull golds. As stunningly
beautiful as it is, the waters are a thin soup of diluted
arsenic, heavy metals and calcites. The best views of the
laguna against the backdrop are on the northern shore,
to the west (right) of your line of approach.

Laguna Verde to San Pedro de Atacama
South and west, 39 miles (62km)
From Laguna Verde to the Chilean/Bolivian border and
the Bolivian customs office is 9 miles (15km) along the
maintained dirt road. Follow the road along the eastern
shore of the lagoon, heading south. The friendly Bolivian
border officials will give you an exit stamp in your
passport before waving you on into Chile.

Just 3 miles (5km) further and you will meet

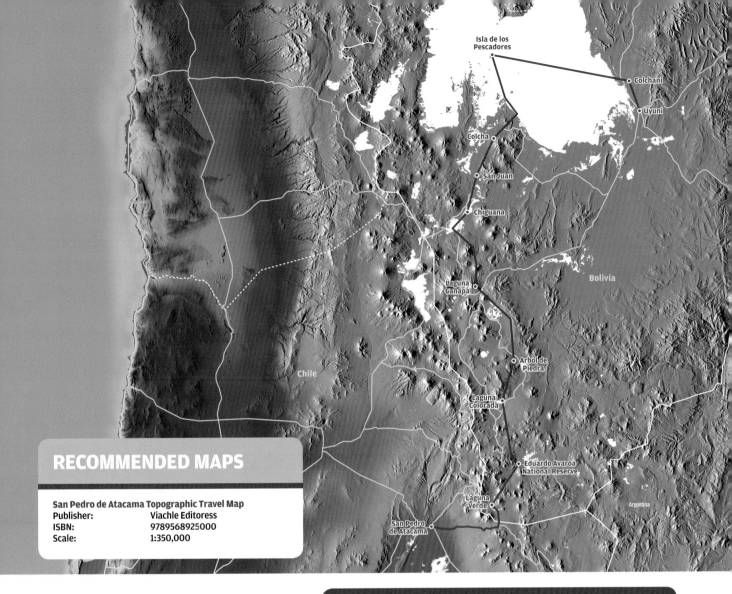

RECOMMENDED MAPS

San Pedro de Atacama Topographic Travel Map
Publisher: Viachle Editoress
ISBN: 9789568925000
Scale: 1:350,000

the paved surface of Route 27. Depending on your disposition you will greet the tarmac either with elation or with a sense of loss at the approaching end of the adventure. Where dirt road meets tarmac, just a little before the junction with Route 27, look back at where you have come from and take in the impressive view of Volcan Licancabur rising up to 19,953ft (5,960m) across the ash fields.

At the junction of Route 27 turn west for the final, fast and smooth 26-mile (42km) stretch downhill to San Pedro de Atacama. At the outskirts of the town, turn right at the junction and stop at the Chilean customs office. The Chilean officials will check your passport for an exit stamp before putting their own entry stamp in and thoroughly checking your bike details. The crossing point can be busy but the soft beds, cool drinks and good food of San Pedro de Atacama are within sight now.

San Pedro de Atacama
San Pedro de Atacama is a well-served small oasis town, which is not short on amenities for any traveller, with a plethora of hotels and hostels to suit any budget, and restaurants to match. The town has become a little touristy in recent years but it still retains its charm.

ABOUT THE AUTHORS

Chris Smith and Liz Peel have travelled all over the world for both work and pleasure, including humanitarian projects in Africa, unsupported expeditions to the Amazon in search of lost villages, and an attempted crossing of the Andes in a three-wheeled motor taxi. The latter didn't work out too well, but they gave a lift to a lot of people. Chris and Liz's first passion is for adventure motorcycle travel, however. They spent three years travelling the length and breadth of the Americas, searching out the more remote and less visited areas of these continents. The unique sense of freedom and the connection to the environment that motorcycle travel offers is what drives them. They also find that riding into a little village in the middle of nowhere on a big overland bike is the best possible icebreaker for meeting the locals. They say: 'It seems everyone is your friend when you're on a bike.'

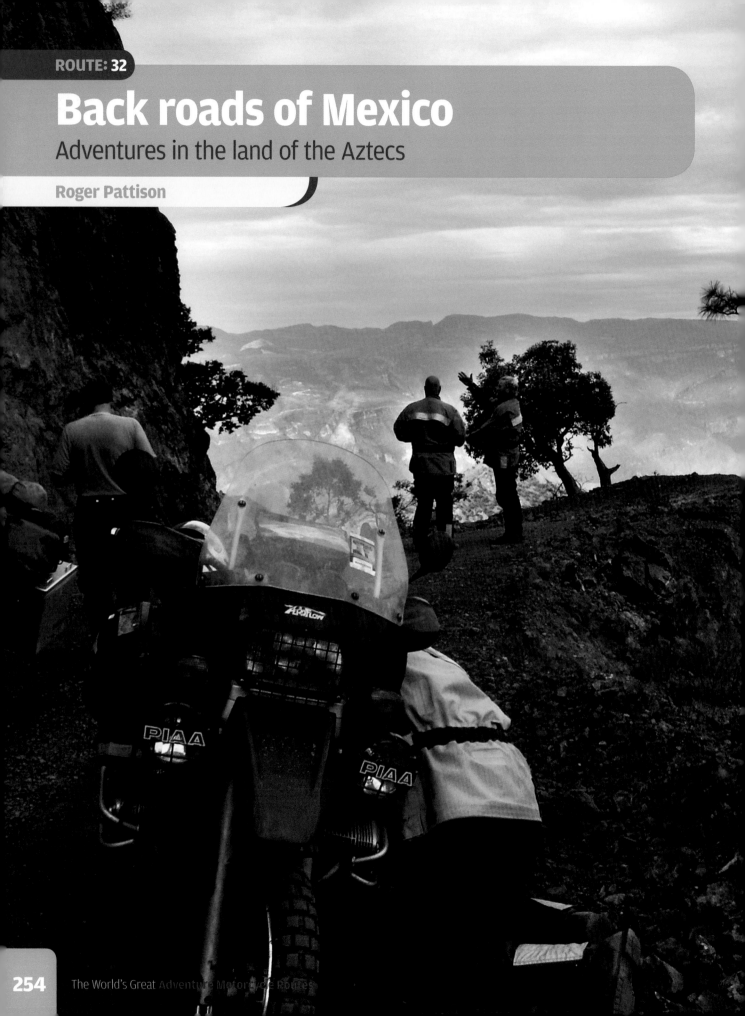

Back roads of Mexico

Adventures in the land of the Aztecs

Roger Pattison

With the proper paperwork in place it is usually easiest for a motorcycle rider to enter and exit Mexico from the north through the bordering states of Texas, New Mexico or Arizona. For the best chance of comfortable temperatures throughout, early spring is an excellent time to travel south. The beginning of most of my journeys into Mexico has meant leaving Las Cruces (New Mexico) early in the morning, riding to the quietly isolated border crossing at Santa Teresa 60 miles (97km) away and spending about an hour and a half or so getting processed to enter Mexico. The ride from there to Casas Grande is a fairly smooth and straight road across the Sonoran Desert.

In Casas Grande a tour of the Anasazi ruins at Paquime is a good way to start soaking up the local history. Paquime was the southern outpost of the ancient Anasazi territory. This mysterious civilisation that at one point in time seemed simply to vanish also left traces of their livelihood in northern New Mexico and southern Colorado.

As you leave the arid desert of northern Mexico, you will begin to see Mennonite family farms and ride through the rolling curves of the northern Sierra Madre foothills. Families that were originally escaping religious persecution have been settled in parts of this area for over a century. Continuing south brings you to the jaw-dropping canyon overlook above Creel, at El Divisadero and the small town of San Rafael.

- **Passport.**
- **Motorcycle-endorsed driver's licence.**
- **Motorcycle registration.**
- **A notarised letter of permission from the lien holder, or from the owner if you are not on your own motorcycle.**
- **Mexico insurance.**
- **A personal credit card to bond the motorcycle.**

Stay a while viewing the deep chasms of Copper Canyon, and then wind back down the mountain road to Creel and turn back south to enter the Barranca del Cobre itself. With several miles of twisted asphalt before the road changes to dirt, you begin to see up close the wonders of the vast erosion that created these amazing cuts in the earth. In the very bottom of this part of the canyon system, just outside the old silver mining town of Batopilas, a new lodge built on a very old foundation clings to the canyon wall, offering a unique place to get a peaceful night's sleep.

Riding on through Batopilas brings you to the lost mission of Satevo. This sixteenth-century cathedral bears no known record of its origin or builders. A short look

← **Roadside adjustments and route discussions are to be expected along the way.**
📷 Roger Pattison

← **The origin of the name 'Copper Canyon' is clearly evident in the colourful and vertiginous geology. Riders drop quickly and deeply into Batopilas Canyon.**
📷 Roger Pattison

⬆ **The low-lying hills near Morelia are home to billions of part-time residents flitting about.**
📷 Roger Pattison

Local industry is a family affair.
📷 Murray Rempel

Standing watch.
📷 Roger Pattison

↗ **Just hanging out at this typical Tarahumara dwelling. No-one home.**
📷 Roger Pattison

at the much newer ruins of the Sheppard Hacienda in Batopilas will tell a story of how hard it is for any building to survive the harsh rainy season in the canyon without diligent maintenance. The route continues as you climb out of the canyon on an obscure dirt and gravel road. This amazing ride to the small woodland town of Guachochic is almost completely on roads surfaced with loose gravel and dirt.

Humble types of accommodation operated by warm and friendly people are available everywhere. They will want to be sure you are well fed before hitting the road again, too. Eggs with beans and potatoes is a typical breakfast dish just about everywhere. Add some chilli (carefully) if you want to spice things up. The road south from here leaves the canyon country going into the mountains, following a smooth yet undulating road on into Hidalgo Del Parral.

The route south from Parral is mostly open highway through remote countryside. Passing along the edge of the city of Durango, the ride continues on into the high mountain region of the Sierra Madre Occidental, to the small mountaintop village of El Salto. This road is tame for now, but will get more interesting as it continues toward the coast. There are many chances to stop for a scenic view into

the distance of the mainland, or later towards the coast.

The Camino del Diablo (Devil's Road), crossing the mountains into Mazatlan, is one of the most famous roads in all of Mexico. Although well improved now, it was once an entire day's trip to travel the 100 miles (160km) or so across this mountain pass from the plains to the coast. This road has seen the demise of many a driver over the years, caught out by paying too little attention to operating their vehicle, with all that is left to remember them a small marker surrounded by flowers alongside the road. This is one section of highway that deserves extra caution.

Once past the steep twisting descent, you can access a stretch of Mexico's new 'Interstate Highway' headed further south. The stretch of four-lane asphalt is a nice quiet break because it is smooth with very little traffic – it is a toll road and the locals rarely drive on it. Bring plenty of extra pesos if you plan to travel the toll roads. At a point several miles along the coast south of Mazatlan divert on to a tiny road through the lush deciduous forest to reach the small sandy beach village of San Blas. It is much less crowded and quieter than the big resort city itself and in early spring the beaches are mostly deserted,

- Take a few pesos to start with, and then get what you need along the way from an ATM.
- Notify your credit/debit card company or bank that you will be on an international trip.
- Temperatures will range from 4ºC (40ºF) to 32ºC (90ºF) in the spring.
- It can be wet in the west and dry in the east.
- Be prepared, motorcycle shops are few and far between.
- If you do break something, there are a lot of creative repair facilities to be found.
- Be nice, no matter how frustrating the slow pace of life may seem at times.
- Take a deep breath and relax, and always remember that you are the foreigner.

offering some time for thoughtful solitude along the peaceful coastline.

As you travel along the coastline the lush green terrain is a jungle-like landscape. The climate is tropical and near sea level it begins to feel wonderfully warm. Further on, the route veers away from the coast at about the most southern point of this route. A reasonable destination for the night is Colima, an older town with modern conveniences and interesting street scenes. Using a wireless receiver, high-speed internet is available right on the plaza, with special covered benches/desks, as you munch a delicious bacon-wrapped hotdog purchased from a nearby street vendor.

Leaving Colima, as the road winds upwards again, beautiful countryside unfolds before you, with fruits and vegetables growing everywhere in the rich fertile soil.

Wherever possible, try to stay off the toll roads in order to see the real country and mix with the locals. The distance is always greater when winding in and out of the remote valleys and villages, but the experience is one of being within the culture rather than flying past above it – you will be in no hurry to get away from the friendly people of rural Mexico.

The historical city of Morelia is a must-see destination in order to experience some of the oldest remaining colonial architecture in the country. Some lodges here have been a destination for travellers since the days of horse and buggy travel. The old downtown is where you will see the finest remaining structures from that era, as well as lively activities of some sort. The cathedral in the main plaza is interesting enough to take up an entire morning, but there are plenty of other wonderful things to see as well.

A pause for systems check at the pass into Guachochic.
Brent Schuster

Many irresistible viewpoints slow down progress.
Roger Pattison

ABOUT THE AUTHOR

Roger Pattison was born and raised on a farm in eastern New Mexico, where he grew up learning to work hard and entertain himself. With school sports too far away for practical involvement, motorcycles filled the void and became his passion and energetic outlet. After many years of off-road competition, Roger became interested in long-distance and endurance challenges. Having participated in and organised numerous such events in the southwestern US and elsewhere, Roger is uniquely qualified for his current position, Tour Director for Aerostich Tours. Roger remains passionate about encouraging and training motorcyclists to learn new skills, particularly off-road skills. Roger currently lives in the high mountains of northern New Mexico with his wife Kerrie Brokaw Pattison, who works with him daily developing the tour business and promoting a variety of rides and events. For more information on adventure riding in Mexico visit www.aerostichtours.com

Just relaxing in the exquisite courtyard of the old carriage house is a wonderful experience to remember.

A short trip eastwards across the hills sees you arrive in alpine forest near the world's only Monarch butterfly migration zone. Zitacuaro is the best base for visiting the butterflies at Cerro Pellon. About 10 miles (16km) north of the town lie the Matlazinca pyramid ruins, and just south in San Pancho is a sixteenth-century church. A wonder-filled morning can be spent hiking through literally billions of butterflies in the remote forest sanctuary, some which travelled 6,000 miles (9,650km) to get to this point. Then continue riding east over wooded hillsides, eventually coming to an overlook displaying the immensity of the second largest city in the world. This is as close as you can get to the maddening traffic snarls and congestion of Mexico City without becoming ensnared. Instead of entering the city, continue meandering on north to the ancient and unique Toltec ruins of Tula.

Tula was an important city from about AD 900 to 1150. Aztec annals tell of the magnificent Toltec capital city with palaces of gold, turquoise, jade and quetzal feathers. Tula was abandoned in the thirteenth century and perhaps the Aztecs looted its treasures. Only a half-day ride back south and east of Mexico City are the most famous and impressive pyramids in the area, at Teotihuacan. You should consider taking an entire day to study these fabulous ruins and their history.

The route turns north again and from here you start to ride through the vast central highland deserts. San Miguel de Allende, founded in about 1550 as a Spanish mission, is a trip into a later and different era of Mexican history. Now the town is a popular art centre with beautiful colonial architecture, and home to many US expatriates.

Further north, after navigating a variety of small back roads, the enigmatic Real de Catorce is as mysterious as it is unique. A long cobblestone paved road and a narrow tunnel provide the only reliable access to this interesting town. Like many old towns in Mexico, this village high on the fringes of the Sierra Madre Oriental has a rich mining history. Although now considered nearly a ghost town for much of the year, the silver boom saw a population of more than 40,000 people living there in the late 1800s.

As the route returns ever northward towards the USA, the country opens up again to long-distance views.

➡ **With so many back roads available to explore, one can spend a lot of time seeing the real Mexico.**
📷 Ed Froese

➡➡ **The 'lost mission' at Satevo stands like a citadel out of place, a simple reminder of Mexico's diverse history.**
📷 Roger Pattison

RECOMMENDED MAPS

Mexico (North)
Publisher:	ITMB – International Travel Maps
ISBN:	9781553415985
Scale:	1:1,300,000

Mexico (South)
Publisher:	ITMB – International Travel Maps
ISBN:	9781553415428
Scale:	1:1,100,000

Mexico (Map Sheet 765)
Publisher:	Michelin
ISBN:	9782067157477
Scale:	1:2,500,000

Mexico: Guja Roji State Road Maps
Publisher:	Guia Roji
ISBN:	9789687140773
Scale:	1:400,000

In springtime it may be necessary to begin adding layers of clothing in order to stay comfortable in the cooler air. Parras is home to the very first winery in the Americas, established in 1597. The now large industrial enterprise lies just north of Parras, in San Lorenzo, and it ships wine called *Casa Madero* all over the world.

The route then begins to pass more quickly through beautiful, open desert scenery. Starting out on back roads, nearer Chihuahua they get larger, and wider, and faster. A large administrative and commercial centre in northern Mexico, the city has a long history of cattle and mining interest. A fast-growing metropolis, Chihuahua still has some old world charm to be found.

The return to the USA will seem like arriving on a different planet after being away for three weeks or so. You will appreciate many things you may never have noticed before, but you will also miss the local hospitality and kindness shown to you in Mexico. Mexico is so close to the modern world – close enough, in fact, to make it a regular place to visit – yet so trapped in history. It would take a while to see all the country has to offer, but this journey of around 3,700 miles (5,950km) is a good start.

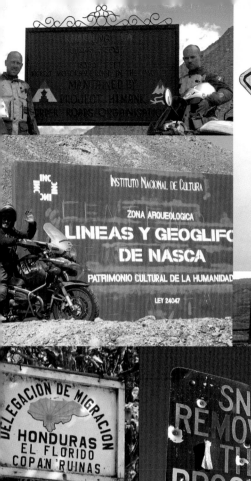

METAL
BRIDGE
DECK

Landmannaleið F 225

INSTITUTO NACIONAL DE CULTURA

ZONA ARQUEOLOGICA

LINEAS Y GEOGLIFO
DE NASCA

PATRIMONIO CULTURAL DE LA HUMANIDAD

LEY 24047

BORDER THAI – MYANMAR

Tropic of Capricorn

DELEGACION DE MIGRACION

HONDURAS
EL FLORIDO
COPAN RUINAS

SNOW NOT
REMOVED BEYOND
THIS POINT
PROCEED AT YOUR
OWN RISK

CHILE
VIA PANAM

Vaðið krefst varúðar
• Hvar er vaðið? – Straumvötn breyta sér.
• Er vélin vatnsvarin?
• Fylgist einhver með þér?
• Hjólför segja ekki alla söguna.
• Kannið sjálf vaðið.
• Notið öryggislínu.
• Klæðist hlýjum fótum í áberandi lit.

Crossing requires caution
• Where is the crossing? – Rivers change.
• Tire tracks do not tell the entire story.
• Has your engine been waterproofed?
• Is somebody watching while you cross?
• Probe the crossing yourself.
• Use a safety line.
• Wear warm clothing in bright colours.

ADDIS TYRE

WELCOME
TO
ETHIOPIA

МЯНГАНЫ ЗАМ

↑ МИРНЫЙ 26
ЯКУТСК 1161 →

العراق →
I R A Q 152 km
التنف →
ATTANF 145 km
↑ تدمر
87 km PALMYRA
حمص ←
123 km HOMS

↑ Kulgera
Adelaide

LASSETER HIGHWAY
Uluṟu (Ayers_Rock) 4 →

इंडियन ऑयल

NEXT FILLING STATION
365 KM AHEAD

Index

Index